Sidney Lanier

English Novel

A study in the development of personaity

Sidney Lanier

English Novel
A study in the development of personaity

ISBN/EAN: 9783337042196

Printed in Europe, USA, Canada, Australia, Japan

Cover: Foto ©Thomas Meinert / pixelio.de

More available books at **www.hansebooks.com**

THE ENGLISH NOVEL

BOOKS BY SIDNEY LANIER.

The English Novel. A Study in the Development of Personality. Cr. 8vo. $2.00.

The Science of English Verse. Cr. 8vo. $2.00.

Poems. Edited by his Wife, with a Memorial by William Hayes Ward. With portrait. 12mo. $2.00.

Select Poems of Sidney Lanier. Edited, with an Introduction and Notes, by Prof. Morgan Callaway, Jr. 12mo, *net*, $1.00.

BOY'S LIBRARY OF LEGEND AND CHIVALRY.

Four volumes. Illustrated. Each cr. 8vo. $2.00.

The Boy's Froissart.	**Knightly Legends of Wales.**
The Boy's King Arthur.	**The Boy's Percy.**

THE

ENGLISH NOVEL

A STUDY IN

The Development of Personality

BY

SIDNEY LANIER

LECTURER IN JOHNS HOPKINS UNIVERSITY
AUTHOR OF "THE SCIENCE OF ENGLISH VERSE"

REVISED EDITION

NEW YORK
CHARLES SCRIBNER'S SONS
1897

𝔘𝔫𝔦𝔳𝔢𝔯𝔰𝔦𝔱𝔶 𝔓𝔯𝔢𝔰𝔰:
JOHN WILSON AND SON, CAMBRIDGE, U.S.A.

Prefatory Note

THE Johns Hopkins lectures delivered in Hopkins Hall during the winter of 1881, and published in 1883 under title of *The English Novel*, were Mr. Lanier's latest literary work excepting his *Introduction* to *The Boy's Mabinogion*, which was dictated at intervals in May and June, 1881, in the Carolina mountains. Their original plan called for twenty lectures; but Mr. Lanier was at the last persuaded to reduce the number to twelve, as President Gilman, with solicitude aroused by the writer's rapid decline, made use of the suggestion that a shorter course would better fit in with the whole schedule of University lectures. To effect this change the entire omission of many subjects and briefer treatment of others became necessary, while George Eliot's death occurring in the middle of the course further modified the plan by urging Mr. Lanier to concentrate upon her work the remaining six lectures.

His own name for the course was "From Æschylus to George Eliot, The Development of Personality," and this better conveys the author's purpose than the compacter book-title, since the novel was preferred for study above other literary forms merely as the fullest exponent of man's growth in the sense of personality, contrasted with its faint and crude expression in the Æschylean drama.   The original title was discarded as too cumbrous, and after thirteen years of circulation the only practicable change is thought to be a clearer statement in a new sub-title.

Immediate publication of these lectures was urged in 1882 by some who had listened to them and who believed that they would require only careful proof-reading.   At this time Mr. Lanier's only companion in their preparation was disabled by illness from taking any part whatever in the editing; so an unrevised first draught of a work shaped and penned — or sometimes dictated — under the weight of a mortal malady was committed to the generous care of a friend who was forbidden to lay any questions before the present editor.   Many mistakes resulted: some from the copyist's unfamiliarity with the feeble handwriting, and others from the former editor's uncertainty regarding Mr. Lanier's final wish at various points. New plates have permitted a thorough revision, the addition of a table of contents and the restoration of several omitted passages.   In addition, some verbal repetitions are suppressed and consistency in external forms has been sought.

One slight alteration the present editor has made with reluctance, upon the assurance that a liberty which the author deliberately claimed the right to exercise would be mistaken for unscholarly carelessness: that is, the interchangeable use of *will* and *shall* as they repeatedly appear in his writings.

He must therefore be put upon record according to his parenthesis " (Observe will and shall here) " that follows the quotation from Sir Thomas Malory on p. 21. He has defined this attitude in a fragmentary note headed " Will and Shall," where he says:

" Who can assume authority on the proper use of *will* and *shall*, when the Wycliffite scriptures have ' I *schal* ryse' and ' I schal go to my fadir' and ' I schal seie to him,' while the modern version has ' I *will* arise' and ' I will say,' etc.? "

So much discretion may fall within the limits of a duty attempted in this revision: to preserve the author's own well-developed sense of personality in its utmost freedom of expression, and to give to his readers the fullest opportunity of studying that rare personality as it is here revealed.

M. D. L.

January, 1897.

Prefatory Note to the First Edition.

THE following chapters were originally delivered as public lectures at John Hopkins University, in the winter and spring of 1881. Had Mr. Lanier lived to prepare them for the press he would probably have recast them to some extent; but the present editor has not felt free to make any changes from the original manuscript, beyond the omission of a few local and occasional allusions, and the curtailment of several long extracts from well known writers.

Although each is complete in itself, this work and its foregoer, *The Science of English Verse*, were intended to be parts of a comprehensive philosophy of formal and substantial beauty, which, unhappily, the author did not live to develop.

W. H. B.

Table of Contents

I

II

IX

X

Table of Contents

The English Novel

A Study in

The Development of Personality

I

THE series of lectures which I last had the pleasure
of delivering in this hall was devoted to the exposition
of what is beyond doubt the most remarkable, the most
persistent, the most wide-spread, and the most noble
of all those methods of arranging words and ideas in
definite relations which have acquired currency among
men — namely, the method of verse, or formal poetry.
That exposition began by reducing all possible phenomena of verse to terms of vibration; and having thus
secured at once a solid physical basis for this science,
and a precise nomenclature in which we could talk
intelligibly upon this century-befogged subject, we advanced gradually from the most minute to the largest
possible considerations upon the matter in hand.

Now wishing that such courses as I might give here
should preserve a certain coherence with each other, I
have hoped that I could secure that end by successively
treating the great forms of modern literature; and,
wishing further to gain whatever advantage of entertainment for you may lie in contrast and variety, I have

thought that inasmuch as we have already studied the verse-form in general, we might now profitably study some great prose-form in particular, and — in still further contrast — that we might study that form not so much analytically — as when we developed the science of formal poetry from a single physical principle — but this time synthetically, from the point of view of literary art rather than of literary science.

I am further led to this general plan by the consideration that so far as I know — but my reading in this direction is not wide and I may be in error — there is no book extant in any language which gives a conspectus of all those well-marked and widely-varying literary forms which have differentiated themselves in the course of time, and of the curious and subtle needs of the modern civilized man which, under the stress of that imperious demand for expression which all man's emotions make, have respectively determined the modes of such expression to be in one case *The Novel*, in another *The Sermon*, in another *The Newspaper Leader*, in another *The Scientific Essay*, in another *The Popular Magazine Article*, in another *The Semi-Scientific Lecture*, and so on : each of these prose-forms, you observe, having its own limitations and fitnesses quite as well-defined as the sonnet-form, the ballad-form, the drama-form, and the like, in verse.

And, with this general plan, a great number of considerations, which I hope will satisfactorily emerge as we go on, lead me irresistibly to select the novel as the particular prose-form for our study.

It happens indeed that over and above the purely literary interest which would easily give this form the first place in such a series as the present, the question of the novel has just at this time become one of the most pressing and vital of all the practical problems which beset our moral and social economy.

The novel — what *we* call the novel — is a new invention. It is customary to date the first English novel with Richardson in 1740; and just as it has been impossible to confine other great inventions to the service of virtue — for the thief can send a telegram to his pal as easily as the sick man to his doctor, and the locomotive spins along no less merrily because ten car-loads of rascals may be profiting by its speed — so vice as well as virtue has availed itself of the novel-form, and we have such spectacles as Scott and Dickens and Eliot and Macdonald using this means to purify the air in one place while Zola in another applies the very same means to defiling the whole earth and slandering all humanity under the sacred names of "naturalism," of "science," of "physiology." Now I need not waste time in descanting before this audience upon the spread of the novel among all classes of modern readers : while I have been writing this, a well-considered paper on "Fiction in our Public Libraries" has appeared in the current *International Review* which, among many suggestive statements, declares that out of pretty nearly five millions (4,872,595) of volumes circulated in five years by the Boston Public Library nearly four millions (3,824,938), that is about four-fifths, were classed as "Juveniles and Fiction;" and — merely mentioning the strength which these figures gain when considered along with the fact that they represent the reading of a people supposed to be more "solid" in literary matter than any other in the country — if we inquire into the proportion at Baltimore, I fancy I have only to hold up this copy of James's *The American*, which I borrowed the other day from the Mercantile Library, and which I think I may say, after considerable rummaging about the books of that institution, certainly bears more marks of "circulation" than any solid book in it. In short, as a people, the novel is educating us. Thus we cannot take any final or secure solace in the discipline and system of our schools and universities until we have also learned to regulate this fascinating universal teacher which has taken such hold upon all minds, from the gravest scholar down to the boot-black shivering on the windy street corner over his dime-novel,— this educator whose principles are fastening themselves upon your boy's mind so that long after he has forgotten his *amo* and his *tupto* they will be controlling his relations to his fellowmen and determining his happiness for life.

But we can take no really effective action upon this matter until we understand precisely what the novel is and means; and it is therefore with the additional pleasure of stimulating you to systematize and extend your views upon a living issue which demands your opinion, that I now invite you to enter with me without further preliminary upon a series of studies in which it is proposed, first, to inquire what is that special relation of the novel to the modern man by virtue of which it has become a paramount literary form, and, secondly, to illustrate this abstract inquiry, when completed, by some concrete readings in the greatest of modern English novelists.

In the course of this inquiry I shall be called on to bring before you some of the very largest conceptions of which the mind is capable, and inasmuch as several of the minor demonstrations will begin somewhat remotely from the novel, it will save me many details which would be otherwise necessary if I indicate in a dozen words the four special lines of development along one or other of which I shall be always travelling.

My first line will concern itself with the enormous
growth in the personality of man which our time reveals
when compared for instance with the time of Æschylus.
I shall insist with the utmost reverence that between
every human being and every other human being exists
a radical, unaccountable, inevitable difference from birth ;
this sacred difference between man and man, by virtue
of which I am I and you are you, this marvellous
separation which we express by the terms " personal
identity," " self-hood," " me," — it is the unfolding of
this, I shall insist, which since the time of Æschylus
(say) has wrought all those stupendous changes in the
relation of man to God, to physical nature, and to his
fellow, which have culminated in the modern cultus.   I
can best bring before you the length and breadth of this
idea of modern personality as I conceive it, by stating it
in terms which have recently been made prominent and
familiar by the discussion as to the evolution of genius,
a phase of which appears in a very agreeable paper by
Mr. John Fiske in the current *Atlantic Monthly* on
" Sociology and Hero Worship."   Says Mr. Fiske, in a
certain part of this article, " Every species of animals or
plants consists of a great number of individuals which
are nearly but not exactly alike.   Each individual varies
slightly in one characteristic or another from a certain
type which expresses the average among all the individuals of the species. . . . Now the moth with his
proboscis twice as long as the average . . . is what we
call a spontaneous variation, and the Darwin or the
Helmholtz is what we call a ' genius ' ; and the analogy
between the two kinds of variation is obvious enough."
He proceeds in another place : " We cannot tell why a
given moth has a proboscis exactly an inch and a quarter
in length any more than we can tell why Shakspere was

a great dramatist," — there being absolutely no precedent conditions by which the most ardent evolutionist
could evolve William Shakspere, for example, from old
John Shakspere and his wife. "The social philosopher
must simply accept geniuses as data, just as Darwin accepts his spontaneous variations."

But now if we reflect upon this prodigious series of
spontaneous variations which I have called the sacred
difference between man and man, — this personality which
every father and mother are astonished at anew every
day when out of six children they perceive that each
one of the six, from the very earliest moment of activity,
has shown his own distinct individuality, differing wholly
from either parent, the child who most resembles the
parent physically often having a personality which
crosses that of the parent at the sharpest angles, — this
radical, indestructible, universal personality which entitles
every " me " to its privacy, which has in course of time
made the Englishman's house his castle, which has developed the Rights of Man, the American Republic, the
supreme prerogative of the woman to say whom she will
love, what man she shall marry, — this personality so precious that not even the miserablest wretch, with no other
possession but his personality, has ever been brought to
say he would be willing to exchange it entire for that of
the happiest being, — this personality which has brought
about that whereas in the time of Æschylus the common
man was simply a creature of the State, like a modern
corporation with rights and powers strictly limited by the
State's charter, now he is a genuine sovereign who makes
the State, a king as to every minutest particle of his individuality so long as that kinghood does not cross the
kinghood of his fellow, — when we reflect upon *this* awful
spontaneous variation of personality, this " mystery in us

which calls itself *I*" (as Thomas Carlyle has somewhere
called it), which makes every man scientifically a human
atom, yet an atom endowed above all other atoms with
the power to choose its own mode of motion, its own
combining equivalent, — when further we reflect upon the
relation of each human atom to each other human atom
and to the great Giver of personalities to these atoms,—
how each is indissolubly bound to each and to Him, and
yet how each is discretely parted and impassably separated from each and from Him by a gulf which is simply
no less deep than the width between the finite and the
infinite, — when we reflect, finally, that it is this simple,
indivisible, radical, indestructible, new force which each
child brings into the world under the name of its self
which controls the whole life of that child, so that its
path is always a resultant of its own individual force on
the one hand, and of the force of its surrounding circumstances on the other, — we are bound to confess, it seems
to me, that such spontaneous variations carry us upon a
plane of mystery very far above those merely unessential
variations of the offspring from the parental type in
physique, and even above those rare abnormal variations
which we call genius.

In meditating upon this matter, I found a short time
ago a poem of Tennyson's floating about the newspapers
which so beautifully and reverently chants this very sense
of personality, that I must read you a line or two from it.
I have since observed that much fun has been made of
this piece, and I have seen elaborate burlesques upon it.
But I think such an attitude could be possible only to
one who had not passed along this line of thought. At
any rate the poem seemed to me a very noble and rapturous hymn to the great Personality above us, acknowledging the mystery of our own personalities as finitely

dependent upon, and yet so infinitely divided from His Personality.

This poem is called *De Profundis — Two Greetings*, and is addressed to a new-born child. I have time to read only a line or two, here and there; you will find the whole poem much more satisfactory. Please observe, however, the ample comforting phrases and summaries with which Tennyson expresses the poetic idea of that personality which I have just tried to express from the point of view of science, of the evolutionist :

> " Out of the deep, my child, out of the deep,
> When all that was to be in all that was
> Whirl'd for a million æons thro' the vast
> Waste dawn of multitudinous-eddying light —
>
> .   .   .   .   .   .
>
> Thro' all this changing world of changeless law,
> And every phase of ever-heightening life
> .   .   .   .   .   Thou comest :
> :   .   .   .   .   .
>
> O, dear Spirit, half-lost
> In thine own shadows and this fleshly sign
> That thou art thou — who wailest, being born
> And banish'd into mystery and the pain
> Of this divisible-indivisible world,   .
>
> . . . Our mortal veil
> And shatter'd phantom of that infinite One
> Who made thee inconceivably thyself
> Out of his whole world — self and all in all —
> Live thou, and of the grain and husk, the grape
> And ivy berry choose ; and still depart
> From death to death thro' life and life, and find
>
> .   .   .   .
>
> This main miracle, that thou art thou,
> With power on thy own act and on the world.
>
> .   .   .   .
>
> We feel we are nothing — for all is Thou and in Thee ;
> We feel we are something — that also has come from Thee ;
> We are nothing, O Thou — but Thou wilt help us to be ;
> Hallowed be Thy name — Hallelujah ! "

I find some expressions here which give me great satisfaction : "The Infinite One who made thee inconceivably thyself, — this divisible-indivisible world, this main miracle that thou art thou," etc.

Now it is with this "main miracle," that I am I, and you, you — with this personality, that my first train of thought will busy itself; and I shall try to show, by several concrete illustrations from the lines and between the lines of Æschylus and Plato and the like writers compared with several modern writers, how feeble the sense and influence of it is in their time as contrasted with ours.

In my second line of development, I shall call your attention to what seems to me a very remarkable and suggestive fact : to-wit, that Physical Science, Music, and the Novel, all take their rise at the same time : of course, I mean what we moderns call science, music, and the novel.   For example, if we select — for the sake of well-known representative names — Sir Isaac Newton (1642), John Sebastian Bach (1685) and Samuel Richardson (1689), the first standing for the rise of modern science, the second for the rise of modern music, the third for the rise of the modern novel, and observe that these three men are born within fifty years of each other, we cannot fail to find ourselves in the midst of a thousand surprising suggestions and inferences.   For in our sweeping arc from Æschylus to the present time, fifty years subtend scarcely any space ; we may say these men are born together.   And here the word accident has no meaning. Time, progress, then, have no accidents.

In this second train of thought I shall endeavor to connect these phenomena with the principle of personality developed in the first train, and shall try to show that this science, music, and the novel, are flowerings-out of that principle in various directions ; for instance, each man, in this growth of personality, feeling himself in direct and personal relations with physical nature (not in relations obscured by the vague intermediary hamadryads and fauns of the Greek system), a general desire to know the exact truth about nature arises, and this desire carried to a certain enthusiasm in the nature of given men — behold the man of science ; a similar feeling of direct personal relation to the Unknown, acting similarly upon particular men, — behold the musician, and the ever-increasing tendency of the modern man to worship God in terms of music ; likewise, a similar feeling of direct personal relation to each individual member of humanity, high or low, rich or poor, acting similarly, gives us such a novel as the *Mill on the Floss*, for instance, where for a long time we find ourselves interested in two mere children — Tom and Maggie Tulliver — or such novels as those of Dickens and his fellow-host who have called upon our human relation to poor, unheroic people.

In my third train of thought I shall attempt to show that the increase of personalities thus going on has brought about such complexities of relation that the older forms of expression were inadequate to them ; and that the resulting necessity has developed the wonderfully free and elastic form of the modern novel out of the more rigid Greek drama, through the transition form of the Elizabethan drama.

And, fourthly, I shall offer copious readings from some of the most characteristic modern novels in illustration of the general principles thus brought forward.

Here, — as the old preacher Hugh Latimer grimly said in closing one of his powerful descriptions of future punishment, — you see your fare.

Permit me, then, to begin the execution of this plan

by bringing before you two matters which will be conveniently disposed of in the outset because they affect all
these four lines of thought in general, and because
I find the very vaguest ideas prevailing about them
among those whose special attention happens not to
have been called this way.

As to the first point : permit me to remind you how
lately these prose-forms have been developed in our literature as compared with the forms of verse.   Indeed,
abandoning the thought of any particular forms of prose,
consider for how long a time good English poetry was
written before any good English prose appears.   It is
historical that as far back as the seventh century Cædmon
is writing a strong English poem in an elaborate form of
verse.   Well-founded conjecture carries us back much
farther than this ; but without relying upon that, we have
clear knowledge that all along the time when *Beowulf*
and *The Wanderer* — to me one of the most artistic
and affecting of English poems — and *The Battle of
Maldon* are being written, all along the time when
Cædmon and Aldhelm and the somewhat mythical
Cynewulf are singing, formal poetry or verse has reached
a high stage of artistic development.   But not only so :
after the Norman change is consummated and our language has fairly assimilated that tributary stock of words
and ideas and influences, the poetic advance, the
development of verse, goes steadily on.   If you examine
the remains of our lyric poetry written along in the
twelfth and thirteenth centuries — short and unstudied
little songs as many of them are, songs which come
upon us out of that obscure period like brief little bird-
calls from a thick-leaved wood — if, I say, we examine
these songs, written as many of them are by nobody in
particular, it is impossible not to believe that a great

mass of poetry, some of which must have been very beautiful, was written in the two hundred years just before Chaucer, and that an extremely small proportion of it can have come down to us.

But, in all this period, where is the piece of English prose that corresponds with *The Wanderer*, or with the daintier Cuckoo-Song of the early twelfth century? In point of fact, we cannot say that even the conception of an artistic prose has occurred to English literary endeavor until long after Chaucer. King Alfred's Translations, the *English Chronicle*, the *Homilies* of Ælfric, are simple and clear enough; and, coming down later, the English Bible set forth by Wyclif and his contemporaries. Wyclif's own sermons and tracts, and Mandeville's account of his travels are effective enough, each to its own end. But in all these the form is so far overridden by the direct pressing purpose, either didactic or educational, that — with exceptions I cannot now specify in favor of the Wyclif Bible — I can find none of them in which the prose seems controlled by considerations of beauty. Perhaps the most curious and interesting proof I could adduce of the obliviousness of even the most artistic Englishmen in this time to the possibility of a melodious and uncloying English prose, is the prose work of Chaucer. While, so far as concerns the mere music of verse, I cannot call Chaucer a great artist, yet he was the greatest of his time; from him, therefore, we have the right to expect the best craftsmanship in words; for all fine prose depends as much upon its rhythms and correlated proportions as fine verse, and, now, since we have an art of prose, it is a perfect test of the real excellence of a poet in verse to try his corresponding excellence in prose. But in Chaucer's time there is no art of English prose. Listen, for example, to

the opening lines of that one of Chaucer's Canterbury
series which he calls *The Parson's Tale*, and which is in
prose throughout.   It happens very patly to my present
discussion that in the Prologue to this tale some conversation occurs which reveals to us quite clearly a
current idea of Chaucer's time as to the proper distinction between prose and verse — or " rym " — and as to the
functions and subject-matter peculiarly belonging to each
of these forms ; and, for that reason, let me preface my
quotation from *The Parson's Tale* with a bit of it.   As
the Canterbury Pilgrims are jogging merrily along,
presently it appears that but one more tale is needed
to carry out the original proposition, and so the ever-
important Host calls on the Parson for it, as follows :

> " As we were entryng at a thropes ende,
> For while our Host, as he was wont to gye,
> As in this caas, our joly compaignye,
> Sayd in this wise : ' Lordyngs, everichoon,
> Now lakketh us no tales moo than oon,' " etc.,

and turning to the Parson,

> " ' Sir Prest,' quod he, ' artow a vicory?
> Or artow a persoun ? Say soth, by thy fay,
> Be what thou be, *ne* breke *thou* nat oure play ;
> For every man, save thou, hath told his tale.
> Unbocle and schew us what is in thy male.
> .   .   .   .   .   .
> Tel us a fable anoon, for cokkes boones ! ' "

Whereupon the steadfast Parson proceeds to assure the
company that whatever he may have in his male [wallet]
there is none of your light-minded and fictitious verse
in it ; nothing but grave and reverend prose.

> " This Persoun him answerede al at oones :
> ' Thow getist fable noon i-told for me ; ' "

(And you will presently observe that " fable " in the Parson's mind means very much the same with verse or poetry, and that the whole business of fiction — that same fiction which has now come to occupy such a command-ing plane with us moderns, and which we are to study with such reverence under its form of the novel — implies downright lying and wickedness.)

> " ' Thow getist fable noon i-told for me ;
> For Poul, that writeth unto Timothé,
> Repreveth hem that weyveth sothfastnesse,
> And tellen fables and such wrecchednesse,
> . . . .
> For which I say, if that yow lust to hiere
> Moralité and vertuous matiere,' "

(that is — as we shall presently see — prose)

> " ' And thanne that ye will yive me audience,
> I wol ful fayne at Cristis reverence,
> Do yow plesaunce leful, as I can.
> But trusteth wel, I am a Suthern man,
> I can nat geste, rum, ram, ruf, by letter,
> Ne, God wot, rym hold I but litel better;
> And therfor, if yow lust, I wol not glose,
> I wol yow telle a mery tale in prose.' "

. Here our honest Parson, (and he was honest : I am frightfully tempted to go clean away from my path and read that heart-filling description of him which Chaucer gives in the general Prologue to the *Canterbury Tales*) sweeps away the whole literature of verse and of fiction with the one contemptuous word " glose " — by which he seems to mean a sort of shame-faced lying all the more pitiful because done in verse — and sets up prose as the proper vehicle for " moralité and vertuous matiere."

With this idea of the function of prose, you will not be surprised to find, as I read these opening sentences

of the Parson's so-called Tale, that the style is rigidly
sententious, and that the movement of the whole is like
that of a long string of proverbs, which of course presently becomes intolerably droning and wearisome.   The
Parson begins :

" Many ben the weyes espirituels that leden folk to oure
Lord Ihesu Crist, and to the regne of glorie ; of whiche
weyes ther is a ful noble wey, which may not faile to no
man ne to womman, that thurgh synne hath mysgon fro
the righte wey of Jerusalem celestial ; and this wey is
cleped penitence.   Of which men schulden gladly herken
and enquere with al here herte, to wyte, what is penitence, and whens it is cleped penitence?   And in what
maner and in how many maneres been the acciones or
workynges of penaunce, and how many spieces ben of
penitences, and whiche thinges apperteynen and byhoven
to penitence, and whiche thinges destourben penitence."

In reading page after page of this bagpipe-bass, one
has to remember strenuously all the moral beauty of the
Parson's character in order to forgive the droning ugliness
of his prose.   Nothing could better realize the description which Tennyson's Northern Farmer gives of *his*
parson's manner of preaching and the effect thereof :

> " An' I hallus coomed to 's choorch afoor moy Sally wur deäd,
> An' 'eärd um a bummin' awaäy loike a buzzard-clock ower
>   my 'eäd.
> An' I niver knaw'd whot a meän'd, but I thowt a 'ad summut
>   to saäy,
> An' I thowt a said whot a owt to 'a said an' I coomed awaäy."

It must be said, however, in justice to Chaucer, that
he writes better prose than this when he really sets about
telling a tale.   What the Parson calls his " Tale " turns
out — to the huge disgust, I suspect, of several other pilgrims besides the Host — to be nothing more than a

homily or sermon, in which the propositions about penitence, with many minor heads and sub-divisions, are un-
sparingly developed to the bitter end.   But in the *Tale
of Melibœus* his inimitable faculty of story-telling comes
to his aid and determines his sentences to a little more
variety and picturesqueness, though the sentions still
predominates.   Here, for example, is a bit of dialogue
between Melibœus and his wife, which I selected because, over and above its applications here as early prose,
we shall find it particularly suggestive presently when we
come to compare it with some dialogue in George Eliot's
Adam Bede where the conversation is very much upon
the same topic.

It seems that Melibœus, being still a young man, goes
away into the fields, leaving his wife Prudence and his
daughter — whose name some of the texts give in its
Greek form as Sophia, while others quaintly enough
call her Sapience, translating the Greek into Latin — in
the house.   Thereupon " three of his olde foos " (says
Chaucer) " have it espyed, and setten laddres to the
walles of his hous, and by the wyndowes ben entred, and
beetyn his wyf, and woundid his daughter with fyve
mortal woundes, in fyve sondry places, that is to sayn, in
here feet, in her handes, in here eres, in her nose, and in
here mouth ; and lafte her for deed, and went away."
Melibœus assembles a great council of his friends, and
these advise him to make war, with an interminable dull
succession of sentious maxims and quotations which
would surely have maddened a modern person to such
a degree that he would have incontinently levied war
upon his friends as well as his enemies.   But after awhile
Dame Prudence modestly advises against the war.
"'This Melibœus answerde unto his wyf Prudence : ' I
purpose not,' quod he, ' to werke by thy counseil, for

many causes and resouns; for certes every wight wolde holde me thanne a fool, this is to sayn, if I for thy counseil wolde chaunge things that affirmed ben by so many wise.

"'Secondly, I say that alle wommen be wikked, and noon good of hem alle. For of a thousand men, saith Solomon, I fond oon good man; but certes of alle wommen good womman fond I never noon. And also certes, if I governede me by thy counseil, it schulde seme that I hadde yiven to the over me the maistry; and God forbid er it so were. For Ihesus Syrac saith,'" etc., etc.

You observe how, although this is dialogue between man and wife, the prose nevertheless tends to the sententious, and every remark must be supported with some dry old maxim or epigrammatic saw. Observe too, by the way, — and we shall find this point most suggestive in studying the modern dialogue in George Eliot's novels, etc. — that there is absolutely no individuality or personality in the talk; Meliboeus drones along exactly as his friends do, and his wife quotes old authoritative saws just as he does. But Dame Prudence replies, — and all those who are acquainted with the pungent Mrs. Poyser in George Eliot's *Adam Bede* will congratulate Meliboeus that his foregoing sentiments concerning woman were uttered five hundred years before that lady's tongue began to wag, — "When Dame Prudence, ful debonerly and with gret pacience, hadde herd al that hir housbande likede for to seye, thanne axede sche of him licence for to speke, and sayde in this wise: 'My Lord,' quod sche, 'as to your firste resoun, certes it may lightly be answered; for I say it is no foly to chaunge counsel whan the thing is chaungid, or elles whan the thing semeth otherwise than it was biforn.'" This very wise position she supports with argument and authority, and then goes on boldly to attack not exactly Solomon's wisdom but the number of data from which he drew it : " ' And though that Solomon say he fond never good womman, it fol- with nought therfore that alle wommen ben wicked : for though that *he* fonde noone goode wommen, certes many another man hath founden many a womman ful goode and trewe : ' " (intimating, what is doubtless true, that the finding of a good womam depends largely on the kind of man who is looking for her).

After many other quite logical replies to all of Meli- bœus' positions Dame Prudence closes with the follow- ing argument : " ' And moreover, whan oure Lord hadde creat Adam oure forme fader, he sayde in this wise : Hit is not goode to be a man aloone ; makes we to him an help semblable to himself. Here may ye se that if that a womman were not good, and hir counseil good and profytable, oure Lord God of heven wolde neither have wrought hem, ne called hem help of man, but rather con- fusioun of man. And ther sayde oones a clerk in tuo versus, What is better than gold ? Jasper. And what is better than jasper ? Wisedom. And what is better than wisedom ? Womman. And what is better than a good womman ? No thing.' "

When we presently come to contrast this little scene between man and wife in what may fairly be called the nearest approach to the modern novel that can be found before the fifteenth century, we shall find a surprising number of particulars, besides the unmusical tendency to run into the sententious or proverbial form, in which the modern mode of thought differs from that of the old writer from whom Chaucer got his Melibœus.

This sententious monotune (if I may coin a word) of the prose, when falling upon a modern ear, gives almost a comical tang even to the gravest utterances of the

period. For example, here are the opening lines of a
fragment of prose from a MS. in the Cambridge
University Library, reprinted by the early English Text
Society in the issue for 1870. It is good, pithy reading,
too. It is called *The Six Wise Masters' Speech of
Tribulation*.

Observe that the first sentence, though purely in the
way of narration, is just as sententious in form as the
graver proverbs of each master that follow.

It begins :

" Here begynyth A shorte extracte, and tellyth how þar
ware sex masterys assemblede, ande eche one askede oþer
quhat thing þai sholde spek of gode, and all þei war acordet
to spek of tribulacoun.

" The fyrste master seyde, þat if ony thing hade bene mor
better to ony man lewynge in this werlde þan tribulacoun,
god wald haue gewyne it to his sone. But he sey wyell that
thar was no better, and tharfor he gawe it hum, and mayde
hume to soffer moste in this wrechede worlde than euer dyde
ony man, or euermore shall.

" The secunde master seyde, þat if þar wer ony man þat
mycht be wyth-out spote of sine, as god was, and mycht
levyn bodely þirty yheris wyth-out mete, ande also were
dewote in preyinge at he mycht speke wyth angele in þe
erth, as dyde mary magdalene, yit mycht he not deserve in
þat lyffe so gret meyde as A man deservith in suffring of A
lytyll tribulacoun.

" The threde master seyde, þat if the moder of gode and all
the halowys of hewyn preyd for a man, þei should not get so
gret meyde as he should hymselfe be meknes and suffryng
of tribulacoun."

Now asking you, as I pass, to remember that I have
selected this extract, like the others, with the further
purpose of presently contrasting the substance of it with
modern utterances, as well as the form which now

mainly concerns us — if we cut short this search after artistic prose in our earlier literature, and come down at once to the very earliest sign of a true feeling for the musical movement of prose sentences, we are met by the fact, which I hope to show is full of fruitful suggestions upon our present studies, that the art of English prose is at least eight hundred years younger than the art of English verse. For in coming down our literature from Cædmon — whom, in some conflict of dates, we can safely place at 670 — the very first writer I find who shows a sense of the rhythmical flow and gracious music of which our prose is so richly capable is Sir Thomas Malory; and his one work, *The History of King Arthur and His Knights of the Round Table*, dates 1469-70, exactly eight hundred years after Cædmon's poetic outburst.

Recalling our extracts just read, and remembering how ungainly and awkward was the port of their sentences, listen for a moment to a few lines from Sir Thomas Malory. I think the most unmusical ear, the most cursory attention, cannot fail to discern immediately how much more flowing and smooth is the movement of this. I read from the fifth chapter of King Arthur.

"And King Arthur was passing wroth for the hurt of Sir Griflet. And by and by he commanded a man of his chamber that his best horse and armor be without the city on to-morrow-day. Right so in the morning he met with his man and his horse, and so mounted up and dressed his shield, and took his spear, and bade his chamberlain tarry there till he came again."

Presently he meets Merlin and they go on together.

"So, as they went thus talking, they came to the fountain and the rich pavilion by it. Then King Arthur was ware

where a knight sat all armed in a chair. ' Sir Knight,' said
King Arthur, ' for what cause abidest thou here ? that there
may no knight ride this way but if he do joust with thee ? '
said the King. ' I rede thee leave that custom,' said King
Arthur.

"' This custom,' said the knight, ' have I used and will
use, maugre who saith nay; and who is grieved with my
custom, let him amend it that will.'

"' I will amend it,' said King Arthur. ' And I shall defend
it,' said the knight."

(Observe *will* and *shall* here.)

Here, you observe, not only is there musical flow of
single sentences, but one sentence remembers another
and proportions itself thereto — if the last was long, this
is shorter or longer, and if one calls for a certain tune,
the next calls for a different tune — and we have not only
grace but variety.   In this variety may be found an easy
test of artistic prose.   If you try to read two hundred
lines of Chaucer's *Melibœus* or his *Parson's Tale* aloud,
you are presently oppressed with a sense of bagpipish-
ness in your own voice which becomes intolerable ; but
you can read Malory's *King Arthur* aloud from beginning to end with a never-cloying sense of proportion
and rhythmic flow.

I wish I had time to demonstrate minutely how much
of the relish of all fine prose is due to the arrangement
of the sentences in such a way that consecutive sentences do not call for the same tune : for example, if
one sentence is sharp antithesis — you know the well-
marked speech tune of an antithesis, "do you mean *this*
book, or do you mean *that* book ? " — you must be careful in the next sentences to vary the tune from that of
the antithesis.

In the prose I read you from Chaucer and from the

old manuscript, a large part of the intolerableness is due to the fact that nearly every sentence involves the tune of an aphorism or proverb, and the iteration of the same pitch-successions in the voice presently becomes wearisome. This fault — of the succession of antithetic ideas so that the voice becomes weary of repeating the same contrariety of accents — I can illustrate very strikingly in a letter which I happen to remember of Queen Elizabeth, whom I have found to be a great sinner against good prose in this particular.

Here is part of a letter from her to King Edward VI. concerning a portrait of herself which it seems the king had desired. (Italicized words represent antithetic accents.)

" Like as the rich man that daily gathereth *riches* to *riches*, and to *one* bag of money layeth a great sort till it come to *infinite;* so methinks your majesty, not being sufficed with so many benefits and gentleness shewed to me afore this time, doth now increase them in *asking* and *desiring* where you may *bid* and *command*, requiring a thing not worthy the desiring for *itself*, but *made* worthy for your highness' *request*. My picture I mean : in which, if the *inward* good mind toward your grace might as well be *declared*, as the *outward* face and countenance shall be *seen*, I would not have *tarried* the commandment but *prevented* it, nor have been the *last* to *grant*, but the *first* to *offer* it."

And so on. You observe here into what a sing-song the voice must fall : if you abstract the words, and say over the tune, it is continually : tum-ty-ty tum-ty-ty tum-ty ; tum-ty-ty tum-ty-ty tum-ty.

I wish also that it lay within my province to pass on and show the gradual development of English prose, through Sir Thomas More, Lord Berners, and Roger Ascham, whom we may assign to the earlier half of the sixteenth century, until it reaches a great and beautiful artistic stage in the prose of Fuller, of Hooker, and of Jeremy Taylor.

But the fact which I propose to use as throwing light on the novel is simply the lateness of English prose as compared with English verse; and we have already sufficiently seen that the rise of our prose must be dated at least eight centuries after that of our formal poetry.

But having established the fact that English prose is so much later in development than English verse, the point that I wish to make in this connection now requires me to go on and ask why this is so?

Without the time to adduce supporting facts from other literatures, and indeed wholly unable to go into elaborate proof, let me say at once that upon examining the matter it seems probable that the whole earlier speech of man must have been rhythmical, and that in point of fact we began with verse which is much simpler in rhythm than any prose, and that we departed from this regular rhythmic utterance into more and more complex utterance just according as the advance of complexity in language and feeling required the freer forms of prose.

To adduce a single consideration leading toward this view: reflect for a moment that the very breath of every man necessarily divides off his words into rhythmic periods: the average rate of a man's breath being 17 to 20 respirations in a minute. Taking the faster rate as the more probable one in speaking, the man would, from the periodic necessity of refilling the lungs, divide his words into twenty groups, equal in time, every minute, and if these syllables were equally pronounced at, say, about the rate of 200 a minute, we should have ten syllables in each group, each ten syllables occupying (in the aggregate at least) the same time with any other ten syllables, that is, the time of one breath.

But this is just the rhythm of our English blank verse, in essential type : ten syllables to the line or group : and our primitive talker is speaking in the true English heroic rhythm. Thus it may be that our dear friend M. Jourdain was not so far wrong after all in his astonishment at finding that he had been speaking prose all his life : it would seem at any rate that man, the race, has not been speaking prose all *his* life.

II

PERHAPS I ought here carefully to state that in propounding the idea that the whole common speech of early man may have been rhythmical through the operation of uniformity of syllables and periodicity of breath, and that for this reason prosĕ, which is practically verse of a very complex rhythm, was naturally a later development; in propounding this idea, I say, I do not mean to declare that the prehistoric man, after a hard day's work on a flint arrow-head at his stone-quarry, would dance back to his dwelling in the most beautiful rhythmic figures, would lay down his palæolithic axe to a slow song, and, striking an operatic attitude, would call out to his wife to leave off fishing in the stream and bring him a stone mug of water — all in a most sublime and impassioned flight of poetry. What I do mean to say is that if the prehistoric man's syllables were uniform, and his breath periodic, then the rhythmical results described would follow. Here let me at once illustrate this, and advance a step towards my final point in this connection, by reminding you how easily the most commonplace utterances in modern English, particularly when couched mainly in words of one syllable, fall into quite respectable verse-rhythms. I might illustrate this, but Dr. Samuel Johnson has already done it for me : —
" I put my hat upon my head and walked into the Strand, and there I met another man whose hat was in his hand."
We have only to arrange this in proper form in order to

see that it is a stanza of verse quite perfect as to all
technical requirement.

> " I put my hat upon my head,
>   And walked into the Strand,
>   And there I met another man,
>   Whose hat was in his hand."

Now let me ask you to observe precisely what
happens when by adding words here and there in this
verse we more and more obscure its verse form and
bring out its prose form. Suppose for example we
here write " hastily," and here " rushed forth," and here
"encountered," and here " hanging," so as to make it read :

> " I hastily put my hat upon my head,
>   And rushed forth into the Strand,
>   And there I encountered another man,
>   Whose hat was hanging in his hand."

Here we have made unmitigated prose, but how?
Remembering that the original verse was in iambic 4's
and 3's,

$$\breve{~}\underline{~}\ \breve{~}\underline{~}\ \breve{~}\underline{~}\ \breve{~}\underline{~}$$
I put | my hat | up-on | my head | ,

— by putting in the word "hastily " in the first line,
we have not destroyed the rhythm : we still have the
rhythmic sequence, " my hat upon my head," unchanged ;
but we have merely added another brief rhythmus —
namely that of the word " hastily," which we may call a
modern or logaœdic dactyl (hastily). That is to say :
instead now of leaving our first line all iambic, we have
varied that rhythmus with another ; and in so doing have
converted our verse into prose. Similarly in the second
line, " rushed forth," which an English tongue would here
deliver as a spondee — rushed forth | — varies the rhythm
by this spondaic intervention, but still leaves us the orig-

inal rhythmic cluster, "into the Strand." So of the other introduced words, "encountered" and "hanging": each has its own rhythm — for an English tongue always gives these words with definite time-relations between the syllables, that is, in rhythm. Therefore, in order to make prose out of this verse, we have not destroyed the rhythms: we have added to them. We have not made it formless: we have made it contain more forms.

Now in this analysis, which I have tried to bring to its very simplest terms, I have presented what seems to me the true genesis of prose, and have set up a distinction which, though it may appear abstract and insignificant at present, we shall presently see lies at the bottom of some most remarkable and pernicious fallacies concerning literature. That distinction is: that the relation of prose to verse is not the relation of the formless to the formal: it is the relation of more forms to fewer forms. It is this relation which makes prose a freer form than verse.

When we are writing in verse, if we have started the line with an iambus (say) then our next words or syllables must make an iambus, and we are confined to that form; but if in prose, our next word need not be an iambus because the first was, but may be any one of several possible rhythmic forms: thus, while in verse we must use one form, in prose we may use many forms: and just to the extent of these possible forms is prose freer than verse. We shall find occasion presently to remember that prose is freer than verse, not because prose is formless while verse is formal, but because any given sequence of prose has more forms in it than a sequence of verse.

Here — reserving to a later place the special application of all this to the novel — I have brought my first general point to a stage where it constitutes the basis of the second one. You have already heard much of "forms" — of the verse-form, the prose-form, of form in art, and the like. Now, in the course of a considerable experience in what Shakspere sadly calls "public means," I have found no matter upon which wider or more harmful misconceptions exist among people of culture, and particularly among us Americans, than this matter of the true function of form in art, of the true relation of science — which we may call the knowledge of forms — to art, and most especially of these functions and relations in literary art. These misconceptions have flowered out into widely different shapes.

In one direction, for example, we find a large number of timorous souls who believe that science, in explaining everything — as they singularly fancy — will destroy the possibility of poetry, of the novel, in short of all works of the imagination: the idea seeming to be that the imagination always requires the hall of life to be darkened before it display its magic, like the modern spiritualistic séance-givers who can do nothing with the rope-tying and the guitars unless the lights are put out.

Another form of the same misconception goes pre-cisely to the opposite extreme, and declares that the advance of science with its incidents is going to give a great new revolutionized democratic literature which will wear a slouch hat, and have its shirt open at the bosom, and generally riot in a complete independence of form.

And finally — to mention no more than a third phase — we may consider the original misconception to have reached a climax which is at once absurd and infernal in a professedly philosophical work called *Le Roman Expérimental*, recently published by M. Emile Zola, gravely defending his peculiar novels as the records of scientific experiments and declaring that the whole field of imaginative effort must follow his lead.

Now if any of these beliefs are true we are wickedly wasting our time here in studying the novel — at least any other novels except M. Zola's — and we ought to look to ourselves. Seriously, I do not believe I could render you a greater service than by here arraying such contribution as I can make towards some firm, clear and pious conceptions as to this matter of form, of science, in art, before briefly considering these three concrete errors I have enumerated — to wit, the belief (1) that science will destroy all poetry, all novel-writing and all imaginative work generally; (2) that science (as Walt Whitman would have it) will simply destroy the old imaginative products and build up a new formless sort of imaginative product in its stead; and (3) that science will absorb into itself all imaginative effort (as Zola believes) so that every novel will be merely the plain unvarnished record of a scientific experiment in passion. Let me submit two or three principles whose steady light will leave, it seems to me, but little space for perplexity as to these diverse claims.

Start, then, in the first place, with a definite recalling to yourself of the province of form throughout our whole daily life. Here we find a striking consensus, at least in spirit, between the deliverances of the sternest science and of the straitest orthodoxy. The latter on the one hand tells us that in the beginning the earth was without form and void; and it is only after the earth is formulated — after the various forms of the lights, of land and water, bird, fish and man appear — it is only then that life and use and art and relation and religion become possible. What we call the creation, therefore, is not the making out of nothing, but it is the giving of form to a something which, though existing, existed to no purpose because it had no form.

On the other hand, the widest generalizations of science bring us practically to the same view. Science would seem fairly to have reduced all this host of phenomena which we call the world into a congeries of motions in many forms. What we know by our senses is simply such forms of these motions as our senses have a correlated capacity for. The atoms of this substance, moving in orbits too narrow for human vision, impress my sense with a certain property which I call hardness or resistance, this " hardness " being simply our name for one form of atom-motion when impressing itself on the human sense. So color, shape, &c. ; these are our names representing a correlation between certain other forms of motion and our senses.

Regarding the whole universe thus as a great congeries of forms of motion, we may now go further and make for ourselves a scientific and useful generalization, reducing a great number of facts to a convenient common denominator by considering that Science is the knowledge of these forms, that Art is the creation of beautiful forms, that Religion is the faith in the infinite Form-giver and in that infinity of forms which many things lead us to believe as existing, but existing beyond any present correlative capacities of our senses, — and finally that Life is the control of all these forms to the satisfaction of our human needs.

And now advancing a step : when we remember how all accounts, the scientific, the religious, the historical, agree that the progress of things is from chaos or formlessness to form, — and, as we saw in the case of verse and prose, — afterwards from the one-formed to the many-formed, we are not disturbed by any shouts, how-

ever stentorian, of a progress that professes to be winning freedom by substituting formlessness for form : we
know that the ages are rolling the other way, — who
shall stop those wheels? We know that what they really
do who profess to substitute formlessness for form is to
substitute a bad form for a good one, or an ugly form
for a beautiful one. Do not dream of getting rid of
form : your most cutting stroke at it but gives us two
forms for one. For, in a sense which adds additional
reverence to the original meaning of those words, we
may devoutly say that in form we live and move and
have our being. How strange, then, the furtive apprehension of danger lying behind too much knowledge of
form, too much technic, which one is amazed to find
prevailing so greatly in our own country.

But, advancing a further step from the particular consideration of science as the knowledge of forms, let us
come to the fact that as all art is a congeries of forms,
each art must have its own peculiar science : and always
we have, in a true sense, the art of an art and the science
of that art. For example : correlative to the art of
music we have the general science of music, which
indeed consists of several quite separate sciences. If a
man desire to become a musical composer, he is absolutely obliged to learn (1) the science of Musical Form,
(2) the science of Harmony, and (3) the science of
Orchestration or Instrumentation.

The science of musical form concerns this sort of
matter, for instance. A symphony has generally four
great divisions, called movements, separated usually from
each other by a considerable pause. Each of these
movements has a law of formation : it consists of two
main subjects, or melodies, and a modulation-part. The
sequence of these subjects, the method of varying them

by causing now one and now another of the instruments to come forward and play the subject in hand
while subordinate parts are assigned to the others, the
interplay of the two subjects in the modulation-part,
— all this is the subject-matter of a science which every
composer must laboriously learn.

But again : he must learn the great science of harmony, and of that wonderful tonality which has caused
our music to be practically a different art from what preceding ages called music : this science of harmony having its own body of classifications and formulated laws
just as the science of geology has, and a voluminous
literature of its own.   Again, he must painfully learn the
range and capacities of each orchestral instrument, — lest
he write passages for the violin which no violin can play,
&c., — and further, the particular ideas which seem to
associate themselves with the tone-color of each instrument, as the idea of women's voices with the clarinet,
the idea of tenderness and childlikeness with the oboe,
and so on.   This is not all : the musical composer may
indeed write a symphony if he has these three sciences
of music well in hand ; but a fourth science of music,
namely, the physics of music, or musical acoustics, has
now grown to such an extent that every composer will
find himself lame without a knowledge of it.

And so the art of painting has its correlative science
of painting, involving laws of optics, and of form ; the art
of sculpture, its correlative science of sculpture, involving
the science of human anatomy, &c. ; and each one of the
literary arts has its correlative science — the art of verse
its science of verse, the art of prose its science of prose.
Lastly, we all know that no amount of genius will supply
the lack of science in art.   Phidias may be all afire with
the conception of Jove, but unless he is a scientific man

to the extent of a knowledge of anatomy, he is no better
artist than Strephon who cannot mould the handle of a
goblet.   What is Beethoven's genius until Beethoven has
become a scientific man to the extent of knowing the
sciences of Musical Form, of Orchestration, and of
Harmony?

But now if I go on and ask what would be the worth
of Shakspere's genius unless he were a scientific man to
the extent of knowing the science of English verse, or
what would be George Eliot's genius unless she knew
the science of English prose or the science of novel-
writing, a sort of doubtful stir arises, and it would seem
as if a suspicion of some vague esoteric difference between the relation of the literary arts to their correlative
sciences and the relation of other arts to their correlative
sciences influenced the general mind.

I am so unwilling you should think me here fighting
a mere man of straw who has been arranged with a view
to the convenience of knocking him down: and I find
such mournful evidences of the complete misconception
of form, of literary science, in our literature : that, with a
reluctance which every one will understand, I am going
to draw upon a personal experience, to show the extent
of that misconception.

Some of you may remember that a part of the course
of lectures which your present lecturer delivered here
last year were afterwards published in book-form, under
the title of *The Science of English Verse*.   Happening
in the publisher's office some time afterwards, I was
asked if I would care to see the newspaper notices and
criticisms of the book, whereof the publishers had collected a great bundle.   Most curious to see if some
previous ideas I had formed as to the general relation
between literary art and science would be confirmed, I

read these notices with great interest. Not only were my suspicions confirmed : but it is perfectly fair to say that nine out of ten, even of those which most generously treated the book in hand, treated it upon the general theory that a work on the science of verse must necessarily be a collection of rules for making verses. Now not one of these writers would have treated a work on the science of geology as a collection of rules for making rocks ; or a work on the science of anatomy as a collection of rules for making bones or for procuring cadavers. In point of fact, a book of rules for making verses might very well be written, but then it would be a hand-book of the art of verse, and would take the whole science of verse for granted, — like an instruction-book for the piano, or the like.

If we should find the whole critical body of a continent treating (say) Prof. Huxley's late work on the crayfish as really a cookery-book, intended to spread intelligent ideas upon the best methods of preparing shell-fish for the table, we should certainly suspect something wrong : but this is precisely parallel with the mistake already mentioned.

But even when the functions of form, of science, in literary art have been comprehended, one is amazed to find among literary artists themselves a certain apprehension of danger in knowing too much of the forms of art. A valued friend who has won a considerable place in contemporary authorship, in writing me not long ago, said, after much abstract and impersonal admission of a possible science of verse — in the way that one admits there may be griffins but feels no great concern about it — "*as for me I would rather continue to write verse from pure instinct.*"

This fallacy — of supposing that we do a thing by instinct simply because we learned to do it unsystematic-

ally and without formal teaching — seems a curious
enough climax to the misconceptions of literary science.
You have only to reflect a moment in order to see that
not a single line of verse was ever written by instinct
alone since the world began.   For — to go no farther —
the most poetically-instinctive child is obliged at least to
learn the science of language — the practical relation of
noun and verb and connective — before the crudest line of
verse can be written ; and since no child talks by instinct,
since every child has to learn from others every word it
uses, — with an amount of diligence and of study which
is really stupendous when we think of it — what wild absurdity to forget these years passed by the child in learning even the rudiments of the science of language which
must be well in hand, mind you, before even the rudiments of the science of verse can be learned — what wild
absurdity to fancy that one is writing verse by instinct
when even the language of verse, far from being instinctive, had to be painfully, if unsystematically, learned as
a science.

Once, for all, remembering the dignity of form as we
have traced it, remembering the relations of Science as
the knowledge of forms, of Art as the creator of beautiful
forms, of Religion as the aspiration towards unknown
forms and the unknown Form-giver, let us abandon this
unworthy attitude towards form, towards science, towards
technic, in literary art, which has so long sapped our
literary endeavor.

The writer of verse is afraid of having too much form,
of having too much technic ; he dreads it will interfere
with his spontaneity.   No more decisive confession of
weakness can be made.   It is only cleverness and small
talent which is afraid of its spontaneity ; the genius, the
great artist, is forever ravenous after new forms, after

technic; he will follow you to the ends of the earth if you will enlarge his artistic science, if you will give him a fresh form. For indeed genius, the great artist, never works in the frantic vein vulgarly supposed; a large part of the work of the poet, for example, is selective: a dozen ideas in a dozen forms throng to his brain at once, he must choose the best; even in the extremest heat and sublimity of his *raptus* he must preserve a god-like calm, and order thus and so, and keep the rule so that he shall to the end be master of his art and not be mastered by his art.

Charlotte Cushman used often to tell me that when she was, as the phrase is, carried out of herself, she never acted well: she must have her inspiration, she must be in a true *raptus*, but the *raptus* must be well in hand, and she must retain the consciousness, at once sublime and practical, of every act.

There is an old aphorism — it is twelve hundred years old — which covers all this ground of the importance of technic, of science, in the literary art, with such completeness and compactness that it always affects me like a poem. It was uttered, indeed, by a poet, — and a rare one he must have been, — an old Armorican named Hervé, of whom all manner of beautiful stories have survived. This aphorism is: "He who will not answer to the rudder, must answer to the rocks." If any of you have read that wonderful description of shipwreck on these same Armorican rocks which occurs in the autobiography of Millet, the painter, and which was recently quoted in a number of *Scribner's Magazine*, you can realize that one who lived in that old Armorica — the modern Brittany from which Millet comes — knew full well what it meant to answer to the rocks.

Now it is precisely this form, this science, this technic,

which is the rudder of the literary artist, whether he
work at verse or novels.   I wish it were everywhere
written, even in the souls of all our young American
writers, that he who will not answer to the rudder shall
answer to the rocks.   This was the belief of the greatest
literary artist our language has ever produced.

We have direct contemporary testimony that Shakspere was supremely solicitous in this matter of form.
Ben Jonson, in that hearty testimonial, "To the Memory of My Beloved, the Author, Mr. William Shakspeare,
and What He Hath Left Us," which was prefixed to the
edition of 1623, says, after praises which are lavish even
for an Elizabethan eulogy :

> "Yet must I not give Nature all: thy art,"

(meaning here thy technic, thy care of form, thy science)

> "My gentle Shakspeare, must enjoy a part ;
>   For though the poet's matter Nature be,
> His art doth give the fashion ; and that he
>   Who casts to write a living line must sweat,
>   (Such as thine are) and strike the second heat
>   Upon the Muses' anvil ; turn the same
> (And himself with it) that he thinks to frame ;
>   Or for the laurel he may gain a scorn,
> *For a good poet's made as well as born,*
>   *And such wert thou.*   Look how the father's face
> Lives in his issue, even so the race
>   Of Shakespeare's mind and manners brightly shines
> *In his well-turnèd* and *true-filèd lines,*
>   *In each of which he seems to shake a lance,*
> As brandished at the eyes of Ignorance."

No fear with Shakspere of damaging his spontaneity :
he shakes a lance at the eyes of Ignorance in every line.

With these views of the progress of forms in general,
of the relations of Science — or the knowledge of all forms
— to Art, or the creation of beautiful forms, we are pre-

pared, I think, to maintain much equilibrium in the midst of the discordant cries, already mentioned, (1) of those who believe that Science will destroy all literary art, (2) of those who believe with Whitman that art is to advance by becoming democratic and formless, (3) and lastly of those who think that the future novelist is to enter the service of science as a police-reporter in ordinary for the information of current sociology.

Let us therefore inquire if it is really true — as I am told is much believed in Germany, and as I have seen not unfrequently hinted in the way of timorous apprehension in our own country — that science is to abolish the poet and the novel-writer and all imaginative literature. It is surprising that in all the discussions upon this subject the matter has been treated as belonging solely to the future. But surely life is too short for the folly of arguing from prophecy when we can argue from history : and it seems to me this question is determined. As matter of fact, science (to confine our view to English science) has been already advancing with prodigious strides for two hundred and fifty years, and side by side with it English poetry has been advancing for the same period. Surely whatever effect science has upon poetry can be traced during this long companionship. While Hooke and Wilkins and Newton and Horrox and the Herschels and Franklin and Davy and Faraday and the Darwins and Dalton and Huxley and many more have been penetrating into physical nature, Dryden, Pope, Byron, Burns, Wordsworth, Keats, Tennyson, Emerson, Longfellow, have been singing ; while gravitation, oxygen, electromagnetism, the atomic theory, the spectroscope, the siren, are being evolved, the *Ode to St. Cecilia*, the *Essay on Man, Manfred, A man's a man for a' that*, the *Ode on Immortality*, *In Memoriam*, the *Ode to a Nightingale*,

Brahma, The Psalm of Life, are being written.   If indeed
we go over into Germany, there is Goethe, at once pursuing science and poetry.

If we examine the course and progress of this poetry,
born thus within the very grasp and maw of this terrible science, it seems to me that we find — as to the
substance of poetry — a steadily increasing confidence and
joy in the mission of the poet, in the sacredness of faith
and love and duty and friendship and marriage, and in
the sovereign fact of man's personality ; while as to the
form of the poetry, we find that just as science has pruned
our faith (to make it more fruitful) so it has pruned our
poetic form and technic, cutting away much unproductive
wood and efflorescence and creating finer reserves and
richer yields.   Since it would be simply impossible in
the space of these lectures to illustrate this by any
detailed view of all the poets mentioned, let us confine
ourselves to one, Alfred Tennyson, and let us inquire how
it fares with him.   Certainly no more favorable selection
could be made for those who believe in the destructive-
ness of science.   Here is a man born in the midst of scientific activity, brought up and intimate with the freest
thinkers of his time, himself a notable scientific pursuer
of botany, and saturated by his reading with all the scientific conceptions of his age.   If science is to sweep
away the silliness of faith and love, to destroy the whole
field of the imagination and make poetry folly, it is a
miracle if Tennyson escape.   But if we look into his own
words this miracle beautifully transacts itself before our
eyes.   Suppose we inquire : Has science cooled this poet's
love?   We are answered in No. 60 of *In Memoriam.*

“ If, in thy second state sublime,
        Thy ransomed reason change replies
        With all the circle of the wise,
    The perfect flower of human time ;

"And if thou cast thine eyes below,
　　How dimly character'd and slight,
　　How dwarf'd a growth of cold and night,
　How blanch'd with darkness must I grow!

"Yet turn thee to the doubtful shore,
　　Where thy first form was made a man,
　　I loved thee, Spirit, and love, nor can
　The soul of Shakspeare love thee more."

Here is precisely the same loving gospel that Shakspere
himself used to preach, in that series of sonnets which
we may call *his* In Memoriam to his friend: the same
loving tenacity, unchanged by three hundred years of
science. It is interesting to compare this No. 60 of
Tennyson's poem with Sonnet 32 of Shakspere's series,
and note how both preach the supremacy of love over
style or fashion.

"If thou survive my well-contented day,
　When that churl Death my bones with dust shall cover,
　And shalt by fortune once more re-survey
　These poor rude lines of thy deceased lover,
　Compare them with the bettering of the time;
　And though they be outstripped by every pen,
　Reserve them for my love, not for their rhyme,
　Exceeded by the height of happier men.
　O then vouchsafe me but this loving thought:
　　'Had my friend's muse grown with this growing age,
　A dearer birth than this his love had brought,
　To march in ranks of better equipage:
　But since he died, and poets better prove,
　Theirs for their style I'll read, his for his love.'"

Returning to Tennyson: has science cooled his yearning for human friendship? We are answered in No. 90
of *In Memoriam*. When was ever such an invocation to
a dead friend to return!

" When rosy plumelets tuft the larch,
      And rarely pipes the mounted thrush;
      Or underneath the barren bush
Flits by the sea-blue bird of March;

"Come, wear the form by which I know
      Thy spirit in time among thy peers;
      The hope of unaccomplish'd years
Be large and lucid round thy brow.

" When summer's hourly-mellowing change
      May breathe, with many roses sweet,
      Upon the thousand waves of wheat,
That ripple round the lonely grange :

" Come : not in watches of the night,
      But where the sunbeam broodeth warm,
      Come, beauteous in thine after-form,
And like a finer light in light."

Or still more touchingly, in No. 49, for here he writes
from the depths of a sick despondency, from all the darkness of a bad quarter of an hour.

" Be near me when my light is low,
      When the blood creeps, and the nerves prick
      And tingle; and the heart is sick,
And all the wheels of Being slow.

"Be near me when the sensuous frame
      Is racked with pains that conquer trust;
      And Time, a maniac scattering dust,
And Life, a fury, slinging flame.

" Be near me when my faith is dry,
      And men the flies of latter spring,
      That lay their eggs, and sting and sing,
And weave their petty cells and die.

" Be near me when I fade away,
      To point the term of human strife,
      And on the low dark verge of life
The twilight of eternal day."

Has it diminished his tender care for the weakness of others?   We are wonderfully answered in No. 33.

" O thou that after toil and storm
    Mayst seem to have reach'd a purer air,
    Whose faith has centre everywhere,
Nor cares to fix itself to form,

" Leave thou thy sister when she prays,
    Her early Heaven, her happy views;
    Nor thou with shadow'd hint confuse
A life that leads melodious days.

" Her faith thro' form is pure as thine,
    Her hands are quicker unto good.
    Oh, sacred be the flesh and blood
To which she links a truth divine!

" See thou, that countest reason ripe
    In holding by the law within,
    Thou fail not in a world of sin,
And ev'n for want of such a type."

Has it crushed out his pure sense of poetic beauty ? Here in No. 86 we have a poem which, for what I can only call absolute beauty, is simply perfect.

" Sweet after showers, ambrosial air,
    That rollest from the gorgeous gloom
    Of evening over brake and bloom
And meadow, slowly breathing bare

" The round of space, and rapt below
    Thro' all the dewy-tassell'd wood,
    And shadowing down the horned flood
In ripples, fan my brows and blow

" The fever from my cheek, and sigh
    The full new life that feeds thy breath
    Throughout my frame, till Doubt and Death,
Ill brethren, let the fancy fly

" From belt to belt of crimson seas
  On leagues of odour streaming far
  To where in yonder orient star
 A hundred spirits whisper ' Peace.' "

And finally we are able to see from his own words
that he is not ignorantly resisting the influences of science,
but that he knows science, reveres it and understands its
precise place and function.   What he terms in the following poem (113 of *In Memoriam*) Knowledge and Wisdom
are what we have been speaking of as Science and
Poetry.

" Who loves not Knowledge?   Who shall rail
  Against her beauty ?   May she mix
  With men and prosper !   Who shall fix
 Her pillars ?   Let her work prevail.

 . . . .
 . . . .
  . . . . Let her know her place;
She is the second, not the first.

" A higher hand must make her mild,
  If all be not in vain ; and guide
  Her footsteps, moving side by side
 With wisdom, like the younger child :

" For she is earthly of the mind,
  But Wisdom heavenly of the soul.
  O friend, who camest to thy goal
 So early, leaving me behind,

 " I would the great world grew like thee
  Who grewest not alone in power
  And knowledge, but by year and hour
 In reverence and in charity."

If then, regarding Tennyson as fairly a representative
victim of science, we find him still preaching the poet's
gospel of beauty, as comprehending the evangel of faith,

hope and charity, only preaching it in those newer and
finer forms with which science itself has endowed him;
if we find his poetry just so much stronger and richer
and riper by as much as he has been trained and beaten
and disciplined with the stern questions which scientific
speculation has put — questions which you will find presented in their most sombre terribleness in Tennyson's
Two Voices; if finally we find him steadily regarding
science as knowledge which only the true poet can vivify
into wisdom : — then I say, life is too short to waste any
of it in listening to those who, in the face of this history,
still prophesy that Science is to destroy Poetry.

Nothing, indeed, would be easier than to answer all
this argument upon *a priori* grounds. The argument is,
in brief, that wonder and mystery are the imagination's
matériel, and that science is to explain away all mystery.
But what a crude view is this of explanation ! The moment you examine the process, you find that at bottom
explanation is simply the reduction of unfamiliar mysteries to terms of familiar mysteries. For simplest example : here is a mass of conglomerate ; science explains
that it is composed of a great number of pebbles which
have become fastened together by a natural cement. But
after all, is not one pebble as great a mystery as a mountain of conglomerate? though we are familiar with the
pebble, and unfamiliar with the other. Now to the wise
man, the poet, familiarity with a mystery brings no contempt : to him every explanation of science, supremely
fascinating as it is, but opens up a new world of wonders,
but adds to old mysteries. Indeed, the wise searcher
into nature always finds, as a poet has declared, that

>   . . . " In seeking to undo
> One riddle, and to find the true
> I knit a hundred others new."

And so, away with this folly: science, instead of being the enemy of poetry, is its quartermaster and commissary — it forever purveys for poetry; and just so much more as it shall bring man into contact with nature, just so much more large and intense and rich will be the poetry of the future in its contents, just so much finer and more abundant in its forms.

And here we may advance to our second class who believe that the poetry of the future is to be democratic and formless.

Here let me first carefully disclaim and condemn all that flippant and sneering tone which dominates so many discussions of Whitman. While I differ from him utterly as to every principle of artistic procedure; while he seems to me the most stupendously mistaken man in all history as to what constitutes true democracy, and the true advance of art and man; while I am immeasurably shocked at the sweeping invasions of those reserves which depend on the very personality I have so much insisted upon, and which the whole consensus of the ages has considered more and more sacred with every year of growth in delicacy; yet, after all these prodigious allowances, I owe some keen delights to a certain combination of bigness and naïvety which make some of Whitman's passages so strong and taking, and indeed, on the one occasion when Whitman has abandoned his theory of formlessness and written in form he has made *My Captain, O my Captain* surely one of the most tender and beautiful poems in any language.

I need quote but a few scraps from characteristic sentences here and there in a recent paper of Whitman's in order to present a perfectly fair view of his whole doctrine. When, for instance, he declares that Tennyson's poetry is not the poetry of the future because, although

it is "the highest order of verbal melody, exquisitely
clean and pure and almost always perfumed like the tube-
rose to an extreme of sweetness," yet it has "never one
democratic page," and is "never free, naïve poetry, but
involved, labored, quite sophisticated;" when we find
him bragging of "the measureless viciousness of the
great radical republic" (the United States, of course)
"with its ruffianly nominations and elections; its loud,
ill-pitched voice, utterly regardless whether the verb
agrees with the nominative; its fights, errors, eructations,
repulsions, dishonesties, audacities; those fearful and
varied, long and continued storm-and-stress stages (so
offensive to the well-regulated, college-bred mind) wherewith nature, history and time block out nationalities more
powerful than the past;" and when finally we hear him
tenderly declaring that "meanwhile democracy waits the
coming of its bards in silence and in twilight — but 'tis
the twilight of dawn": — we are in sufficient possession
of the distinctive catch-words which summarize his
doctrine.

In examining it, a circumstance occurs to me at the
outset which throws a strange but effective light upon
the whole argument.   It seems curious to reflect that the
two poets who have most avowedly written for the people,
who have claimed most distinctively to represent and
embody the thought of the people, and to be bone of the
people's bone and flesh of the people's flesh, are precisely the two who have most signally failed of all popular acceptance and who have most exclusively found
audience at the other extreme of culture.   These are
Wordsworth and Whitman.   We all know how strenuously and faithfully Wordsworth believed that in using
the simplest words and treating the lowliest themes, he
was bringing poetry back near to the popular heart; yet

Wordsworth's greatest admirer is Mr. Matthew Arnold, the apostle of culture, the farthest remove from anything that could be called popular : and in point of fact it is probable that many a peasant who would feel his blood stir in hearing *A man's a man for a' that*, would grin and guffaw if you should read him Wordsworth's *Lambs* and *Peter Grays*.

And a precisely similar fate has met Whitman. Professing to be a mudsill and glorying in it, chanting democracy and shirt-sleeves and equal rights, declaring that he is nothing if not one of the people, nevertheless the people, the democracy, will yet have nothing to do with him, and it is safe to say that his sole audience has lain among such representatives of the highest culture as Emerson and the English *illuminated*.

The truth is, that if closely examined, Whitman, instead of being a true democrat, is simply the most incorrigible of aristocrats masquing in a peasant's costume, and his poetry, instead of being the natural outcome of a fresh young democracy, is a product which would be impossible except in a highly civilized society.

III

AT our last meeting we endeavored to secure some solid basis for our ideas of form in general, and to develop thereupon some conceptions of form in art, and specially of literary form, which would enable us to see our way clear among misconceptions of this subject which prevail. We there addressed ourselves towards considering particularly three of these misconceptions. The first we examined was that which predicts the total death of imaginative literature — poetry, novels and all — in consequence of a certain supposed quality of imagination by virtue of which, like some ruin-haunting animals, it cannot live in the light, so that the destructive explanations of advancing science — it was apprehended — would gradually force all our imaginative energies back into the dark crevices of old fable and ruined romance until finally, penetrating these also, it would exterminate the species. We first tested this idea by laying it alongside the historic facts in the case : confining our view to England, we found that science and poetry had been developing alongside of each other ever since early in the seventeenth century ; inquiring into the general effect of this long contact, we could only find that it was to make our general poetry greatly richer in substance and finer in form ; and upon testing this abstract conclusion by a concrete examination of Tennyson — as a poet most likely to show the influence of science because himself most exposed to it, indeed most saturated with it — we found from several readings in *In Memoriam* that whether as to love, or friendship, or the sacredness of marriage, or the pure sense of beauty, or the true relation of knowledge to wisdom, or faith in God, — the effect of science had been on the whole to broaden the conceptions and to clarify the forms in which they were expressed by this great poet.

And having thus appealed to facts, we found further that in the nature of things no such destruction could follow : that what we call explanation in science is at bottom only a reduction of unfamiliar mysteries to terms of familiar mysteries, and that, since to the true imaginative mind, whether of poet or novelist, the mysteries of this world grow all the greater as they grow more familiar, the necessary effect of scientific explanations is at last the indefinite increase of food for the imagination. The modern imagination, indeed, shall still love mystery ; but it is not the shallow mystery of those small darks which are enclosed by caves and crumbling dungeons, it is the unfathomable mystery of the sunlight and the sun, it is this inexplicable contradictory shadow of the infinite which is projected upon the finite, it is this multitudinous flickering of all the other *egos* upon the tissue of my *ego :* these are the lights and shades and vaguenesses of mystery in which the modern imaginative effort delights. And here I cannot help adding to what was said on this subject in the last lecture, by declaring to every young man who may entertain the hope of poethood, that at this stage of the world you need not dream of winning the attention of sober people with your poetry unless that poetry, and your soul behind it, are informed and saturated at least with the largest final conceptions of current science.   I do not mean that you are to write *Loves of the Plants*, I do not mean that you are to

4

versify Biology, but I mean that you must be so far instinct with the scientific thought of the time that your poetic conceptions will rush as it were from under these pure cold facts of science like those Alpine torrents which flow out of glaciers.   Or, — to change the figure for the better — just as the chemist, in causing chlorine and hydrogen to form hydrochloric acid, finds that he must not only put the chlorine and hydrogen together, but must put them together in the presence of light in order to make them combine : so the poet of our time will find that his best poetic combinations, his greatest syntheses of wisdom, own this law, and they too must be effected in the presence of the awful light of science.

Returning to our outline of the last lecture : After we had discussed this matter, we advanced to the second of the great misconceptions of the function of form in art — that which holds that the imaginative effort of the future will be better than that of the present, and that this improvement will come through a progress towards formlessness.   After quoting several sentences from Whitman which seemed to contain the substantial argument — to-wit, that the poetry of the future is to be signalized by independence of form, and is, by virtue of this independence, to gain strength, and become a democratic poetry, as contrasted with the supposed weak and aristocratic poetry of the present — I called your attention to a notable circumstance which seems to throw a curious light along this inquiry : that circumstance being that the two English poets who have most exclusively laid claim to represent the people in poetry, to express nothing but the people's heart in the people's words, namely, Wordsworth and Whitman, are precisely the two whose audience has been most exclusively confined to the other

extreme of culture. Wordsworth, instead of appealing
to Hodge, Nokes, and Stiles, instead of being found in
penny editions on the collier's shelves, is most cherished
by Mr. Matthew Arnold, the high-priest of culture. And
so with Whitman. We may say with safety that no
preacher was ever so decisively rejected by his own :
continually crying democracy in the market-place, and
crying it in forms or no-forms professing to be nothing
but products of the democratic spirit, nevertheless the
democracy everywhere have turned a deaf ear, and
it is only with a few of the most sober and retired
thinkers of our time that Whitman has found even a
partial acceptance.

And finally by way of showing a reason for this state
of things in Whitman's case, the last lecture closed with
the assertion that Whitman's poetry, in spite of his
belief (which I feel sure is most earnest) that it is
democratic, is really aristocratic to the last degree ; and
instead of belonging, as he claims, to an early and
fresh-thoughted stage of a republic, is really poetry
which would be impossible except in a highly civilized
state of society.

Here, then, let us take up the thread of that argument.
In the quotations which were given from Whitman's
paper, we have really the ideal democracy and democrat
of this school. It is curious to reflect in the first place
that in point of fact no such democracy, no such democrat, has ever existed in this country. For example :
when Whitman tells us of "the measureless viciousness
of the great radical republic, with its ruffianly nominations and elections ; its loud ill-pitched voice ; its fights,
errors, eructations, dishonesties, audacities, those fearful
and varied storm-and-stress stages (so offensive to the
well-regulated, college-bred mind) wherewith nature,

history and time block out nationalities more powerful than the past;" when he tells us this, with a sort of caressing touch upon all the bad adjectives, rolling the "errors" and the "audacities" and the "viciousness" under his tongue and faithfully believing that the strength which recommends his future poetry is to come out of viciousness and ruffianly elections and the like: let us inquire, to what representative facts in our history does this picture correspond, what great democrat who has helped to block out this present republic sat for this portrait? Is it George Washington, that beautiful, broad, tranquil spirit whom, I sometimes think, even we Americans have never yet held quite at his true value, — is it Washington who was vicious, dishonest, audacious, combative? But Washington had some hand in blocking out this republic. Or what would our courtly and philosophic Thomas Jefferson look like if you should put this slouch hat on him, and open his shirt-front at the bosom, and set him to presiding over a ruffianly nomination? Yet he had some hand in blocking out this republic. In one of Whitman's poems I find him crying out to Americans, in this same strain : "O lands ! would you be freer than all that has ever been before? If you would be freer than all that has been before, come listen to me." And this is the deliverance :

" Fear grace — fear elegance, civilization, delicatesse,
  Fear the mellow sweet, the sucking of honey-juice;
  Beware the advancing mortal ripening of nature,
  Beware what precedes the decay of the ruggedness of States
    and men."

And in another line, he rejoices in America because —
"Here are the roughs, beards, . . . combativeness,"
and the like.

But where are these roughs, these beards, and this combativeness? Were the Adamses and Benjamin Franklin roughs? was it these who taught us to make ruffianly nominations? But they had some hand in blocking out this republic. In short, leaving each one to extend this list of names for himself, it may be fairly said that nowhere in history can one find less of that ruggedness which Whitman regards as the essential of democracy, nowhere more of that grace which he considers fatal to it, than among the very representative democrats who blocked out this republic. In truth, when Whitman cries " fear the mellow sweet," and " beware the mortal ripening of nature," we have an instructive instance of the extreme folly into which a man may be led by mistaking a metaphor for an argument. The argument here is, you observe, that because an apple in the course of nature rots soon after it mellows, *argal* a man cannot mellow his spirit with culture without decaying soon afterwards. Of course it is sufficient only to reflect *non sequitur:* for it is precisely the difference between the man and the apple that whereas every apple must rot after ripeness no man is bound to.

If therefore after an inquiry ranging from Washington and Jefferson down to William Cullen Bryant (that surely unrugged and graceful figure who was so often called the finest American gentleman) and Lowell and Longfellow and the rest who are really the men that are blocking out our republic, — if we find not a single representative American democrat to whom any of these pet adjectives apply, — not one who is measurelessly vicious, or ruffianly, or audacious, or purposely rugged, or contemptuous towards the graces of life, — then we are obliged to affirm that the whole ideal drawn by

Whitman is a fancy picture with no counterpart in nature. It is perfectly true that we have ruffianly nominations; but we have them because the real democrats who govern our republic, who represent our democracy, stay away from nominating conventions and leave them to the ruffians. Surely no one can look with the most cursory eye upon our everyday American life without seeing that the real advance of our society goes on not only without, but largely in spite of that ostensible apparatus, legislative, executive, judicial which we call the Government, — that really the most effective legislation in our country is that which is enacted in the breasts of the individual democrats who compose it. And this is true democratic growth: every day, more and more, each man perceives that the shortest and most effectual method of securing his own rights is to respect the rights of others, and so every day do we less and less need outside interference in our individual relations; so that every day we approach nearer and nearer towards that ideal government in which each man is mainly his own legislator, his own governor or president, and his own judge, and in which the public government is mainly a concert of measures for the common sanitation and police.

But again: it is true as Whitman says that we have dishonesties; but we punish them, they are not representative, they have no more relation to democracy than the English thief has to English aristocracy.

From what spirit of blindness is it alleged that these things are peculiar to our democracy? Whitman here explicitly declares that the over-dainty Englishman " cannot stomach the high-life below stairs of our social status so far," this high-life consisting of the measureless viciousness, the dishonesty, and the like. Cannot

stomach it, no : who could? But how absurd to come
down to this republic, to American society for these
things ! Alas, I know an Englishman, who, three
hundred years ago, found these same things in that
aristocracy there : and he too, thank heaven, could not
stomach them, for he has condemned them in a sonnet
which is the solace of all sober-thoughted ages. I mean
Shakspere, and his sonnet :

LXVI.

"Tired with all these, for restful death I cry, —
  As, to behold desert a beggar born,
  And needy nothing trimmed in jollity,
  And purest faith unhappily foresworn,
  And gilded honor shamefully misplaced,
  And maiden virtue rudely strumpeted,
  And right perfection wrongfully disgraced,
  And strength by limping sway disabled,
  And art made tongue-tied by authority,
  And folly (doctor-like) controlling skill,
  And simple truth miscalled simplicity,
  And captive good attending captain ill :
    Tired of all these, from these would I be gone,
    Save that, to die, I leave my love alone."

It is true that we have bad manners ; yet among the
crowds at the Centennial Exposition it was universally
remarked that in no country in the world could such
vast multitudes of people have assembled day after day
with so few arrests by the police, with so little disorder,
and with such an apparent universal and effective sentiment of respect for decorum and law.

Now if we carry the result of this inquiry over into
art ; if we are presented with a poetry which professes to
be democratic because it — the poetry — is measurelessly
vicious, purposely eructant, striving after ruggedness,
despising grace, like the democracy described by Whit-

man ; then we reply that as matter of fact there never was any such American democracy and that the poetry which represents it has no constituency. And herein seems a most abundant solution of the fact just now brought to your notice, that the actually existing democracy have never accepted Whitman's poetry. But here we are met with the cry of strength and manfulness. Everywhere throughout Whitman's poetry the "rude muscle," the brawn, the physical bigness of the American prairie, the sinew of the Western backwoodsman, are apotheosized, and all these, as Whitman claims, are fitly chanted in his "savage song."

Here, then, is a great stalwart man, in perfect health, all brawn and rude muscle, set up before us as the ideal of strength. Let us examine this strength a little. For one, I declare that I do not find it impressive. Yonder, in a counting-room — alas, in how many counting-rooms ! — a young man with weak eyes bends over a ledger, and painfully casts up the figures day by day, on pitiful wages, to support his mother, or to send his younger brother to school, or some such matter. If we watch this young man when he takes down his hat, lays off his ink-splotched office-coat, and starts home for dinner, we perceive that he is in every respect the opposite of the stalwart Whitman ideal ; his chest is not huge, his legs are inclined to be pipe-stems, and his dress is like that of any other book-keeper. Yet the weak-eyed pipe-stem-legged young man impresses me as more of a man, more of a democratic man, than the tallest of Whitman's roughs ; to the eye of my spirit there is more strength in this man's daily endurance of petty care and small weariness, for love, more of the sort of stuff which makes a real democracy and a sound republic, than in an army of Whitman's unshaven loafers.

I know — and count it among the privileges of my life
that I do — a woman who has spent her whole life in bed
for twenty years past, confined by a curious form of
spinal disease which prevents locomotion and which in
spite of constant pain and disturbance leaves the system
long unworn. Day by day she lies helpless, at the
mercy of all those tyrannical small needs which become
so large under such circumstances ; every meal must be
brought to her, a drink of water must be handed ; and
she is not rich, to command service. Withal her nature
is of the brightest and most energetic sort. Yet, surrounded by these unspeakable pettinesses, enclosed in
this cage of contradictions, this woman has made herself
the centre of an adoring circle of the brightest people ;
her room is called " Sunnyside : " when brawny men are
tired they go to her for rest, when people in the rudest
physical health are sick of life they go to her for the cura-
tive virtue of her smiles. Now this woman has not so
much rude muscle in her whole body as Whitman's man
has in his little finger : she is so fragile that long ago
some one called her " White Flower," and by this name
she is much known : it costs her as much labor to press a
friend's hand as it costs Whitman's rough to fell a tree :
regarded from the point of view of brawn and sinew, she
is simply absurd ; yet to the eye of my spirit there is more
manfulness in one moment of her loving and self-sacri-
ficing existence than in an æon of muscle-growth and
sinew-breeding : and hers is the manfulness which is the
only solution of a true democrat, hers is the manfulness
of which only can a republic be built. A republic is the
government of the spirit ; a republic depends upon the
self-control of each member ; you cannot make a republic
out of muscles and prairies and Rocky mountains : re-
publics are made of the spirit.

Nay, when we think of it, how little is it a matter of the future, how entirely is it a matter of the past, when people come running at us with rude muscle and great mountains and such matters of purely physical bigness to shake our souls? How long ago is it that they began to put great bearskin caps on soldiers with a view to make them look grisly and formidable when advancing on the enemy? It is so long ago that the practice has survived mainly as ceremonial, and the little boys on the streets now laugh at this ferociousness when the sappers and miners come by who affect this costume.

Yet here in the nineteenth century we behold artists purposely setting bearskin caps upon their poetry to make it effective. This sort of thing never yet succeeded as against Anglo-Saxon people. I cannot help thinking here of old Lord Berners' account translated from Froissart, of how the Genoese cross-bowmen attempted to frighten the English warriors at the battle of Crécy. "Whan the genowayes were assembled togayder, and beganne to aproche, they made a great leape and crye, to abasshe thenglysshmen, but they stode styll, and styredde not for all that; thane the genowayes agayne the seconde tyme made another leape, and a fell crye, and stepped forward a lytell, and thenglysshmen remeved not one fote; thirdly, agayne they leapt and cryed, and went forthe tyll they come within shotte; thane they shot feersley with their crosbowes; than thenglysshe archers stept forthe one pase, and lette fly their arowes so hotly, and so thycke, that it semed snowe; when the genowayes felt the arowes persynge through heedes, armes, and brestes, many of them cast downe their crosbowes, and dyde cutte their strynges, and retourned dysconfited."

And so the Poetry of the Future has advanced upon us

with a great leap and a fell cry, relying upon its loud,
ill-pitched voice, but the democracy have stirred not for
all that.   Perhaps we may fairly say, gentlemen, it is five
hundred years too late to attempt to capture Englishmen with a yell.

I think it interesting to compare Whitman's often
expressed contempt for poetic beauty — he taunts the
young magazine writers of the present time with having
the beauty-disease — with some utterances of one who
praised the true function of ruggedness in works the
world will not soon forget.   I mean Thomas Carlyle,
who has so recently passed into the Place where the
strong and the virtuous and the beautiful souls assemble
themselves.   In one of Carlyle's essays he speaks as
follows of Poetic Beauty.   These words scarcely sound
as if they came from the lover of Danton and Mirabeau.

"It dwells and is born in the inmost Spirit of Man,
united to all love of Virtue, to all true belief in God ; or
rather, it is one with this love and this belief, another
phase of the same highest principle in the mysterious
infinitude of the human Soul.   To apprehend this beauty
of poetry, in its full and purest brightness, is not easy,
but difficult ; thousands on thousands eagerly read poems,
and attain not the smallest taste of it ; yet to all uncor-
rupted hearts, some effulgences of this heavenly glory
are here and there revealed ; and to apprehend it clearly
and wholly, to acquire and maintain a sense of heart that
sees and worships it, is the last perfection of all humane
culture."

In the name of all really manful democracy, in the
name of the true strength that only can make our republic reputable among the nations, let us repudiate the
strength that is no stronger than a human biceps, let us
repudiate the manfulness that averages no more than six

feet high. My democrat, the democrat whom I contemplate with pleasure, the democrat who is to write or to read the poetry of the future, may have a mere thread for his biceps, yet he shall be strong enough to handle hell, he shall play ball with the earth ; and albeit his stature may be no more than a boy's, he shall still be taller than the great redwoods of California ; his height shall be the height of great resolution and love and faith and beauty and knowledge and subtle meditation ; his head shall be forever among the stars.

But here we are met with the cry of freedom. This poetry is free, it is asserted, because it is independent of form. But this claim is also too late. It should have been made at least before the French Revolution. We all know what that freedom means in politics which is independent of form, of law. It means myriad-fold slavery to a mob. As in politics, so in art. Once for all, in art, to be free is not to be independent of any form, it is to be master of many forms. Does the young artist of the Whitman school fancy that he is free because under the fond belief that he is yielding himself to nature, stopping not for words lest he may fail to make what Whitman proudly calls "a savage song," he allows himself to be blown about by every wind of passion? Is a ship free because, without rudder or sail, it is turned loose to the winds, and has no master but nature? Nature is the tyrant of tyrants. Now, just as that freedom of the ship on the sea means shipwreck, so independence of form in art means death. Here one recurs with pleasure to the aphorism cited in the last lecture : in art, as elsewhere, "he who will not answer to the rudder shall answer to the rocks." I find all the great artists of time striving after this same freedom ; but it is not by destroying, it is by extending the forms of art, that

all sane and sober souls hope to attain. In a letter of
Beethoven's to the Archduke Rudolph, written in 1819,
I find him declaring "But freedom and progress are our
true aim in the world of art, just as in the great creation
at large."

We have seen how in the creation at large progress is
effected by the continual multiplication of new forms.
It was this advance which Beethoven wished : to become
master of new and more beautiful forms, not to abolish
form. In a letter of his to Matthisson, as early as 1800,
accompanying a copy of *Adelaide*, we may instructively
gather what he thought of this matter : "Indeed even
now I send you *Adelaide* with a feeling of timidity.
You know yourself what changes the lapse of some years
brings forth in an artist who continues to make progress ;
the greater the advances we make in art the less are we
satisfied with our works of an early date." This unstudied declaration becomes full of significance when we
remember that this same *Adelaide* is still held, by the
common consent of all musicians, to be the most perfect
song-form in music ; and it is given to young composers
as a type and model from which all other forms are to
be developed. We may sum up the whole matter by
applying to these persons who desire formlessness, words
which were written of those who have been said to desire
death :

> " Whatever crazy Sorrow saith,
>   No life that breathes with human breath
>   Has ever truly longed for death.

> " 'Tis life whereof our nerves are scant,
>   O life, not death, for which we pant ;
>   More life, and fuller, that I want."

In art, form and chaos are so nearly what life and

death are in nature, that we do not greatly change this
stanza if we read :

> 'Tis form whereof our art is scant,
> O form, not chaos, for which we pant,
> More form, and fuller, that I want.

I find some deliverances in Epictetus which speak so
closely to more than one of the points just discussed
that I must quote a sentence or two. " What then," he
says in the chapter " About Freedom," " is that which
makes a man free from hindrance and makes him his
own master? For wealth does not do it, nor consulship,
nor provincial government, nor royal power; but something else must be discovered. What then is that which
when we write makes us free from hindrance and unim-
peded? The knowledge of the art of writing. What
then is it (which gives freedom) in playing the lute?
The science of playing the lute." If Whitman's doctrine
is true, the proper method of acquiring freedom on the
lute is to bring lute-music to that point where the loud
jangling chord produced by a big hand sweeping at random across the strings is to take the place of the finical
tunes and harmonies now held in esteem. " Therefore,"
continues Epictetus, " in life, also, it is the science of
life. . . . When you wish the body to be sound, is it in
your power or not? — It is not. When you wish it to be
healthy? Neither is this in my power." (I complain of
Whitman's democracy that it has no provision for sick,
or small, or puny, or plain-featured, or hump-backed, or
any deformed people, and that his democracy is really
the worst kind of aristocracy, being an aristocracy of
nature's favorites in the matter of muscle.) And so of
estate, house, horses, life and death, — Epictetus continues ; these are not in our power, they cannot make us

free. So that, in another chapter, he cries: "This is the true athlete, the man who exercises himself against such appearances. Stay, wretch, do not be carried away. Great is the combat, divine is the work: it is for kingship, for freedom, for happiness."

And lastly, the Poetry of the Future holds that all modern poetry, Tennyson particularly, is dainty and over-perfumed, and Whitman speaks of it with that contempt which he everywhere affects for the dandy. But surely — I do not mean this disrespectfully — what age of time ever yielded such a dandy as the founder of this school, Whitman himself? The simpering beau who is the product of the tailor's art is certainly absurd enough ; but what difference is there between that and the other dandy-upside-down who from equal motives of affectation throws away coat and vest, dons a slouch hat, opens his shirt so as to expose his breast, and industriously circulates his portrait, thus taken, in his own books. And this dandyism — the dandyism of the roustabout — I find in Whitman's poetry from beginning to end. Everywhere it is conscious of itself, everywhere it is analyzing itself, everywhere it is posing to see if it cannot assume a naïve and striking attitude, everywhere it is screwing up its eyes, not into an eyeglass like the conventional dandy, but into an expression supposed to be fearsomely rough and barbaric and frightful to the terror-stricken reader, and it is almost safe to say that one half of Whitman's poetic work has consisted of a detailed description of the song he is going to sing. It is the extreme of sophistication in writing.

But if we must have dandyism in our art, surely the softer sort, which at least leans toward decorum and gentility, is preferable ; for that at worst becomes only laughable, while the rude dandyism, when it does acquire a factitious interest by being a blasphemy against real manhood, is simply tiresome.

I have thus dwelt upon these claims of the Whitman school, not so much because of any intrinsic weight they possess, as because they are advanced in such taking and sacred names, — of democracy, of manhood, of freedom, of progress.   Upon the most earnest examination, I can find it nothing but wholly undemocratic ; not manful, but dandy ; not free, because the slave of nature ; not progressive, because its whole momentum is derived from the physical-large which ceased to astonish the world ages ago, in comparison with spiritual greatness.

Indeed, this matter has been pushed so far, with the apparent, but wholly unreal sanction of so many influential names, that in speaking to those who may be poets of the future, I cannot close these hasty words upon the Whitman school without a fervent protest, in the name of all art and all artists, against a poetry which has painted a great scrawling picture of the human body and has written under it, " *This is the soul;* " which shouts a profession of religion in every line, but of a religion that, when examined, reveals no tenet, no rubric, save that a man must be natural, must abandon himself to every passion ; and which constantly roars its belief in God, but with a camerado air as if it were patting the Deity on the back and bidding Him *Cheer up* and hope for further encouragement.

It seems like a curious sarcasm of time that even the form of Whitman's poetry is not poetry of the future but tends constantly into the rhythm of

" Brimmanna boda abeod eft ongean,"

which is the earliest rhythm of our poetry. The only difference which Whitman makes is in rejecting the allit-

eration, in changing the line-division, so as to admit
longer lines, and the allowance of much liberty in inter-
rupting this general rhythm for a moment. It is remarkable indeed that this old rhythm is still distinctly the
prevalent rhythm of English prose. Some years ago
Walter Savage Landor remarked that the dactyl was
"the bindweed of English prose," and by the dactyl he
means simply a word of three syllables with the accent
on the first, like *Brimmanna*. For example:

"I loaf and invite my soul;
I lean and loaf at my ease, observing a spear of summer grass.
I exist as I am — that is enough;
If no other in the world be aware, I sit content;
And if each and all be aware I sit content.
Washes and razors for foofoos, and for me freckles and a
bristling beard."

"Walt Whitman am I, a cosmos of mighty Manhattan the
sun."

We are here arrived at a very fitting point to pass on
and consider that third misconception of the relation
between science and art which has been recently formulated by M. Émile Zola in his work called *Le Roman
Expérimental*. Zola's name has been so widely associated with a certain class of novels that I am unfortunately
under no necessity to describe them, and I need only
say that the work in question is a formal reply to a great
number of objections which have come from many quar-
ters as to the characters and events which Zola's novels
have brought before the public.

His book, though a considerable volume, may be said
to consist of two sentences which the author has varied
with great adroitness into many forms. These two sentences I may sum up as follows: (1) every novel must
hereafter be the entirely unimaginative record of an ex-

periment in human passion; and (2) every writer of the
Romantic school in France, particularly Victor Hugo, is
an ass. You are not to suppose that in this last sentiment
I have strengthened Zola's expressions. A single quotation will show sufficient authority. As for example
where M. Zola cries out to those who are criticising
him: "Every one says: 'Ah yes, the naturalists! they
are those men with dirty hands who want all novels to
be written in slang, and choose the most disgusting subjects.' Not at all! you lie! . . . Do not say that I
am idiot enough to wish to paint nothing but the
gutter."

But with this quarrel we are not here concerned; I
simply wish to examine in the briefest way Zola's
proposition to convert the novel into a work of science.
His entire doctrine may be fairly, indeed amply gathered
in the following quotations:

"We continue by our observations and experiments the
work of the physiologist, who has himself employed that of
the physicist and the chemist. We after a fashion pursue
scientific psychology in order to complete scientific physiology; and in order to complete the evolution, we need only
carry to the study of nature and man the invaluable tool of
the experimental method. In a word, we should work upon
characters, passions, human and social facts, as the physicist and chemist work with inorganic bodies, as the physiologist works with living organisms. Determinism controls
everything.

"This, then, is what constitutes the experimental novel,—
to understand the mechanism of human phenomena, to show
the machinery of intellectual and emotional manifestations
as physiology shall explain them to us under the influence
of heredity and surrounding circumstances; then to show
man living in the social *milieu* which he has himself produced,
and which he modifies every day, while at the same time
experiencing in his turn a continual transformation. So we

rest on physiology ; we take man isolated from the hands of
the physiologist to continue the solution of the problem and
to solve scientifically the question, How men live as members
of society. — We are, in a word, experimental philosophers,
showing by experiment how a passion exhibits itself in certain
social surroundings. The day when we shall understand the
mechanism of this passion, it may be treated, reduced, made
as inoffensive as possible."

These propositions need not detain us long. In the
first place, let us leave the vagueness of abstract assertions
and, coming down to the concrete, let us ask who
is to make the experiment recorded in the novel? Zola
says, " We (we novelists) are experimental philosophers,
showing by experiment how a passion exhibits itself in
certain social surroundings." Very well ; in one of
Zola's most popular novels, the heroine Nana, after a
remarkable career, dies of small-pox ; and a great naturalistic ado is made over this death. A correspondent of
the *Herald*, writing from Paris, says : " In a very few
days we are to be treated to the stage version of *Nana*,
at the Ambigu. . . . Nana, it will be remembered, dies at
the end of the story, of small-pox. We are to be given
every incident of the agony — every mark of the small-pox.
Pretty Mlle. Massin (who is to play this death-scene) is to
be the crowning attraction of the new play. . . . We shall
be shown a real death of small-pox, or the nearest possible
approach to it. Mlle. Massin, who is to sustain the pleasing
part of the ' heroine ' will make her pretty face hideous
for the occasion. At half past 11 every evening she will
issue from behind the drapery of a bed, clad only in the
most indispensable of nightly raiment — and that ' in most
admired disorder '— her neck, cheeks and forehead dis-
figured, changed and unrecognizable for simulated pustules. At twenty minutes to 12 the pustules will be too

much for her, and she will expire. At a quarter to 12
the deafening applause of the public will call her to life
again, and she will bow her acknowledgments."

Applying Zola's theory, sociology is to find here a
very instructive record of how a woman such as Nana
would comport herself when dying of small-pox; and
furthermore, his description of it must be an exact record
of an experiment in death from small-pox conducted by
M. Zola in person. But now recurring to our question
let us ask, how could M. Zola conduct this experiment?
It would certainly be inconvenient for him to catch the
small-pox and die, with a view to recording his sensations; and yet it is perfectly apparent that the conditions
of scientific experiment could not be satisfied in any
other way. M. Zola would probably reply with effusion,
that he had taken pains to go to a small-pox hospital and
to study with great care the behavior of a patient dying
with that disease. But, we immediately rejoin, this is
very far from what his theory bound him to show us: his
theory bound him to show us not some person, any
person, dying of small-pox, but Nana with all her individuality derived from heredity and from her own spontaneous variation — it was Nana dying of small-pox that
he must set before us; one person dies one way and
another person dies another way, even of the same disease; Smith, a very tragic person, would make a death-
scene full of tragic message and gesture; Brown might
close his eyes and pass without a word; Nana, particularly, with her peculiar career and striking individuality,
would naturally make a peculiar and striking death.
Now since Nana is purely a creation of Zola, (unless indeed the novel is a biography, which is not pretended)
Zola is the only person in the world who understands
Nana's feelings in death or on any occasion; and this

being so it is simply impossible that Zola could make a scientific experiment of Nana's death from small-pox without dying himself. This seems so absurd that one goes back to *Le Roman Expérimental* to see if Zola's idea of a scientific experiment has not something peculiar about it; and one quickly finds that it has. It is in fact interesting to observe that though Zola has this word experiment continually on his lips, yet he never means that the novelist is to conduct a real, gross, downright, actual brute of an experiment; and the word with him is wholly Pickwickian, signifying no more than that the novelist, availing himself of such realistic helps as he can find in hospitals and the like, is to evolve therefrom something which he believes to be the natural course of things. Examine the book wherever you may, the boasted experiment, the pivot of the whole system, fades into this.

The experiment of Zola is as if a professor of chemistry, knowing something of the properties of given substances, desiring to see how a certain molecule would behave itself in the presence of a certain other molecule, hitherto untried in this connection, instead of going into his laboratory and bringing the molecules together and observing what they actually did, should quietly sit before his desk and write off a comfortable account of how he thought these molecules would behave, judging from his previous knowledge of their properties. It is still more interesting to find that Zola is apparently unconscious of the difference between these two modes of experiment. About this unconsciousness I have my own theory, I think it entirely probable that if these two kinds of experiment were described to Zola he would maintain with perfect good faith that they were exactly the same. There is a phase of error — perhaps

we may call it hallucination — in which certain sorts of
minds come to believe that two things which have been
habitually associated are always the same.   For instance,
a friend of mine has told me that a certain estimable
teacher of the French language, who, after carrying on
his vocation for many years during which English and
French became equally instinctive tongues to him, was
accustomed to maintain that English and French were
absolutely one and the same language.   "When you
say *water*," he was accustomed to argue to my friend,
"you mean water: when I say *l'eau* I mean water:
water — l'eau, l'eau — water, do you not see?   We
mean the same thing, it is the same language."

However this may be, nothing is clearer than that
Zola's conception of an experiment is what I have
described it — namely, an evolving, from the inner
consciousness, of what the author thinks the experimental
subjects would do under given circumstances.   Here are
some of Zola's own words: and surely nothing more
naïve was ever uttered.   "The writer" (of the novel)
"employs both observation and experiment.   The observer gives the facts as he has observed them . . .
and establishes the solid ground on which his characters
shall march, and the phenomena shall develop themselves.   *Then the experimenter appears and conducts the
experiment; that is to say*" (I am quoting from M. Zola)
"*he moves the characters in a particular story to show
that the sequence of facts will be such as is determined by
the study of phenomena.*"   That is to say, to carry Zola's
"experiment" into chemistry: knowing something of
chlorine and something of hydrogen separately, a chemist
who wishes to know their behavior under each other's
influence may "experiment" upon that behavior by
giving his opinion as to what chlorine and hydrogen
would likely do under given circumstances.

It seems incredible, but it is logically beyond question, that by this short process we have got to the bottom of this whole elaborate system of the Experimental Novel and have found that it is nothing but a repetition of the old, old trick of the hand of Jacob and the voice of Esau. Think how much self-sacrifice and labor, of how many noble and brave spirits, from Horrox and Hooke in the seventeenth century down to the hundreds of scientific men who at this moment are living obscure and laborious lives in the search of truth, — think, I say, how much fervent and pious labor has gone to invest the mere name of scientific experiment with that sacredness under which the Zola school is now claiming the rights and privileges of science for what we have seen is *not* science, and what, we might easily see if it were worth showing, *is* mere corruption. The hand is the hand of science : but the voice is the voice of a beast.

To many, this animal voice has seemed a portentous sound. But if we think what kind of beast it is, we cease to fear. George Eliot, somewhere in *Adam Bede*, has a *mot :* when a donkey sets out to sing, everybody knows beforehand what the tune will be. This voice has been heard many times before. Long before Zola came on the stage, I find Schiller crying in his sweet silver tones to some who were likewise misusing both art and science : " Unhappy mortal, that, with science and art, the noblest of all instruments, effectest and attemptest nothing more than the day-drudge with the meanest ; that in the domain of perfect Freedom bearest about in thee the spirit of a slave." In these words, Schiller has at once prophesied and punished the Experimental Novel.

But there is another view of Zola's claims which leads us into some thoughts particularly instructive at the present time, and will carry us very directly to the more special studies which will engage our attention.

After the views of form which have been presented to you, it will not be necessary for me to argue that even if Zola's Experimental Novel were a physical possibility, it would be an artistic absurdity. If you *could* make a scientific record of actual experiments in human passion, very well : but why should we call that record a novel, if we do not call Professor Huxley's late work on the crayfish a novel, or if we do not call any physician's report of some specially interesting clinical experience to the *Medical and Surgical Journal* a novel?

Here we are put upon securing for ourselves perfectly clear conceptions as to certain relations between that so-called poetic activity and scientific activity of the human mind which find themselves in a singularly interesting contact in the true and worthy novel which we are going to study. Merely reminding you of the distinction with which every one is more or less familiar theoretically, that that activity which we variously call " poetic," " imaginative," or " creative," is essentially synthetic, is a process of putting together, while the scientific process seems distinctively analytic, or a tearing apart ; let us pass from this idea to those applications of the poetic faculty which are made whenever a scientific searcher goes further than the mere collection of facts, to classify them and to effect generalizations. This is an activity of what is well called the scientific imagination. Now what is the difference between a work of the scientific imagination and a work of the poetic imagination? Without going into subtleties, I think the shortest way to gain a perfectly clear working-idea of this difference is to confine our attention to the differing results of these activities : the scientific imagination results in a formula, whose

paramount purpose is to be as short and as comprehensive as possible ; the poetic imagination results in a
created form or forms, whose paramount purpose is to
be as beautiful and as comprehensive as possible. For
example, the well-known formula of evolution : that
evolution is a process from the uniform and indefinite to
the multiform and definite : that is a result of long efforts
of the scientific imagination : while on the other hand
Tennyson's *In Memoriam*, in which we have deep matters discussed in the most beautiful words and the most
musical forms of verse, is a poetic work.

And now if we pass one step farther and consider
what would happen if the true scientific activity and the
true poetic activity should engage themselves upon one
and the same set of facts, we arrive at the novel.

The great modern novelist is at once scientific and
poetic : and here, it seems to me, in the novel, we have
the meeting, the reconciliation, the kiss, of science and
poetry. George Eliot, having with those keen eyes of
hers collected and analyzed and sorted many facts of
British life, binds them together into a true poetic
synthesis, in, for instance, *Daniel Deronda*, where instead
of giving us the ultimate relations of all her facts in the
shape of a formula, like that of evolution, she gives them
to us in the creation of beautiful Gwendolen Harleth and
all the other striking forms which move through the
book as embodiments in flesh and blood of the scientific
relations between all her facts.

Perhaps we shall find it convenient here, too, to base
perfectly clear ideas of the three existing schools of
novel-writing upon these foregoing principles. It has
been common for some time to hear of the Romantic and
the Realistic school, and lately a third term has been
brought into use by the Zola section who call themselves

the Naturalistic school.   It is easy to see that these terms have arisen from the greater or less prominence given now to the poetic activity, now to the scientific activity, in novel writing ; those who most rely on the poetic being the Romantic, those on a combination of the poetic and scientific the Realistic, and those who entirely reject the imagination (as Zola professes to do) the Naturalistic school.   At all events, then, not troubling ourselves with the Naturalists who, as we have seen, call that an experiment which is only an imaginative product, we are prepared to study the novel as a work in which science is carried over into the region of art.   We are not to regard the novel therefore as aught else but a work of art, and the novelist as an artist.

One rejoices to find our wise Emerson discussing the novel in this light purely, in his very suggestive essay on *Books*.   "Whilst the prudential and economical tone of society starves the imagination, affronted Nature gets such indemnity as she may.   The novel is that allowance and frolic the imagination finds.   Everything else pins it down, and men flee for redress to Byron, Scott, Disraeli, Dumas, Sand, Balzac, Dickens, Thackeray and Reade.

"The imagination infuses a certain volatility and intoxication.   It has a flute which sets the atoms of our frame in a dance, like planets ; and, once so liberated, the whole man reeling drunk to the music, they never quite subside to their old stony state."

Nay, we have such beautiful novels in the world, novels far from the experimental romances by which we are not perfected but infected (*non perficitur, inficitur*), as old Burton quotes in the *Anatomy*, novels in which scientific harmony has passed into its heavenly after-life of wisdom, novels in which the pure sense of poetic

beauty is so tenderly drawn out that I love to think of
them in the terms which our most beauty-loving of
modern poets has applied to beauty, in the opening
of *Endymion*:

" A thing of beauty is a joy forever:
    Its loveliness increases ; it will never
    Pass into nothingness ; but still will keep
    A bower quiet for us, and a sleep
    Full of sweet dreams, and health, and quiet breathing.
    Therefore, on every morrow, are we wreathing
    A flowery band to bind us to the earth,
    Spite of despondence, of the inhuman dearth
    Of noble natures, of the gloomy days,
    Of all the unhealthy and o'erdarkened ways
    Made for our searching : yes, in spite of all,
    Some shape of beauty moves away the pall
    From our dark spirits.   Such the sun, the moon,
    Trees old and young, sprouting a shady boon
    For simple sheep ; and such are daffodils
    With the green world they live in ; and clear rills
    That for themselves a cooling covert make
    'Gainst the hot season ; the mid-forest brake,
    Rich with a sprinkling of fair musk-rose blooms ;
    And such too is the grandeur of the dooms
    We have imagined for the mighty dead ;
    All lovely tales that we have heard or read :
    An endless fountain of immortal drink,
    Pouring unto us from the heaven's brink."

IV

THE points discussed at our last meeting were mainly of such a nature that I need not occupy your time with the detailed review which has seemed advisable heretofore.

You will remember, in a general way, that we finished examining the claims of the poetry of the future, as presented by Whitman, and found reason to believe from several trains of argument that its alleged democratic spirit was based on a political misconception, its religious spirit was no more than that general feeling of good fellowship and *cameraderie* which every man of the world knows to be the commonest of virtues among certain classes, its strength rested upon purely physical qualifications which have long ago practically ceased to be strength, its contempt for dandyism was itself only a cruder dandyism, and its proposed substitution of power for beauty not only an artistic blindness but a historical error as to the general progress of this world, which has been *from* strength *to* beauty ever since the ponderous old gods Ouranus and Gæa — representatives of rude strength — gave way to the more orderly (that is, more beautiful) reign of Saturn, and he in turn to the still more orderly and beauty-representing Jupiter, whom Chaucer has called the "fadyr of delicacye."

Passing thus from the Whitman school, we attacked that third misconception of literary form which had taken the shape of the so-called naturalistic school, as led by Zola in his novels and defended by him in his recent work, *The Experimental Novel.* Here we quickly discovered that if the term "experiment" were used by this school in its ordinary and scientific sense, it would in a large number of cases involve conditions which would exterminate the authors of the projected experimental novels often at an early stage of the plot; but that secondly, this inconvenience was avoided through the very peculiar meaning which was attached to the word by this school, and which reveals that they make no more use of experiment, in point of fact, than any one of the numerous novelists who have for years been in the habit of studying real life and nature as the basis of their work. In short, it appeared that to support the propriety of circulating such books by calling them experimental novels, was as if a man should sell profitable poison under the name of scientific milk, and claim therefor both the gratitude of society and the privileges of science. Finally, supplying ourselves with clear ideas as to the difference between what has become so well known in modern times as the scientific imagination and the poetic imagination, we determined to regard the novel as a true work of art, and the novelist as an artist, by reason of the created forms in the novel which were shown to be the distinctive outcome of the poetical imagination as opposed to the formula which is the distinctive outcome of the scientific imagination. Nevertheless, in view of the circumstance that the facts embodied in these forms are facts which must have been collected by a genuine exercise of the true scientific faculty of observing and classifying, we were compelled to regard the novel as a joint product of science and art, ranking as art by virtue of its final purely artistic outcome in the shape of beautiful created forms.

It is with a sense of relief that one turns away from what I fear has seemed the personal and truculent tone of the last lecture — an appearance almost inseparable from the fact that certain schools of writing have become represented by the names of their living founders, and which would, indeed, have prevented your present lecturer from engaging in the discussion had not his reluctance been overwhelmed by the sacred duty of protesting against all this forcible occupation of the temple of art by those who have come certainly not for worship — it is with a sense of relief that one turns from this to pursue the more gracious and general studies which will now occupy us.

According to the plan already sketched : having now acquired some clear fundamental conceptions of the correlations among form, science, art, and the like notions often so vaguely used, we are next to inquire, as our first main line of research : Is it really true that what was explained as the growth in human personality is the continuing single principle of human progress, is it really true that the difference between the time of Æschylus and the time of (say) George Eliot is the difference in the strength with which the average man feels the scope and sovereignty of his *ego ?* For upon this fundamental point necessarily depends our final proposition that the modern novel is itself the expression of this intensified personality, and an expression which could only be made by greatly extending the form of the Greek drama. Pursuing our custom of leaving the abstract and plunging into the concrete as soon as possible, let us determine this question by endeavoring to find some special notable works of antique and of modern times in which substantially the same subject matter has been treated ; let us then compare the difference in treatment, let us summarize the picture of things evidently existing in the old, as contrasted with the modern author's and reader's minds; and finally let us see whether the differences thus emerging will not force themselves upon us as differences growing out of personality. For the purposes of this comparison I have thought that the *Prometheus Bound* of Æschylus, the *Prometheus Unbound* of Shelley, and the *Prince Deukalion* of Bayard Taylor offered inviting resources as works which treat substantially the same story, although the first was written some two thousand three hundred years before the last two. Permit me then, in beginning this comparison, to set before you these three works in the broadest possible sketch by reading from each here and there a line such as may bring the action freshly before you and at the same time elucidate specially the differences in treatment we are in search of. As I now run rapidly through the *Prometheus* of Æschylus, I ask you to bear along in mind the precise nature of this spontaneous variation between man and man which I was at some pains to define in my first lecture; and perhaps I may profitably extend the partial idea there given by adopting a pretty fancy which I find in No. 44 of Tennyson's *In Memoriam*, and carrying it to a larger sphere than there intended. The poet is here expressing the conception that perhaps the main use of this present life of ours is for each one to learn himself — possibly as preparatory to learning other things hereafter. He says:

> " The baby new to earth and sky
>   What time his tender palm is prest
>   Against the circle of the breast,
> Has never thought that 'this is I:'

> " But as he grows he gathers much,
>   And learns the use of 'I' and 'me,'
>   And finds 'I am not what I see,
> And other than the things I touch.'

" So rounds he to a separate mind
From whence clear memory may begin,
As thro' the frame that binds him in
His isolation grows defined.

" This use may lie in blood and breath,
Which else were fruitless of their due,
Had man to learn himself anew
Beyond the second birth of Death."

If we extend the process of growth here described as of a single child passing through a single life to the collective process of growth effected by humanity from age to age, we have quite clearly the principle whose light I wish to shed upon our comparison of the works I have named. Just as the child learns to know himself — " that I am I " — so man comes in the course of time to feel more and more distinctly, I am I ; and the growth of this feeling continually uproots his old relations to things and brings about new relations with new forms to clothe them in.

One may say indeed that this recognition of the supreme finality of the *ego* feeling among modern men seems a curious and not unrelated counterpart of the theory by which the modern physicist, in order to explain his physical world, divides it into atoms which atoms are themselves indivisible. We have here the perplexing problem which in the poem *De Profundis*, partially read to you, was poetically called " the pain of this divisible-indivisible world." To explain the world, whether the moral or the physical world, we must suppose it divisible into atoms ; to explain the atom, we must suppose that indivisible. Let us see then in what form this " pain of the divisible-indivisible world " with all its attendant pains of contradiction between fate and free will, — between the Infinite Personality, which should

seem boundless, and the finite personality which nevertheless seems to bound it, — let us see, I say, under what
explicit forms this pain appears in the *Prometheus Bound*,
for alas it was an old grief when Æschylus was a baby.
Here, then, in the centre of the stage lies the gigantic
figure of Prometheus, (let us fancy,) stark, prostrate,
proud, unmoving throughout the whole action.   Two
ministers of Jove, Might and Force, have him in charge,
and Hephæstus — the god more commonly known as
Vulcan — stands by with chain, hammer and bolt.   Might
acquaints us at once with what is toward.

> " At length the utmost bound of earth we've reached,
> This Scythian soil, this wild untrodden waste.
> Hephæstus, now Jove's high behests demand
> Thy care; to these steep, cliffy rocks bind down
> With close-linked chains of during adamant
> This daring wretch.   For he the bright rayed fire,
> Mother of arts   .   .   .   .   .
> Filched from the gods and gave to mortals.   Here
>
> .   , ...
> Let his pride learn to bow to Jove supreme,
> And love men well but love them not too much."

Hephæstus proceeds to chain him, but with many pro-
tests, not only because Prometheus' act seems over-
punished, but because he is Prometheus' kinsman.

> " Would that some other hand,"

he cries,

> " Had drawn the lot
> To do this deed ! "

To which Might replies

> " All things may be, but this :
> To dictate to the gods.   There's one that's free,
> One only — Jove."

6

And Hephæstus sullenly acquiesces, as he beats away at his task,

"I know it, and am dumb."

Amid similar talk — of protest from Vulcan and pitiless menace from Might — the great blacksmith proceeds to force an adamantine bolt through the breast of Prometheus, then to nail his feet to the rock, and so at last cries, in relief,

"Let us away. He's fettered, limb and thew."

But Might must have his last pitiless speech.

"There lie,"

he exults, —

"And feed thy pride on this bare rock,
   Filching gods' gifts for mortal men.   What man
   Shall free thee from these woes? Thou hast been called
   In vain the Provident:"

(*pro-vident*, same as pro-metheus, he who looks ahead, who provides, the provident)

"had thy soul possessed
   The virtue of thy name, thou had'st foreseen
   These cunning toils, and had'st unwound thee from them."

Here all depart but Prometheus.   Up to this time the Titan has maintained a proud silence.   He now breaks into that large invocation which seems still to assault our physical ears across the twenty odd centuries.

"O divine Æther, and swift-winged Winds,
   And Fountains of the rivers and multitudinous
   Laughter of ocean, and thou Earth,
   Born mother of us all, and thou bright round
   Of the all-seeing Sun, you I invoke!
   Behold what ignominy of causeless wrongs
   I suffer from the gods, myself a god!"

(This, by the way, is one of those passages which our elder poets seem to have regarded as somehow lying outside the pale of moral law—like umbrellas—and which they have therefore appropriated without a thought of blushing. Byron, in *Manfred*, and Shelley, in his *Prometheus Unbound*, have quite fairly translated parts of it.)

Enter now a chorus of Oceanides, and these continue throughout the play to perform the functions of exciting sympathy for the Protagonist, and of calling upon him for information when it becomes necessary that the audience should know this and that fact essential to the intelligibility of the action.

For example, after the Oceanides have alighted from their wind-borne car, and have condoled with the sufferer, Æschylus makes them the medium of drawing from Prometheus the recital of his wrongs, and thus of freshly placing that whole tremendous story before the minds of his audience.

"Speak now,"

say the Chorus,

> "And let us know the whole offence
> Jove charges thee withal."

And Prometheus relates :

> "When first the gods their fatal strife began,
> And insurrection raged in heaven, some striving
> To cast old Kronos from his hoary throne
> That Jove might reign, and others to crush i' the bud
> His swelling mastery — I wise counsel gave
> To the Titans, sons of primal Heaven and Earth;
> But gave in vain.   .   .   .   .   .
> Thus baffled in my plans, I deemed it best,
> As things then were, leagued with my mother Themis,

To accept Jove's proffered friendship. By my counsels
From his primeval throne was Kronos hurled
Into the pit Tartarean, dark, profound,
With all his troop of friends.   .   .

"Soon as he sat on his ancestral throne
He called the gods together, and assigned
To each his fair allotment, and his sphere
Of sway; but, ah! for wretched man!
To him no portion fell: Jove vowed
To blot his memory from the Earth, and mould
The race anew. I only of the gods
Thwarted his will; and, but for my strong aid,
Hades had whelmed, and hopeless ruin swamped
All men that breathe. Such were my crimes:

.   .   .   .   .   .

"And here I lie, in cunning torment stretched,
A spectacle inglorious to Jove."

Presently Ocean appears, and advises Prometheus to yield. Prometheus scornfully refuses, and Ocean, fearful of being found in bad company, prudently retires, whereupon, after a mournful hymn from the Chorus, reciting the sympathy of all nations and things with Prometheus, he proceeds to relate in detail his ministry in behalf of mankind. The account which he gives of the primal condition of the human race is very instructive upon our present research, as embodying, or rather as unconsciously revealing, the complete unconsciousness of personality — of what we call personality — among Æschylus and his contemporaries.

Prometheus begins by calling the whole human race at that time a babe, and goes on to declare that

"Having eyes to see, they saw not,
And hearing, heard not, but, like dreamy phantoms,
A random life they led from year to year,
All blindly floundering on. No craft they knew"

(to build)

" But in the dark earth burrowed.   .   .   .
Numbers too I taught them   .   .   and how
To fix their shifting thoughts by marshalled signs."

He brings the ox, the ass, and the horse into service, launches the first boat on the sea, teaches medicine, institutes divination, and finally

"I probed the earth
To yield its hidden wealth   .   .   .
Iron, copper, silver, gold;   .   .   .
And thus, with one short word to sum the tale,
Prometheus taught all arts to mortal men."

CHORUS.

" Do good to men, but do it with discretion.
Why shouldst thou harm thyself?   Good hope I nurse
To see thee soon from these harsh chains unbound,
As free, as mighty, as great Jove himself."

PROMETHEUS.

" This may not be; the destined course of things
Fate must accomplish.   .   .   .
Though art be strong, necessity is stronger."

CHORUS.

" And who is lord of strong necessity ? "

PROMETHEUS.

" The triform Fates and the sure-memoried Furies."

CHORUS.

" And mighty Jove himself must yield to them ? "

PROMETHEUS.

" No more than others Jove can 'scape his doom."

CHORUS.

.   .   .   .

" There's some dread mystery in thy speech
Close-veiled "

PROMETHEUS.

"The truth thou'lt know
In fitting season ; now it lies concealed
In deepest darkness ; for relenting Jove
Himself must woo this secret from my breast."

(This secret — so it is told in the old myths — is that
Jove is to meet his own downfall through an unfortunate
marriage, and Prometheus is in possession of the details
which would enable Jove to avoid the doom.)

After a choral hymn, recommending submission to
Jove, we have suddenly the grotesque apparition of Io
upon the stage. Io had been beloved by Jove, but the
jealousy of Hera, or Juno, had transformed her into a
cow, and had doomed her to wander over the world
stung by an inexpugnable gadfly and watched by the
hundred-eyed Argus. Thus suddenly upon the spectacle of a man suffering from the hatred of Jove Æschylus
brings the spectacle of a woman suffering from the love
of Jove.   Io enters with this fine outburst :

"What land is this ?   What race of mortals
Owns this desert ?   Who art thou,
Rock-bound with these wintry fetters,
And for what crime tortured thus?
Worn and weary with far travel,
Tell me where my feet have borne me !
O pain ! pain ! pain ! it stings and goads me again,
The fateful gadfly ! — save me, O Earth ! — avaunt
Thou horrible shadow of the earth-born Argus !
Could not the grave close up thy hundred eyes,
But thou must come,
Haunting my path with thy suspicious look,
Unhoused from Hades ?
Avaunt ! avaunt ! why wilt thou hound my track,
The famished wanderer on the waste sea-shore?"

After much talk Io now relates her mournful story
and, supported by the Chorus, persuades Prometheus to

prophesy the very eventful future which awaits her when her wanderings are over. In this prophetic account of her travels Æschylus gives a soul-expanding review of land after land according to the geographic and ethnic notions of his time ; and here Mr. Blackie, whose translation of the *Prometheus* I have been partly quoting from, sometimes reproduces his author in very large and musical measures. For example, Prometheus chants :

" When thou hast crossed the narrow stream that parts
The continents, to the far flame-faced East
Thou shalt proceed, the highway of the sun ;
Then cross the sounding ocean, till thou reach
Cisthene and the Gorgon plains, where dwell
Phorcys' three daughters, maids with frosty eld,
White as the swan, with one eye and one tooth
Shared by the three ; them Phœbus, beamy-bright
Beholds not, nor the nightly moon. Near them
Their wingéd sisters dwell, the Gorgons dire,
Man-hating monsters, snaky-locked, whom eye
Of mortal ne'er might look upon and live.
　　.　　.　　.　　One more sight remains
That fills the eye with horror.　　.　　.　　.
The sharp-beaked Griffins, hounds of Jove, avoid,
Fell dogs that bark not ; and the one-eyed host
Of Arimaspian horsemen with swift hoofs
Beating the banks of golden-rolling Pluto.
A distant land, a swarthy people next
Receives thee : near the fountains of the sun
They dwell by Ethiop's wave. This river trace
Until thy weary feet shall reach the pass
Whence from the Bybline heights the sacred Nile
Pours his salubrious flood. The winding wave
Thence to triangled Egypt guides thee, where
A distant home awaits thee, fated mother
Of no unstoried race."

In this strain Prometheus continues to foretell the adventures of Io until her son Epaphus, monarch of

Egypt, is born, who will be — through the fifty daughters
celebrated in *The Suppliants* of Æschylus — the ancestor
of Hercules, which Hercules is to be the deliverer of
Prometheus himself.

Then, in a frenzy of pain, Io departs, while the Chorus
bursts into a hymn deploring such ill-matched unions as
that of Io with Jove and extolling marriage between
equals.

After the exit of Io — to finish our summary of the
play — the action hastens to the end ; the Chorus implores
Prometheus to submit ; presently Hermes or Mercury
appears and tauntingly counsels surrender, only to be
as tauntingly repulsed by Prometheus ; and, after a sharp
passage of wits between these two, accompanied by indignant outbursts from the Chorus at the pitilessness of
Hermes, the play ceases with a speech from Prometheus
describing the new punishment of Jove :

> " Now in deed and not in discourse,
>   The firm earth quakes.
>   Deep and loud the ambient thunder
>   Bellows, and the flaring lightning
>   Wreathes his fiery curls around me
>   And the whirlwind rolls his dust,
>   And the winds from rival regions
>   Rush in elemental strife,
>   And the sky is destroyed with the sea.
>   Surely now the tyrant gathers
>   All his hoarded wrath to whelm me.
>   Mighty Mother, worshipped Themis,
>   Circling Æther that diffusest
>   Light, the common joy of all,
>   Thou beholdest these my wrongs ! "

Thus in the crash of elements the play ends.   Fortunately our purpose with this huge old story thus treated
by Æschylus lays us under no necessity to involve our-

selves in endless discussions of Sun-myths, of the connection between ox-horned Io and the sacred Egyptian cow Isis, of moral interpretations which vary with every standpoint.   The extent to which these do vary is amusingly illustrated in an interpretation of the true significance of Prometheus which I recently happened to light upon, made by a certain Mr. Newton who published an elaborate work a few years ago in defence of the strictly vegetable diet.   Mr. Newton would not have us misapply fire to cookery ; and in this line of thought he interprets the old fable that Prometheus stole fire from heaven and was punished by being chained to Caucasus with a vulture to gnaw his liver.   The simple fact, says our vegetarian, is that " Prometheus first taught the use of animal food, and of fire with which to render it more pleasing, etc., to the taste.   Jupiter, and the rest of the gods, foreseeing the consequences of the inventions" (these consequences being all manner of gastric and other diseases which Newton attributes to the use of animal food) " were amused or irritated at the short-sighted devices of the . . . creature, and left him to experience the sad effects of them."   In short, the chaining to a rock, with a vulture to gnaw his liver, is simply a very satisfactory symbol for dyspepsia.

Untroubled by these entanglements, which thus reach from Max Müller with his Sun-wanderings, to the dyspeptic theory of our vegetarian, our present concern is less with what Æschylus or his fable meant than with the frame of mind of the average man who sat in his audience and who listened to these matters with favor, who accepted this picture of gods and men without rebellion.   My argument is that if this average man's sense of personality had not been most feeble he could not have accepted this picture at all.   Permit me then to specify three or four of the larger features of it before we go on to contrast the treatment of this fable by Æschylus with that by Shelley and Taylor in a later age.

In the first place, since we are mainly meditating upon the growth of human personality, I beg you to observe the complete lack of all provision for such growth either among the gods or the men of this presentation. Consider Hephæstus, for example, or Vulcan. Vulcan may hammer away, immortal as he is, for a million æons upon the thunderbolts of Jove, he may fashion and forge until he has exhausted the whole science and art of offensive and defensive armament; but how much better off is Vulcan for that? he can never step upon a higher plane, — he is to all eternity simply Vulcan, armorer to Jove. And so Hermes or Mercury may carry messages eternally, but no more; his faculty and apparatus go to that end and no farther. But these limitations are intolerable to the modern personality. The very conception of personality seems to me to imply a conception of growth. If I do one thing to-day, another to-morrow, I am twice as much to-morrow as I was to-day, by virtue of the new thing; or, even if I do only the same thing to-morrow that I did to-day, I do it easier, — that is, with a less expenditure of force, which leaves me a little surplus; and by as much as this surplus (which I can apply to something else) I am more than I was yesterday. This " more " represents the growth which I said was implied in the very conception of personality, of the continuous individual.

Now the feeling of all this appears to be just as completely asleep in Æschylus himself and in all his precedent old Greek theogonists as it is in the most witless boor who gazes open-mouthed at the gigantic Prometheus. But if we here descend from the gods, to the men, of this picture, we find Prometheus almost in terms asserting this absence of personality among the men whom he taught which we have just found by implication among the gods who tortured him.

You will remember the lines I read from the first long speech of Prometheus in which he describes the utterly brutish, crawling cave-dwellers to whom he communicated the first idea of every useful art. The denial of all power in man himself, once he was created, of originating these inventions — that is, of growing — that is, of personality — is complete.

I find nothing so subtly and inconsolably mournful among all the explicit miseries of the Greek mythology as this fixity of nature in the god or the man, by which the being is suspended, as it were, at a certain point of growth, there to hang forever. And in this view the whole multitudinous people, divine and human, of the whole Greek cyclus, seem to me as if sculptured in a half relief upon the black marble wall of their Fate — in half relief because but half gods and half men, who in the lack of personality cannot grow, cannot move.

When Keats stands regarding the figures sculptured upon the Grecian urn, it is only a cunning sign of the unspeakable misery of his own life that he finds the youth happy because though he can never succeed in his chase he can never fall any farther behind in it; to Keats's teased aspiration a certain sense of rest comes out of the very fixity of a man suspended in marble.

> " Fair youth beneath the trees, thou canst not leave
> Thy song, nor ever can those trees be bare ;
> Bold lover, never, never canst thou kiss
> Though winning near the goal ! Yet do not grieve:
> She cannot fade though thou hast not thy bliss,
> Forever wilt thou love and she be fair."

A true old Greek despair fills these lines with a sorrow which is all the more penetrating when we hear it singing out from among the keen and energetic personalities of modern times, — personalities which will not accept any youth's happiness of being howsoever near to his love if that happiness be coupled with the condition that he is never to be nearer, — personalities which find their whole summary in continuous growth, increase, movement.

And the case grows all the stronger if we consider that the Golden Age, (when the condition of primal man is very far from the miserable state depicted by Prometheus,) in which the antique imagination took such great delight, not all unshared, it must be confessed, by later times, fails to please the modern personality.

How taking seems this simplicity :

> " A blisful lyfe, a peseable and so swete,
>   Leddyn the peplis in the former age ;
>   Thei helde them paied with the frutes they ete,
>   Wich that the feldes gafe them by usage ;
>
> " Thei etyn most hawys and such pownage
>   And dronken watyr of the colde welle.
>
> " Yet was the ground not woundyd with the plough,
>   But corne upsprange onsowe of mannes hand ;
>
> " No man yit knew the furous of hys land ;
>   No man yit fier owt of the flynt fand.
>
> " No flesche ne wyst offence of hegge or spere ;
>   No coyne ne knew man whiche was false or trewe ;
>   No shyppe yit karfe the wawys grene and blewe ;
>   No marchand yit ne fet owtlandische ware.
>
> " Yit were no palys chambris, ne no hallys ;
>   In cavys and in wodes soft and swete
>   Sleptyn thys blessyd folk withowte wallys
>   On grasse or levys in parfite joy and quiete.

" Unforgyd was the hauberke and the plate;
    The lambisshe pepyl, voyd of alle vice,
    Hadden noo fantasye to debate,
    But eche of hem wold oder well cheriche;
    No pride, none envy, none avarice,
    No lord, no taylage by no tyrannye,
    Humblesse, and pease, good fayth the emprise.

" Yit was not Jupiter the likerous,
    That first was fadyr of delicacye
    Come in thys world, ne Nembroth desirous
    To raygne hadde not made hys towrys hyghe.
    Alas! alas! now may men wepe and crye,
    For in owre days is not but covetyse,
    Doublenesse, treson, and envye,
    Poysonne, manslawtyr, mordre in sondri wyse."

Surely this is all soothing and enchanting enough;
one cannot escape the amiable complacencies which
breathe out from this placid scene; but what modern
man would soberly agree to exchange a single moment
of this keen, breezy, energetic, growing existence of ours
for a Methuselah's life in this golden land where nature
does not offer enough resistance to educe manhood or
to furnish material for art, and where there is absolutely
no room, no chance, no need, no conception of this personality that if rightly felt makes the humblest life one
long enchantment of the possible. The modern personality confronted with these pictures, after the first
glamour is gone, is much minded to say with the sharp-
witted Glaucon in Plato's *Republic*, according to Jowett:
" after all, a state of simplicity is a city of pigs."

But secondly, the cumbrous apparatus of power with
which Æschylus presents us in this play is a conception
of people not acquainted with that model of infinite
compactness which every man finds in his own *ego*.
Jove, instead of speaking a word and instantly seeing

the deed result, must rely first upon his two ministers, Might and Force, who in the first scene of our play have hauled in the Titan Prometheus; these, however, do not suffice, but Hephæstus must be summoned in order to nail him to the rocks; and Jove cannot even learn whether or not his prisoner is repentant until Hermes, the messenger, visits Prometheus and returns. The modern *ego* which, though one indivisible, impalpable unit, yet remembers, reasons, imagines, loves, hates, fears and does a thousand more things all within its little scope, without appliances or external apparatus — such an *ego* regards such a Jove much in the light of that old Spanish monarch in whose court various duties were so minutely distributed and punctiliously discharged, that upon a certain occasion (as is related), the monarch being seated too near the fire and the proper functionary for removing him being out of call, his majesty was roasted to death in the presence of the entire royal household.

And as the third feature of the unpersonality revealed in this play, consider the fact that it is impossible for the modern reader to find himself at all properly terror-stricken by the purely physical paraphernalia of thunder, of storms, of chains, of sharp bolts, and the like, which constitute the whole resources of Jove for the punishment of Prometheus.

The modern direct way of looking at things — the perfectly natural outcome of the habit of every man's dealing with a thing for himself and of first necessarily looking to see what the thing actually is — this directness of vision cannot help seeing that Prometheus is a god, that he is immortal, that thunder cannot kill him, that the bolt through his breast makes no wound but will repair itself with ease, that he not only knows all this, but knows further that it is to end (as Prometheus himself

declares in the play) in his own triumph.   Under these
circumstances the whole array of whirlwinds and lightnings becomes a mere pin-scratch ; the whole business is
a matter of that purely physical pain which every man
is ashamed to make a noise of.   We can conceive a
mere man fronting all these terrors of storm and thunder
with unbowed head and serene countenance, in the consciousness that the whitest of these lightnings cannot
singe an eyelash of his immortal personality ; how, then,
can it be expected that we shall be greatly impressed with
the endurance of these ills by a god to whose greater
resistive endowment the whole system of this gross thrust-
and-smite of iron and fire is no more than the momentary
tease of a gnat !   To the audience of Æschylus, not
so ; they shiver and groan ; they know not themselves.

I do not know how I can better show the grossness of
this conception of pain than by opposing to it a subtle
modern conception thereof whose contrast will fairly
open out before us the truly prodigious gulf between
the average personality of the time of Æschylus and
that of ourselves.   The modern conception I refer to is
Keats's *Ode on Melancholy;* which, indeed, if one may
say a word *obiter*, out of the fullness of one's heart — I
am often inclined to think for all-in-all, — that is, for
thoughts most mortally compacted, for words which
come forth, each trembling and giving off light like a
morning-star, and for the pure beauty of the spirit and
strength and height of the spirit, — which, I say, for
all-in-all, I am often inclined to think, reaches the highest
height yet touched in the lyric line.

> "No, no, go not to Lethe, neither twist
>   Wolf's-bane, tight-rooted, for its poisonous wine ;
>   Nor suffer thy pale forehead to be kiss'd
>   By night-shade, ruby grape of Proserpine ;

Make not your rosary of yew-berries,
  Nor let the beetle, nor the death-moth be
  Your mournful Psyche, nor the downy owl
A partner in your sorrow's mysteries;
  For shade to shade will come too drowsily,
  And drown the wakeful anguish of the soul.

" But when the melancholy fit shall fall
  Sudden from heaven like a weeping cloud,
That fosters the droop-headed flowers all,
  And hides the green hill in an April shroud,
Then glut thy sorrow on a morning rose,
  Or on the rainbow of the salt-sand wave,
  Or on the wealth of globed peonies;
Or if thy mistress some rich anger shows,
  Imprison her soft hand, and let her rave,
  And feed deep, deep upon her peerless eyes.

" She dwells with Beauty — Beauty that must die;
  And Joy, whose hand is ever at his lips
Bidding adieu; and aching Pleasure nigh,
  Turning to poison while the bee-moth sips:
Ay, in the very temple of Delight
  Veiled Melancholy has her sovran shrine,
Though seen of none save him whose strenuous tongue
  Can burst Joy's grape against his palate fine;
His soul shall taste the sadness of her might,
  And be among her cloudy trophies hung."

V

THE main direction of our studies has been indicated in the preceding lectures to such an extent that from this point forward our customary review may be omitted. In examining the *Prometheus* of Æschylus we have found three particulars in which not only Æschylus but his entire contemporary time shows complete unconsciousness of the most precious and essential belongings of personality. These particulars were, (1) the absolute impossibility of growth, implicitly affirmed of the gods and explicitly affirmed of men in the passages which were read ; (2) the awkwardness of Jove's apparatus of power — which included a minister for every kind of act — as contrasted with the elasticity and much-in-little which each man must perceive in regarding the action of his own mind ; and (3) the gross and purely physical character of the punishments used by Jove to break the spirit of Prometheus. It was contended, you remember, that if the audience of Æschylus had acquired that direct way of looking phenomena in the face which is one of the incidents of our modern personality they would have perceived such an inadequacy between the thunders and earthquakes of Jove, on the one hand, and the immortal spirit of a Titan and a god like Prometheus, on the other, that the play, instead of being a religious and impressive spectacle to them, as it doubtless was, would have been simply a matter of ridicule, or at best one of those mere *dilettante* entertainments

7

where of our own free will we forgive the grossest
violations of common sense and propriety for the sake
of the music or the scenery with which they are associated, as for example at the Italian opera, or the Christmas pantomime.

This last particular brings us directly upon Shelley's
play of the *Prometheus Unbound*. We have seen that
Æschylus had a fit audience for this fable and was working upon emotions which are as deep as religion; but
now, when we come down 2300 years to a time from
which the Æschylean religious beliefs have long exhaled,
and when the enormous growth of personality has quite
rolled away the old lumpish terror that stood before the
cave of the physical and darkened it: in such a time
it would, of course, be truly amazing if a man like
Shelley should have elaborated this same old Promethean fable into a lyrical drama in the expectation of
shaking the souls of men with this same old machinery
of thunder, whirlwind and earthquake.

Such a mistake — the mistake of tearing the old fable
forcibly away from its old surroundings and of setting
it in modern thoughts before modern men — would be
much the same with that which Emerson has noted in
his poem *Each and All*:

> "I thought the sparrow's note from heaven,
> Singing at dawn on the alder bough;
> I brought him home in his nest at even;
> He sings the song, but it pleases not now,
> For I did not bring home the river and sky —
> He sang to my ear, they sang to my eye.
> The delicate shells lay on the shore;
> Bubbles of the latest wave
> Fresh pearls to their enamel gave;
> And the bellowing of the savage sea
> Greeted their safe escape to me.

I wiped away the weeds and foam
I fetched my sea-born treasures home;
But the poor, unsightly, noisome things
Had left their beauty on the shore
With the sun and the sand and the wild sea-shore."

Accordingly, it is instructive, as we look into Shelley's work, to observe how this inability of his to bring home the river and the sky along with the sparrow — this inability to bring a Greek-hearted audience to listen to his Greek fable — operates to infuse a certain tang of insincerity, of dilettantism, whenever he attempts to reproduce upon us the old terrors of thunder and lightning which Æschylus found so effective. We — we moderns — cannot for our lives help seeing the man in his shirt-sleeves who is turning the crank of the thunder-mill behind the scenes ; nay, we are inclined to ask with a certain proud indignation, How is it that you wish us to tremble at this mere resinous lightning, when we have seen a man (not a Titan nor a god), one of ourselves, go forth into a thunder-storm and send his kite up into the very bosom thereof and fairly entice the lightning by his wit to come and perch upon his finger, and be the tame bird of him and his fellows thereafter and forever? But secondly, it is still more conclusive upon our present point, of the different demands made by the personality of our time from that of Æschylus, to observe how Shelley's own sense of this difference, his own modern instinct, has led him to make most material alterations of the old fable, not only by increasing the old list of physical torments with a number that are purely spiritual and modern, but also by dignifying at once the character of Prometheus and the catastrophe of the play with that enormous motive of forgiveness which seems to be the largest outcome of the developed personality. Many

of you are aware of the scholastic belief that the
Prometheus Bound of Æschylus was but the middle play
of a trilogy, and that the last showed us a compromise
effected between Prometheus and Jove according to
which Prometheus reveals the fatal secret concerning
Jove's marriage, and Jove makes a new league of amity
with the Titan. We have a note of this change in
treatment in the very opening lines of Shelley's play —
which I now beg to set before you in the briefest possible
sketch. Scene I of Act I opens — according to the stage
direction — upon *A ravine of icy rocks in the Indian
Caucasus : Prometheus is discovered bound to the precipice :
Panthea and Ione are seated at his feet: time, night:
during the scene, morning slowly breaks.* Prometheus
begins to speak at once. I read only here and there a
line selected with special reference to showing the change
of treatment I have indicated as due to that intenser
instinct of personality which Shelley shared in common
with his contemporaries over Æschylus and his contemporaries.

Prometheus exclaims :

> " Monarch of gods and demons, and all spirits
> But one, who throng those bright and rolling worlds
> Which thou and I alone of living things
> Behold with sleepless eyes !   .   .   .
> Three thousand years of sleep-unsheltered hours,
> And moments aye divided by keen pangs
> Till they seemed years, torture and solitude,
> Scorn and despair, — these are mine empire,
> More glorious far than that which thou surveyest
> From thine unenvied throne ! "

Here we have the purely spiritual torments of " soli-
tude, scorn and despair " set before us : though Shelley
retains and even multiplies the physical torments of

Æschylus. A few lines further on, in this same long opening speech of Prometheus, we have them thus described :

> " Nailed to this wall of eagle-baffling mountain,
> Black, wintry, dead, unmeasured; without herb,
> Insect, or beast, or shape or sound of life.
>
> .   .   .   .
>
> The crawling glaciers pierce me with the spears
> Of their moon-freezing crystals ; the bright chains
> Eat with their burning cold into my bones.
>
> .   .   .   .
>
> .   .   .   The earthquake fiends are charged
> To wrench the rivets from my quivering wounds
> When the rocks split and close again behind ;
> While from their wild abysses howling throng
> The genii of the storm, urging the rage
> Of whirlwind, and afflict me with keen hail."

And presently, when after the repulse of Mercury Jove begins to stir up new terrors, we hear Ione exclaiming :

> " O, sister, look ! white fire
> Has cloven to the roots yon huge snow-loaded cedar ;
> How fearfully God's thunder howls behind ! "

But even in Shelley's array of these terrors we perceive a cunning outcrop of modernness in a direction which I have not yet mentioned but which we shall have frequent occasion to notice when we come to read the modern novel together : and that is in the detail of the description. Æschylus paints these conclusions with a big brush, and three sweeps of it : Shelley itemizes them.

It is worth while observing, too, that the same spirit of detail in modern criticism forces us to convict Shelley here of an inconsistency in his scene : for how could this " snow-loaded cedar " of Ione exist with propriety in a scene which Prometheus himself has just described as " without herb, insect, or beast, or sound of life ? "

The same instinct of modernness both in the spirituality of the torment and in the minuteness of its description displays itself a little farther on in the curse of
Prometheus.   Prometheus tells us in this same opening
speech that long ago he uttered a certain awful curse
against Jove which he now desires to recall; but it
would seem that in order to recall it he wishes to hear
the exact words of it.   " What was that curse?" — he
exclaims at the end of the speech; " for ye all heard me
speak."   To this question we have page after page of
replies from five voices — namely, the Voice of the Mountains, of the Springs, of the Air, of the Whirlwinds and
of the Earth — embodying such a mass of falsetto sublimity that Shelley himself would surely have drawn his
pen through the whole if he had lived into the term of
manhood.   Finally the whole awkward device for getting
the curse of Prometheus before the reader is consummated by raising up the phantasm of Jupiter which
repeats the curse, word for word.   We have page after
page of talk before this first act is finished; and for our
present purpose it may be dismissed with the single
remark that the very wordiness of it, the detail, the
diffuseness, — which ramble all over the heavens and the
earth, and search the very depths of the spirit, for
similes, until the reader's mind is brought to a condition
like that when one repeats a word over and over until
the word loses all meaning, — all this, I say, may be dismissed with the single remark that the enormity of it is
itself an incident of the very personality we have seen
cropping out in so many other directions.   I think I
know not a single English poet — not even among the
Elizabethans, whose besetting sin is wordiness — who sins
so prodigiously in this respect.   In truth, Shelley appears
always to have labored under an essential immaturity:

it is very possible that if he had lived a hundred years he would never have become a man : he was penetrated with modern ideas, but penetrated as a boy would be, crudely, overmuch, and with a constant tendency to the extravagant and illogical : so that I call him the modern boy.

These considerations quite cover the remaining three acts of his *Prometheus Unbound* and render it unnecessary for me to quote from them in support of the passages already cited.

The first act contains, indeed, nearly the substance of the whole drama.   Act II contains no important motive except the visit of Asia and Panthea to Demogorgon under the earth.   In the third act we have a view of Jove surrounded by his ministers ; but in the midst of a short speech to them he is suddenly swept into hell for everlasting punishment.   Here, of course, Shelley makes a complete departure from the old story of the compromise between Jove and Prometheus ; Shelley makes Prometheus scornfully reject such a compromise and allow Jove to go down to his doom.   Hercules then unbinds Prometheus who repairs to a certain exquisite interlunar cave and there dwells in tranquillity with his beloved Asia. The rest of Act III is filled with long descriptions of the change which comes upon the world with the dethronement of Jove.   Act IV is the most amazing piece of surplusage in literature ; the catastrophe has been reached long ago in the third act, Jove is in eternal duress, Prometheus has been liberated and has gone with Asia and Panthea to his eternal paradise above the earth, and a final radiant picture of the reawakening of man and nature under the new régime has closed up the whole with the effect of a transformation-scene.   Yet, upon all this, Shelley drags in Act IV which is simply leaden

in action and color alongside of Act III and in which
the voices of unseen spirits, the chorus of Hours, Ione,
Panthea, Demogorgon, the Earth and the Moon pelt each
other with endless sweetish speeches that rain like ineffec-
tual comfits in a carnival of silliness.   For example, a
Voice of Unseen Spirits cries :

> " Bright clouds float in heaven,
> Dew-stars gleam on earth,
> Waves assemble on ocean,
> They are gathered and driven
> By the storm of delight, by the panic of glee !
> They shake with emotion,
> They dance in their mirth.
> But where are ye ?

> " The pine boughs are singing
> Old songs with new gladness ;
> The billows and fountains
> Fresh music are flinging
> Like the notes of a spirit from land and from sea ;
> The storms mock the mountains
> With the thunder of gladness.
> But where are ye ? "

The people thus inquired for, being the chorus of
Hours, sleepily reply :

> " The voice of the spirits of air and of earth
> Has drawn back the figured curtain of sleep
> Which covered our being and darkened our birth
> In the deep."

A VOICE.

" In the deep ? "

SEMI-CHORUS.

" Oh, below the deep."

.   .   .   .

SEMI-CHORUS I.

> " We have heard the lute of Hope in sleep ;
> We have known the voice of love in dreams,
> We have felt the wand of power come and leap — "

SEMI-CHORUS II.

" As the billows leap in the morning beams,"

CHORUS.

" Weave the dance on the floor of the breeze,
  Pierce with song heaven's silent light,
  Enchant the day that too swiftly flees,
  To check its flight ere the cave of night.

" Once the hungry Hours were hounds
  Which chased the day like a bleeding deer,
  And it limped and stumbled with many wounds
  Through the nightly dells of the desert year.

" But now oh ! weave the mystic measure
  Of music, and dance, and shapes of light ;
  Let the Hours and the spirits of night and pleasure
      Like the clouds and sunbeams unite."

CHORUS OF SPIRITS.

" We join the throng
  Of the dance and the song,
  By the whirlwind of gladness borne along ;
  As the flying-fish leap
  From the Indian deep
  And mix with the sea-birds half asleep."

This long lyric outburst, wholly unnecessary to an action which was already complete, seems an instructive fact to place before young writers in a time when many souls which might be poetic gardens if they would compact all their energies into growing two roses and a lily — three poems in all, for a lifetime — become instead mere wastes of profuse weeds that grow and are cut down and cast into the oven with each monthly magazine.

But it would not be fair to leave Shelley with this flat taste in our mouths, and I will therefore beg to finish our examination of the *Prometheus Unbound* by three quotations from these last acts, in which his modernness

of detail and of subtlety,— being exercised upon matters
capable of such treatment — has made for us some
strong and beautiful poetry.   Here for instance at the
opening of Scene I, Act II, we have a charming specimen
of the modern poetic treatment of nature and of landscape, full of spirituality and full of detail.   The stage
direction is *Morning; A Lovely Vale in the Indian
Caucasus. Asia, alone.*   Asia, who is the lovely bride
of Prometheus, is awaiting Panthea who is to come with
news of him.   She begins with an invocation of the
Spring.

ASIA.

" From all the blasts of heaven thou hast descended :
     Yes : like a spirit, like a thought, which makes
     Unwonted tears throng to the horny eyes,
     And beatings haunt the desolated heart,
     Which should have learnt repose : thou hast descended
     Cradled in tempests ; thou dost wake, O Spring !
     O child of many winds !   As suddenly
     Thou comest as the memory of a dream,
     Which now is sad because it hath been sweet !
     Like genius, or like joy which riseth up
     As from the earth, clothing with golden clouds
     The desert of our life.
     This is the season, this the day, the hour ;
     At sunrise thou shouldst come, sweet sister mine,
     Too long desired, too long delaying, come !
     How like death-worms the wingless moments crawl !
     The point of one white star is quivering still
     Deep in the orange light of widening morn
     Beyond the purple mountains : through a chasm
     Of wind-divided mist the darker lake
     Reflects it : now it wanes : it gleams again
     As the waves fade, and as the burning threads
     Of woven cloud unravel the pale air :
     'Tis lost ! and through yon peaks of cloud-like snow
     The roseate sunlight quivers : hear I not
     The Æolian music of her sea-green plumes
     Winnowing the crimson dawn ? "

And here we find some limpid details of underwater life which are modern. Two fauns are conversing : one inquires where live certain delicate spirits whom they hear talking about the woods, but never meet. We are here in an atmosphere very much like that of the *Midsummer-Night's Dream*. I scarcely know anything more compact of pellucid beauty : it seems quite worthy of Shakspere.

SECOND FAUN.

> " 'Tis hard to tell :
> I have heard those more skill'd in spirits say,
> The bubbles, which th' enchantment of the sun
> Sucks from the pale faint water-flowers that pave
> The oozy bottom of clear lakes and pools,
> Are the pavilions where such dwell and float
> Under the green and golden atmosphere
> Which noontide kindles through the woven leaves ;
> And when these burst, and the thin fiery air,
> The which they breathed within those lucent domes,
> Ascends to flow like meteors through the night,
> They ride on them, and rein their headlong speed,
> And bow their burning crests, and glide in fire
> Under the waters of the earth again."

Here again, in my third extract, we have poetry which is as strong as the other is dainty, and which is as modern as geology. Asia is describing a vision in which the successive deposits in the crust of the earth are revealed to her. The whole treatment is detailed, modern, vivid, powerful.

> " The beams flash on
> And make appear the melancholy ruins
> Of cancell'd cycles : anchors, beaks of ships ;
> Planks turn'd to marble ; quivers, helms, and spears,
> And gorgon-headed targes, and the wheels
> Of scythed chariots, and the emblazonry
> Of trophies, standards, and armorial beasts,

Round which death laugh'd, sepulchred emblems
Of dread destruction, ruin within ruin!
The wrecks beside of many a city vast,
Whose population which the earth grew over
Was mortal, but not human; see, they lie,
Their monstrous works and uncouth skeletons,
Their statues, domes, and fanes, prodigious shapes
Huddled in gray annihilation, split,
Jamm'd in the hard, black deep; and over these
The anatomies of unknown winged things,
And fishes which were isles of living scale,
And serpents, bony chains, twisted around
The iron crags, or within heaps of dust
To which the torturous strength of their last pangs
Had crushed the iron crags; and over these
The jagged alligator, and the might
Of earth-convulsing behemoth, which once
Were monarch-beasts, and on the slimy shores,
And weed-overgrown continents of earth,
Increased and multiplied like summer worms
On an abandoned corpse, till the blue globe
Wrapt deluge round it like a cloak, and they
Yelled, gasped, and were abolished; or some God,
Whose throne was in a comet, past, and cried
Be not! And like my words they were no more."

Shelley appears not to have been completely satisfied
with the Promethean story. This dissatisfaction displays
itself in a characteristic passage of his preface to the
Prometheus which happens very felicitously to introduce the only other set of antique considerations I shall
offer you on this subject. " Let this opportunity " (he
says in one place) " be conceded to me of acknowledging
that I have what a Scotch philosopher characteristically
terms ' a passion for reforming the world.' . . . But
it is a mistake to suppose that I dedicate my poetical
compositions solely to the direct enforcement of reform,
or that I consider them in any degree as containing a
reasoned system on the theory of human life. . . .

" . . . Should I live to accomplish what I purpose, that is, produce a systematical history of what appear to me to be the genuine elements of human society, let not the advocates of injustice and superstition flatter themselves that I should take Æschylus rather than Plato as my model."

In Shelley's poem we have found much of the modernness between the lines, or appearing as the result, merely, of that spirit of the time which every writer must . share to a greater or less extent with his fellow-beings of the same period. But as we proceed now to examine Bayard Taylor's poem, *Prince Deukalion*, we find a man not only possessed with modernness, but consciously possessed, so that what was implicit in Shelley — and a great deal more — here becomes explicit and formulated.

As one opens the book a powerful note of modernness in the drama, as opposed to the drama of Æschylus, strikes us at the outset in the number of the actors. One may imagine the amazement of old Æschylus as he read down this truly prodigious array of *dramatos prosopa:*

Eos, Goddess of the Dawn; Gæa, Goddess of the Earth; Eros; Prometheus; Epimetheus; Pandora; Prince Deukalion; Pyrrha; Agathon; Medusa; Calchas; Buddha; Spirits of Dawn; Nymphs; Chorus of Ghosts; Charon; Angels; Spirits; The Nine Muses; Urania; Spirit of the Wind; Spirit of the Snow; Spirit of the Stream; Echoes; the Youth; the Artist; the Poet; the Shepherd; the Shepherdess; the Mediæval Chorus; Mediæval Anti-Chorus; Chorus of Builders; Four Messengers. With these materials Mr. Taylor's aim is to array before us the whole panorama of time, painted in symbols of the great creeds which have characterized each epoch. These epochs are four; and one act is devoted to each. In the first act we have the passing away of nymph and satyr and the whole antique Greek mythos; and we are shown the coming man and woman in the persons of Prince Deukalion and Pyrrha, his wife-to-be, whose figures, however, are as yet merely etched upon a mist of prophecy.

In Act II we have the reign and fall of the mediæval faith, all of which is mysteriously beheld by these same shadowy personalities, Deukalion and Pyrrha. In Act III the faith of the present is similarly treated. In Act IV we have at last the coming man, or developed personality fairly installed as ruler of himself and of the world, and Prince Deukalion and Pyrrha, the ideal man and the ideal woman now for the first time united in deed as well as in aspiration, pace forth into the world to learn it and to enjoy it. Mr. Taylor, as I said, is so explicit upon the points of personality and modernness as compared with the Æschylean play, that few quotations would be needed from his work, and I will not attempt even such a sketch of it as that of Shelley's. For example, in Scene I, Act I, of *Prince Deukalion*, Scene I being given in the stage direction as

"*A plain sloping from high mountains towards the sea; at the bases of the mountains lofty, vaulted entrances of caverns; a ruined temple on a rocky height; a shepherd asleep in the shadow of a clump of laurels; the flock scattered over the plain,*" — a shepherd awakes and wonderingly describes his astonishment at certain changes which have occurred during his sleep. This shepherd, throughout the book, is a symbol of the mass of the common people, the great herd of men. Voices from various directions interrupt his ejaculations : and amongst other utterances of this sort we have presently one from the

nymphs — as representative of the Greek nature-mythos
— which is quite to our present purpose.

NYMPHS

(Who are to the shepherd voices and nothing more)

" Our service hath ceased for you, shepherds !
    We fade from your days and your dreams,
    With the grace that was lithe as a leopard's,
    The joy that was swift as a stream's !
    To the musical reeds, and the grasses ;
    To the forest, the copse, and the dell ;
    To the mist, and the rainbow that passes,
    The vine, and the goblet, farewell !
    Go, drink from the fountains that flow not !
    Our songs and our whispers are dumb:
    But the thing ye are doing ye know not,
    Nor dream of the thing that shall come."

In Scene IV, Deukalion, leading Pyrrha, passes into
a cavern, the last mouth of Hades left on the earth.
Presently the two emerge upon "a shadowy, colorless
landscape," and are greeted by a chorus of ghosts which
very explicitly formulates that dreary impossibility of
growth which I pointed out in the last lecture as incident
to the old conception of personality.

CHORUS OF GHOSTS.

" Away !
    Ashes that once were fires,
    Darkness that once was day,
    Dead passions, dead desires,
    Alone can enter here !
    In rest there is no strife,

    .   .   .   .

    Like some forgotten star,
    What first we were, we are.
    The past is adamant :
    The future will not grant
    That, which in all its range
    We pray for — change."

In spite of these warnings they push on, find Charon at his old place by the dark river, but are left to row themselves across, Charon pleading age and long unused joints, and after many adventures find Prometheus who very distinctly declares to Prince Deukalion and Pyrrha their mission.

" Since thou adrift,"

says Prometheus,

" And that immortal woman by thy side
 Floated above submerged barbarity
 To anchor, weary, on the cloven mount,
 Thou wast my representative."

Prince Deukalion — as perhaps many will remember — is the Noah of the old Promethean cyclus, and the story ran that the drowned world was miraculously repeopled by him and Pyrrha. In the same speech Prometheus introduces to Deukalion as a future helper his brother Epimetheus — one of the most striking conceptions of the old fable and one of the most effective characters in Mr. Taylor's presentation. We saw in the last lecture that Prometheus was called the Provident, — the *pro-metheus* being a looking forward. Precisely opposite is Epimetheus, that is, he who looks *epi* — upon or backward. Perhaps it is a fair contrast to regard Prometheus as a symbol of striving onward, or progress; and Epimetheus as a symbol of the historic instinct, the instinct which goes back and clears up the past as if it were the future; which with continual effort reconstructs it; which keeps the to-be in full view of what has been; which reconciles progress and conservation. Accordingly the old story reports Epimetheus as oldest at his birth and growing younger with the progress of the ages.

"Take one new comfort,"

continues Prometheus,

> "Epimetheus lives!
> Though here beneath the shadow of the crags
> He seems to slumber, head on nerveless knees,
> His life increases; oldest at his birth,
> The ages heaped behind him shake the snow
> From hoary locks, and slowly give him youth.
> 'Tis he shall be thy helper: Brother, rise!"

EPIMETHEUS — (*coming forward*)

"I did not sleep: I mused.   Ha! comest thou, Deukalion?"

PROMETHEUS.

> "Soon thy work shall come!
>   Shame shall cease
> When midway on their paths our mighty schemes
> Meet, and complete each other!   Yet my son,
> Deukalion — yet one other guide I give,
> Eos!"

And presently Prometheus leads Deukalion and Pyrrha to what is described in the stage-direction as "*The highest verge of the rocky table-land of Hades, looking eastward.*" Eos is summoned by Prometheus, much high conversation ensues, and this, the sixth and last scene of the first act ends thus:

Eos (*addressing young Deukalion and Pyrrha*)

> "Faith, when none believe;
>   Truth, when all deceive;
>   Freedom, when force restrains;
>   Courage to sunder chains;
>   Pride, when good is shame;
>   Love, when love is blame, —
>   These shall call me in stars and flame!
>   Thus if your souls have wrought,
>   Ere ye approach me, I shine unsought."

8

But Eos proceeds to warn Deukalion and Pyrrha of long trial, and of many disappointments, closing thus:

> "When darkness falls,
> And what may come is hard to see;
>   When solid adamant walls
> Seem built against the Future that shall be;
> When Faith looks backward, Hope dies, Life appals,
>   Think most of Morning and of me!"

[The rosy glow in the sky fades away]

PROMETHEUS (to *Prince Deukalion*)

"Go back to Earth, and wait!"

PANDORA (to *Pyrrha*)

" Go: and fulfil our fate!"

This sketch of the first act of Taylor's work is so typical of the remainder that I need not add quotations from the second, or third, or fourth act: the explicit modernness of the treatment, the spirituality, the personality of it, everywhere forms the most striking contrast to the treatment of Æschylus; and I will close the case as to *Prince Deukalion* by quoting the subtle and wise words of Prometheus which end the play. The time is the future: the coming man and woman, Deukalion and Pyrrha, after long trial and long separation are at last allowed to marry and to begin their earthly life. These are Prometheus's parting words to them. It would be difficult to imagine one plane of thought farther removed from another than is that of the time-spirit which here speaks through Taylor, from the time-spirit which speaks through Æschylus. Remembering the relations between man and inexorable nature, between man and the exterminating god which we saw revealed by the Prometheus of Æschylus, listen to these relations prophesied by the Prometheus of Taylor.

> "Retrieve perverted destiny!"

(In Æschylus, once "destiny" is about, all retrieval grows absurd.)

> "'Tis this shall set your children free.
> The forces of your race employ
> To make sure heritage of joy;
> Yet feed, with every earthly sense,
> Its heavenly coincidence, —
> That, as the garment of an hour;
> This, as an everlasting power.
> For Life, whose source not here began,
> Must fill the utmost sphere of Man
> And, so expanding, lifted be
> Along the line of God's decree,
> To find in endless growth all good, —
> In endless toil, beatitude.
> Seek not to know Him; yet aspire
> As atoms toward the central fire!
> Not lord of race is He, afar, —
> Of Man, or Earth, or any star,
> But of the inconceivable All;
> Whence nothing that there is can fall
> Beyond Him, — but may nearer rise,
> Slow-circling through eternal skies.
> His larger life ye cannot miss,
> In gladly, nobly using this.
> Now, as a child in April hours
> Clasps tight its handful of first flowers,
> Homeward, to meet His purpose, go! —
> These things are all ye need to know."

We have seen that Shelley thought of producing a history of "the genuine elements of human society," taking Plato as his model, instead of Æschylus. Had he done so, how is it likely he would have fared? It so happens that of all the monstrosities of thought which

we find in the whole Greek cultus, based upon the failure
to conceive personality, the most monstrous are those
which originated with Plato.   And since you have now
heard this word personality until your patience must be
severely taxed, I am glad to say that I can now close
this whole pending argument which I have announced
as our first line of research in a short and conclusive
way by asking you to consider for a moment the complete massacre and deliberate extermination of all
those sacred bases of personality upon which the fabric
of our modern society rests in that ideal society which
Plato has embodied in his *Republic*.   Nothing is more
irresistible than the conviction that the being who planned
Plato's *Republic* could neither have had the least actual
sense of his own personality nor have recognized even
theoretically the least particle of its real significance.
Fortunately this examination can be made with great
brevity by confining our attention to the three quite conclusive matters of marriage, children, and property, as
they are provided for in Book V of Plato's *Republic*.

At line 460 of that book we find Socrates inquiring:
" And how can marriages be made most beneficial " in
our ideal republic? and presently answering his own
question in due form.   I quote here and there, to make
the briefest possible showing of the plan.   " Why the
principle has been already laid down, that the best of
either sex should be united with the best as often as
possible ; and that inferiors should be prevented from
marrying at all."   " Now these goings on must be a
secret which the rulers only know, . . . or there will be
a farther danger of our herd . . . breaking into rebellion."   To these ends we had " better appoint certain
festivals at which the brides and bridegrooms " (whom
the rulers have previously selected with care and secrecy)

"will be brought together, and sacrifices will be offered and suitable hymeneal songs composed by our poets;" . . . and we "invent some ingenious kind of lots which the less worthy may draw." In short, the provision for marriage is that the rulers shall determine each year how many couples shall marry, and shall privately designate a certain number of the healthiest couples for that purpose; at the annual festival all marriageable couples assemble and draw lots, these lots having previously been so arranged that all unhealthy or in any way inferior couples shall draw blanks. Of course this is fraud, but Plato defends it against Glaucon's objection thus : since " our rulers will have to practice on the body corporate with medicines "; and since " falsehood and deceit " may " be used with advantage as medicines ; our rulers will find a considerable dose of these " (that is, of falsehood and deceit) " necessary for the good of their subjects ; . . . and this lawful use of them seems likely to be often needed in the regulations of marriages." The couples thus married eat at a common table. A brave youth, as a reward of valor, is allowed more than one wife.

Such are the marriage-arrangements of Plato's ideal republic, except that I have omitted all the most monstrous provisions, giving only the rosiest view of it. Reserving comment, let us see how the children are provided for. Immediately after birth " The proper officers will take the offspring of the good " (or healthy) " parents to " a certain common " fold, and there . . . deposit them with certain nurses ; but the offspring of the inferior, or of the better where they chance to be deformed, will be put away in some mysterious unknown place, as decency requires ; " the mothers are afterwards allowed to come to the fold to nourish the children, but the officers are to take "the greatest care that no mother recognizes her own child:" of course these children, when they grow up are to be also bridegrooms and brides, and the problem of how to prevent unknown brothers and sisters, and the like, from marrying is duly attended to; but the provisions for this purpose are at once so silly and so beastly — nay, they out-beast the beasts — that surely no one can read them without wishing to blot out the moment in which he did so.

And lastly property is thus disposed of. "Then" (line 482, Bk. V, *Republic*) " the community of wives and children is clearly the source of the greatest good to the State, . . . and agrees with the other principle that the guardians " — the guardians are the model citizens of this ideal republic — " are not to have houses or lands or any other property; their pay is to be their food and they are to have no private expenses; . . . Both the community of property and the community of families . . . tend to make them more truly guardians; they will not tear the city in pieces by differing about *meum* and *tuum;* the one dragging any acquisition which he has made into a house of his own, where he has a separate wife and children, . . . and another into another; . . . but all will be affected as far as may be by the same pleasures and pains; . . . and, as they have nothing but their persons which they can call their own, suits and complaints will have no existence among them."

Now as soon as these ideal dispositions of Plato are propounded to a modern hearer they send an instantaneous shock to the remotest ends of his nature; and what I will ask you to do at present is to formulate this shock in terms of personality. Taking for example the Platonic provision with regard to marriage (how grotesquely, by the way, these provisions show alongside of what have gained great currency as " Platonic attachments ") : perhaps the two thousand years since Plato have taught us nothing so clearly as that one of the most mysterious and universal elements of personality is that marvellous and absolutely inconsequential principle by which a given man finds himself determined to love a certain woman, or a given woman determined to love a certain man ; and if we look back we find that the most continuous travail of the ages has been to secure perfect freedom for these determinations.

Does it not seem as if Time grinned at us in some horrible dream when we remind ourselves that here the divine Plato, as he has been called, and the unspeakable Zola (as some of us have learned to call him) have absolutely come cheek by jowl, and that the physiological marriage of Zola is no more nor less than the ideal marriage of Plato?

Rejecting comment on the child-nursing arrangement of Plato it is instructive to pass on and regard from a different point of view, though still from the general direction of personality, the Platonic community of property. If men desire property, says Plato, "one man's desire will contravene another's and we shall have trouble. How shall we remedy it? Crush out the desire : and to that end abolish property."

But no, cries modern personality to Plato, cannot you imagine such an extension of personality as to make each man see that on the whole the shortest way to carry out his desires for property is to respect every other man's desire for property, and thus, in the regulations which will necessarily result from this mutual respect, to secure everything he acquires by spiritual considerations infinitely more effective than spears and bars?

We had occasion to observe the other day how complete has been the success of this doctrine here in the United States: we found that the real government now going on is individual, personal, — not at Washington — and that we have every proper desire, — of love in marriage, of having one woman to wife, of cherishing our own children, of accumulating property, — secured by external law apparently, and really by respect for that law and the principles of personality it embodies.

It seems curious to me here to make two further points of contact which, taken with the Zola point just made, seem to tax the extremes of the heavens and the earth. Plato's organic principle appears to emerge from some such consideration as this. A boy ten years old is found to possess a wondrous manual deftness: he can do anything with his fingers: word is brought to Plato: what shall the State do with this boy? Why, says Plato, if he be manually so adroit, likely he will turn pickpocket: the plain course is to chop off his hands, — or to expose him to die in one of those highly respectable places such as decency requires for generally unavailable children.

No, says the modern man: you are destroying his manifest gift, the very deepest outcome of his personality; he might be a pickpocket, true, but then he might be a great violinist, he might be a great worker in all manner of materials requiring deftness: instead of cutting off his hands, let us put him at an industrial school, let us set him to playing the violin, let us cherish him, let us develop his personality. So, Plato takes the gift of acquiring property — for it is a real gift and blessing to man if properly developed — and he will chop it off, that is, he will crush out the desire of property by destroying the possibility of its exercise.

And what is this in its outcome but the Nirvana of the

Buddhistic religion?   My passions keep me in fear and hope : therefore I will annihilate them ; when I neither think nor desire, then I shall rest, then I shall enjoy Nirvana.   Plato institutes a Nirvana for the ills of marriage, of offspring, of property ; and he realizes it by the slow death through inanition of the desire for love, for children, for property.

And as we have found the Platonic Plato arguing himself into a Zola, the dialectic Plato arguing himself into a dreaming Buddha, all for lack of the sense of personality, we now find the ideal Plato arguing himself, for the same lack, into a sturdy Whitman.   Think of Plato's community of property, and listen to Whitman's reverie, as he looks at some cattle.   It is curious to notice how you cannot escape a certain sense of naïvety in this, and how you are taken by it, — until a moment's thought shows you that the naïvety is due to a cunning and bold contradiction of every fact in the case.

> "I think I could turn and live with
>   animals, they are so placid and self-contain'd:
> I stand and look at them long and long.
>
> "Not one is dissatisfied — not one is demented
>   with the mania of owning things:
> Not one is respectable or industrious over the
>   whole earth."

The Whitman method of reaching naïvety is here so funnily illustrated that it seems worth while to stop a moment and point it out.   Upon the least reflection, one must see that "animals" here must mean cows, and well-fed cows; for they are about the only animals in the world to whom these items would apply.   For, says Whitman, "not one is dissatisfied, not one is demented with the mania of owning things : " but suppose he were taking one of his favorite night-strolls in the woods of Bengal rather than of New Jersey, is it not more than probable that the first animal he met would be some wicked tiger not only dissatisfied, but perfectly demented with the mania of owning Mr. Whitman, the only kind of property the tiger knows? Seriously, when we reflect that property to the animal means no more than food or nest or lair, and that the whole wing-shaken air above us, the earth-surface about us, the earth-crust below us, the seas, and all, are unceasingly agog day and night with the furious activity of animals quite as fairly demented with the mania of owning their property as men theirs; and that it is only the pampered beast who is not so demented, — the cow, for instance, who has her property duly brought to her in a pail so many times a day, and no more to do but to enjoy the cud thereof until next feed-time, — we have a very instructive model of methods by which poetry can make itself naïve.

And finally what a conclusive light is shed upon the principles supporting Plato's community of property, when we bring forward the fact, daily growing more and more notable, that along with the modern passion for acquiring property has grown the modern passion of giving away property, that is, of charity? What ancient scheme ever dreamed of the multitudinous charitable organizations of some of our large cities? Charity has become organic and a part of the system of things: it has sometimes overflowed its bounds so that great social questions now pend as to how we shall direct the overflowing charitable instincts of society so as really to help the needy and not pamper the lazy: its public manifestations are daily, its private ministrations are endless.

Plato would have crushed the instinct of property; but the instinct, vital part of man's personality, as it is, has

taken care of itself, has been cherished and encouraged
by the modern cultus, and behold, instead of breeding a
wild pandemonium of selfishness as Plato argued, it has
in its orderly progress developed this wonderful new out-
growth of charity which fills every thoughtful man's
heart with joy, because it covers such a multitude of the
sins of the time.

I have been somewhat earnest — I fear tediously so —
upon this matter, because I have seen what seem the
greatest and most mischievous errors concerning it
receiving the stamp of men who usually think with
clearness and who have acquired just authority in many
premises.

It would not be fair to the very different matters which
I have now to treat, to detail these errors; and I will
only mention that if, with these principles of personality
fairly fixed in one's mind, one reads for example the
admirable Introduction of Professor Jowett to his translation of Plato's *Republic*, one has a perfect clew to many
of the problems over which that translator labors with
results which, I think, cannot be conclusive to his own
mind.

Here, too, no one can be satisfied with the otherwise
instructive chapter on Individuality in Professor Eucken's
Fundamental Concepts of Modern Philosophic Thought.
Eucken's direct reference to Plato's *Republic* is evidently
made upon only a very vague recollection of Plato's
doctrine, which is always dangerous. "The complete
subordination and sacrifice of the individual expressed
in Plato's idea of a state arose from his opposition to a
tendency of the times which he considered pernicious,
and so is characterized rather by moral energy and
intensity of feeling than by the quiet and simple resig-
nation to the objective which we find in the great men

of the preceding period." But a mere "opposition to a
tendency of the times" could never have bred this elaborate and sweeping annihilation of individuality; and it is
forgotten that Plato is not here legislating for his times
or with the least dream of the practical establishment of
his Republic: again and again he declares his doubts as
to the practicability of his plans for any time. No, he
is building a republic for all time, and is consistently
building upon the ruins of that personality which he was
not sensible of except in its bad outcome as selfishness.

I must add that there was an explicit theory of
what was called Individuality among the Greeks; the
phenomenon of the unaccountable differences of men
from birth early attracted those sharp eyes, and the
Stoics and others soon began to build in various directions from this basis. But just as the Greeks had a
theory of harmony, though harmony was not developed
until the last century, — as Richter says somewhere that
a man may contemplate the idea of death for twenty
years, and only in some moment of the twenty-first
suddenly have the realization of death come upon him,
and shake his soul — so their theory of individuality
must have been wholly amateur, not a working element,
and without practical result. Surely, we seem in condition to say so with confidence if you run your minds
back along this line of development which now comes
to an end. For what have we done? We have inter-
rogated Æschylus and Plato, whom we may surely call
the two largest and most typic spirits of the whole Greek
cultus, upon the main fact of personality; we have
verified the abstract with the concrete by questioning
them upon the most vital and well-known elements
of personality: what do you believe about spiritual
growth, about spiritual compactness, about true love,

marriage, children, property? and we have received answers which show us that they have not yet caught a conception of what personality means, and that when they explicitly discuss individuality in their theories, it is a discussion of blind men about colors.

VI

WE are now to enter upon the second of our four lines of study by concentrating our attention upon three historic details in the growth of this personality whose general advance has been so carefully illustrated in our first line. These details are found in the sudden rise of Physical Science, of Modern Music, and of the Modern Novel, at periods of time so little separated from each other that we may consider these great fields of human activity as fairly opening simultaneously to the entrance of man about the seventeenth and eighteenth centuries.

Addressing ourselves first then to the idea of Science, let us place ourselves at a point of view from which we can measure with precision the actual height and nature of the step which man took in ascending from the plane of, say, Aristotle's " science " to that of Sir Isaac Newton's " science." And the only possible method of placing ourselves at this point of view is to pass far back and fix ourselves in the attitude which antiquity maintained towards physical nature, and in which succeeding ages comfortably dozed, scarcely disturbed even by Roger Bacon's feeble protest in the thirteenth century, until it was shocked out of all future possibility by Copernicus, Galileo and Sir Isaac Newton.

Accordingly, in pursuance of our custom of abandoning abstract propositions at the earliest moment when we can embody them in terms of the concrete, let us spend a quiet hour in contemplating some of the specific absurdities of our ancestors in scientific thought and in generalizing them into the lack of personality.   Let us go and sit with Socrates on his prison-bed, in the *Phædo*, and endeavor to see this matter of man's scientific relation to physical nature, with his sight.   Hear Socrates talking to Simmias : he is discussing the method of acquiring true knowledge : it is well we are invisible as we sit by him, for we cannot keep back a quiet smile, — we who come out of a beautiful and vast scientific acquirement all based upon looking at things with our eyes, we whose very intellectual atmosphere is distilled from the proverb, " seeing is believing " — when we hear these grave propositions of the wisest antique man.   " But what of the acquisition of wisdom," says Socrates : . . . " do the sight and hearing convey any certainty to mankind, or are they such as the poets incessantly report them, who say that we neither hear nor see anything as it is? . . . Do they not seem so to you?"

"They do, indeed," replied Simmias.   " When, then," continued Socrates, " does the soul attain to the truth? For when it attempts to investigate anything along with the body, it is plain that the soul is led astray by the body. . . . Is it not by reasoning, if by anything, that reality is made manifest to the soul?"

" Certainly."

But now Socrates advances a step to show that not only are we misled when we attempt to get knowledge by seeing things, but that nothing worth attention is capable of being physically seen.   I shall have occasion to recur in another connection to the curious fallacy involved in this part of Socrates' argument.   He goes on to inquire of Simmias: "Do we assert that Justice is anything, or not?"

" We say that it is."

" And beauty and goodness, also ? "

" Surely."

" Did you ever see anything of the kind with your eyes ? "

" Never," replied Simmias.

. . . " Then," continues Socrates, " whoever amongst us prepares, with the greatest caution and accuracy, to reflect upon that particular thing by itself upon which he is inquiring" and . . . " using reflection alone, endeavors to investigate every reality by itself, . . . abstaining as much as possible from the use of the eyes . . . is not such an one, if any, likely to arrive at what really exists ? "

" You speak, Socrates," answered Simmias, " with amazing truth."

It is curious to note in how many particulars this process of acquiring knowledge is opposed to that of the modern scientific man. Observe specially that Socrates wishes to investigate every reality by itself, while we on the contrary fly from nothing with so much vehemence as from an isolated fact ; it maddens us until we can put it into relation with other facts, and delights us in proportion to the number of facts with which we can relate it. In that book of multitudinous suggestions which Novalis (Friedrich Von Hardenberg) calls *The Pupil at Sais*, one of the most modern sentences is that where, after describing many studies of his wondrous pupil, Novalis adds that " erelong he saw nothing alone."

Surely one of the earliest and most delightful sensations one has in spiritual growth, after one has acquired the true synthetic habit which converts knowledge into wisdom, is that delicious, universal impulse which accompanies every new acquisition as it runs along like a warp across the woof of our existing acquisition, making a pleasant tang of contact, as it were, with each related fibre.

But Plato speaks even more directly upon our present point, in advocating a similar attitude towards physical science. In Book VII, of the *Republic*, he puts these words into the mouth of Socrates : " And whether a man gapes at the heavens, or blinks on the ground, seeking to learn some particular of sense, I would deny that he can learn, for nothing of that sort is matter of science."

Of course these, as the opinions of professed idealists, would not be representative of the Greek attitude towards physical science. Yet when we turn to those who are pre-eminently physical philosophers we find that the mental disposition, though the reverse of hostile, is nearly always such as to render the work of these philosophers unfruitful. When we find, for example, that Thales in the very beginning of Greek philosophy holds the principle, or beginning, ἡ ἀρχή of all things to be moisture, or water ; that Anaximenes a little while after holds the beginning of things to be air ; that Heraclitus holds the *arche* to be fire : this sounds physical, and we look for a great extension of men's knowledge in regard to water, air and fire, upon the idea that if these are really the organic principles of things thousands of keen inquiring eyes would be at once levelled upon them, thousands of experiments would be at once set on foot, all going to reveal properties of water, air and fire. But perhaps no more expressive summary of the real relation between man and nature, not only during the Greek period but for many centuries after it, could be given than the fact that these three so-called elements which begin the Greek physical philosophy remained themselves unknown for more than two thousand years after Thales and Anaximenes and Heraclitus, until the very last century when, with the discovery of oxygen, men are able to prove that they are not elements at all, but that what we call fire is merely an effect of the rapid union of oxygen with bodies, while water and air are compounds of it with other gases. It is perfectly true that in the years between Thales and the death of Aristotle a considerable body of physical facts had been accumulated; that Pythagoras had observed a number of acoustic phenomena and mathematically formulated their relations; it is true that — without detaining you to specify intermediate inquirers — we have that wonderful summary of Aristotle — wonderful for one man — which is contained in his *Physics*, those *Physics* from which the name " metaphysics " originated, through the circumstance that he placed the other books *after* those on physics, calling them Τὰ μετὰ τὰ φυσιχὰ βιβλία, the meta-physical, or over and above physical, books.

When we read the titles of these productions — here are " Eight Books of Physical Lectures," " Four Books of the Heavens," " Two Books of Production and Destruction," Treatises "On Animals," "On Plants," " On Colors," " On Sound " — we feel that we must be in a veritable realm of physical science. But if we examine these lectures and treatises, which probably contain the entire body of Greek physical learning, we find them hampered by a certain disability which seems to me characteristic not only of Greek thought, but of all man's early speculation, and which excludes the possibility of a fruitful and progressive physical science. I do not know how to characterize this disability otherwise than by calling it a lack of that sense of personal relation to fact which makes the thinker passionately and

supremely solicitous about the truth, that is, the existence of his facts and the soundness of his logic : solicitous
of these not so much with reference to the value of his
conclusions as because of an inward tender inexorable
yearning for the truth and nothing but the truth.   In
short, I find that early thought everywhere, whether
dealing with physical facts or metaphysical problems, is
lacking in what I may call the intellectual conscience —
the conscience which makes Mr. Darwin spend long
and patient years in investigating small facts before
daring to reason upon them, and which makes him
state the facts adverse to his theory with as much care as
the facts which make for it.

Part of the philosophy of this personal relation between
a man and a fact is very simple.   For instance what do
you know at present of the inner life of the Patagonians?
Probably no more than your Mitchell's or Cornell's
Geography told you at school.   But if a government
expedition is soon to carry you to the interior of that
country, a personal relation arises which will probably
set you to searching all the libraries at your command
for such travels or treatises as may enlarge your
knowledge of Patagonia.

It is easy to give a thousand illustrations of this lack
of intellectual conscience in Greek thought which continued indeed up to the time of the Renaissance.   For
example : it would seem that nothing less than a sort of
amateur mental attitude towards nature, an attitude which
does not bind the thinker to his facts with such iron con-
scientiousness that if one fact were out of due order it
would rack him, could account for Aristotle's grave exposition of the four elements.   " We seek," he says, " the
principles of sensible things, that is of tangible bodies.
We must take therefore not all the contrarieties of quality

but those only which have reference to the touch. . . .
Now the contrarieties of quality which refer to the touch
are these : hot, cold ; dry, wet ; heavy, light ; hard, soft ;
unctuous, meagre ; rough, smooth ; dense, rare." Aristotle then rejects the last three couplets on several
grounds and proceeds : " Now in four things there are
six combinations of two ; but the combinations of two
opposites, as hot and cold, must be rejected ; we have
therefore four elementary combinations which agree with
the four apparently elementary bodies. Fire is hot and
dry ; air is hot and wet ; water is cold and wet ; earth is cold
and dry." And thus we comfortably fare forward with fire,
air, earth and water for the four elements of all things.

But Aristotle argues that there must be a fifth element :
and our modern word quintessence is, by the way, a relic
of this argument, this fifth element having been called by
later writers *quinta essentia* or quintessence. The argument is as follows : " the simple elements must have simple
motions, and thus fire and air have their natural motions
upwards and water and earth have their natural motions
downwards ; but besides these motions there is motion
in a circle which is unnatural to these elements, but
which is a more perfect motion than the other, because a
circle is a perfect line and a straight line is not ; and there
must be something to which this motion is natural. From
this it is evident that there is some essence or body different from those of the four elements, . . . and superior
to them. If things which move in a circle move contrary
to nature it is marvelous, or rather absurd that this the
unnatural motion should alone be continuous and eternal ;
for unnatural motions decay speedily. And so from all
this we must collect that besides the four elements which
we have here and about us there is another removed far
off and the more excellent in proportion as it is more
distant from us."

Or take Aristotle's dealing with the heaviness and lightness of bodies.

After censuring former writers for considering these as merely relative, he declares that lightness is a positive or absolute property of bodies just as weight is ; that earth is absolutely heavy, and therefore tends to take its place below the other three elements ; that fire has the positive property of lightness, and hence tends to take its place above the other three elements ; (the modern word *empyrean* is a relic of this idea from the *pyr* or fire, thus collected in the upper regions), and so on ; and concludes that bodies which have the heavy property tend to the centre, while those with the light property tend to the exterior, of the earth, because " Exterior is opposite to Centre, as heavy is to light."

This conception, or rather misconception, of opposites appears most curiously in two of the proofs which Socrates offers for the immortality of the soul, and I do not know how I can better illustrate the infirmity of antique thought which I have just been describing than by citing the arguments of Socrates in that connection according to the *Phædo*. Socrates introduced it with special solemnity.

" I do not imagine," he says, " that any one, not even if he were a comic poet, would now say that I am trifling. . . . Let us examine it in this point of view, whether the souls of the dead survive or not.

" Let us consider this, whether it is absolutely necessary in the case of as many things as have a contrary, that this contrary should arise from no other source than from a contrary to itself. For instance, where anything becomes greater, must it not follow that from being previously less it subsequently became greater ? "

" Yes."

" So too, if anything becomes less, shall it become so subsequently to its being previously greater ? "

"Such is the case," said Cebes.

"And weaker from stronger, swifter from slower, . . . worse from better, juster from more unjust?"

"Surely."

"We are then sufficiently assured of this, that all things are so produced, contraries from contraries?"

"Sufficiently so."

" . . . Do you now tell me likewise in regard to life and death. Do you not say that death is the contrary of life?"

"I say so."

"And that they are produced from each other?"

"Yes."

"What then is that which is produced from life?"

"Death," said Cebes.

"And that which is produced from death?"

"I must allow," said Cebes, "to be life."

"Therefore, our souls exist after death."

This is one formal argument of Socrates. He now goes on speaking to his friends during that fatal day at great length, setting forth other arguments in favor of the immortality of the soul. Finally he comes to the argument which he applies to the soul, that magnitude cannot admit its contrary, the small, but that one retires when the other approaches. At this point he is interrupted by one who remembers his former position. Plato relates:

Then some one of those present (but who he was I do not clearly recollect) when he heard this said, "In the name of the gods, was not the very contrary of what is now asserted laid down in the previous part of the discussion, that the greater is produced from the less and the less from the greater, and this positively was the mode of generating contraries from contraries?" Upon which Socrates said . . . "Then it was argued that a contrary thing was produced from a contrary; but now, that contrary itself can never become its own contrary. . . . But observe further if you will agree with me in this. Is there anything you call heat and cold ? "

" Certainly."

" The same as snow and fire ? "

" Assuredly not."

" Is heat, then, something different from fire, and cold something different from snow ? "

" Yes."

" But this I think is evident to you, that snow while it is snow can never, having admitted heat, continue to be what it was, snow and hot, but on the approach of heat will either give way to it or be destroyed."

" Certainly so."

" And fire, on the other hand, on the approach of cold, must either give way to it or be destroyed, nor can it ever endure, having admitted cold, to continue to be what it was, fire and cold. . . . Such I assert to be the case with the number 3 and many other numbers. Shall we not insist that the number 3 shall perish first . . . before it would endure while it was yet 3 to become even ? . . . What, then ? what do we now call that which does not admit the idea of the even ? "

" Odd," replied he.

" And that which does not admit the just, nor the graceful ? "

" The one, ungraceful, and the other, unjust."

" Be it so.   But by what name do we call that which does not admit death ? "

" Immortal."

" Does the soul, then, not admit death ? "   (Socrates has already suggested that whatever the soul occupies it brings life to.)

" No."

" Is the soul, therefore, immortal ? "

" Immortal."

Socrates' argument drawn from the number 3 brings before us a great host of these older absurdities of scientific thought, embracing many grave conclusions drawn from fanciful considerations of number, everywhere occurring. For briefest example : Aristotle in his book *On the Heavens* proves that the world is perfect by the following complete argument : " 'The bodies of which the world is composed . . . have three dimensions ; now 3 is the most perfect number ; . . . for of 1 we do not speak as a number ; of 2 we say *both;* but 3 is the first number of which we say *all;* moreover, it has a beginning, a middle and an end." You may instructively compare with this the marvelous matters which the school of Pythagoras educed out of their perfect number which was 4, or the *tetractys;* and Plato's number of the *Republic* which commentators to this day have not settled.

These illustrations seem sufficient to show a mental attitude towards facts which is certainly like that one has towards a far-off country which one does not expect to visit. The illustration I have used is curiously borne out by a passage in Lactantius, writing so far down as the fourth century : in which we have a picture of mediæval relations towards nature, and of customary discussions.

" To search," says he, " for the causes of natural things ; to inquire whether the sun be as large as he seems, whether the moon is convex or concave, whether the stars are fixed in the sky or float freely in the air ; of what size and what material are the heavens ; whether they be at rest or in motion ; what is the magnitude of the earth ; on what foundations it is suspended and balanced ; — to dispute and conjecture on such matters is just as if we chose to discuss what we think of a city in a remote country of which we never heard but the name."

Perhaps this defect of thought, this lack of personality towards facts, is most strikingly perceived in the slowness with which most primary ideas of the form and motion of the earth made their way among men. Although astronomy is the oldest of sciences and the only progressive science of antiquity; and although the idea that the earth was a sphere was one of the earliest in Greek philosophy; yet this same Lactantius in the fourth century is vehemently arguing as follows: " Is it possible that men can be so absurd as to believe that the crops and trees on the other side of the earth hang downwards, and that men there have their feet higher than their heads?   If you ask of them how they defend these monstrosities — how things do not fall away from the earth on that side? they reply that the nature of things is such that heavy bodies tend towards the centre, like the spokes of a wheel, while light bodies, as clouds, smoke, fire, tend from the earth towards the heavens on all sides.   Now I am really at a loss what to say of those who, when they have once gone wrong, steadily persevere in their folly and defend one absurd opinion by another."

And coming on down to the eighth century, the anecdote is well known of honest Bishop Virgil of Salisbury, who shocked some of his contemporaries by his belief in the real existence of the antipodes, to such an extent that many thought he should be censured by the Pope for an opinion which involved the existence of a whole " world of human beings out of reach of the conditions of salvation."

And finally we all know the tribulations of Columbus on this point far down in the fifteenth century, at the very beginning of the Renaissance.

Now this infirmity of mind is, as I have said, not distinctive of the Greek.   To me it seems simply a natural incident of the youth of reason, of the childhood of personality.   At any rate, for a dozen centuries and more after Aristotle's death, to study science means to study Aristotle; in vain do we hear Roger Bacon in the thirteenth century — that prophet-philosopher who first announces the two rallying cries of modern science, mathematics and experiment — in vain do we hear Roger Bacon crying: "If I had power over the works of Aristotle I would have them all burnt; for it is only a loss of time, a course of error, and a multiplication of ignorance beyond expression, to study in them."

Various attempts have been made to account for the complete failure of Greek physical science by assigning this and that specific tendency to the Greek mind : but it seems a perfect confirmation of the view I have here presented — to wit that the organic error was not Greek but simply a part of the general human lack of personality — to reflect that for 1,500 years after Aristotle things are little better, and that when we do come to a time when physical science begins to be pursued upon progressive principles, we find it to be also a time when all other departments of activity begin to be similarly pursued, so that we are obliged to recognize not the correction of any specific error in Greek ratiocination, but a general advance of the spirit of man along the whole line.

And perhaps we have now sufficiently prepared ourselves, as was proposed at the outset of this sketch of Greek science, to measure precisely the height of the new plane which begins with Copernicus, Kepler and Galileo in the sixteenth century, over the old plane which ended with Aristotle and his commentators. Perhaps the true point up to which we should lay our line in making this measurement is not to be found until we pass nearly through the seventeenth century and arrive fairly at Sir Isaac Newton. For while each one of the

great men who preceded him had made his contribution
weighty enough, as such, yet each brings with him some
old darkness out of the antique period.

When we come to examine Copernicus we find that
though the root of the matter is there, a palpable envi-
ronment of the old cycle and epicycle still hampers
it; Galileo disappoints us at various emergencies; Kepler
puts forth his sublime laws amid a cluster of startling
absurdities; Francis Bacon is on the whole unfruitful;
Descartes will have his vortices or eddies as the true
principles of motion of the heavenly bodies; and so it
is not until we reach Sir Isaac Newton at the end of the
seventeenth century that we find a large, quiet, wholesome
thinker, de-Aristotleized, de-Ptolemized, de-Cartesianized,
pacing forth upon the domain of reason as if it were his
own orchard, and seating himself in the centre of the
universe as if it were his own easy chair, observing the
fact and inferring the law as if with a personal passion
for truth and a personal religion towards order. In
short, and in terms of our present theory, with Sir Isaac
Newton the growth of man's personality has reached a
point when it has developed a true personal relation
between man and nature.

Let us now sum these matters. Up to the time of
Newton one seems to find everywhere some chilly trace
of the old inexorable pre-Promethean enmity of nature
towards man. Even from out the ancient Titanic times
of geologic convulsion — times of upheaval, of flood, of
the grind of glaciers, — times when nature as if in a
nightmare swarms with the great Saurians and grotesque
forms that make terrible the air and the oozy earth, —
times of huge-backed monsters, " isles of living scale,"
looming up in the swash of muddy waves, — times that
have filled the crust of the earth with bones, the rem-

nants and reminders of death, — times which seem to
have somehow crept into the memory of man to appear
in those wars of the Titans of which Prometheus told us,
or in the visions of griffins and monsters which haunt
the human imagination, — or perhaps in the marsh-
monsters, Grendel and his mother, of our own old
Beowulf epic, — even from out these times a vast cone
of shadow seems to project itself and to extend far
beyond the time when nature's mood itself has become
more gentle, when instead of the ptero-dactyl she gives
us the antelope, and instead of tree-fern and club-moss
she gives us the lily and the rose. It seems part of the
chill operations of this shadow that the Greek cannot
go directly to his vine, his mountain, his stream, his
tree, but can approach these only through the intermediary Bassarid, the Oread, the Hamadryad, the
Nymph. It is as if, in the absence of Prometheus,
some one must still stand between man and this old
inimical nature which for so many centuries has frozen
him with her snows, burned him with her heats, and
racked him with her hungers : hence, Faun, Nymph,
Hamadryad. I have fancied, too, that the same stern
note is to be found in the very highest antique moral
conceptions. When Plato is developing the monstrous
doctrines which we have seen concerning marriage, &c.,
he is doing so from the purest religious motives. His
loftiest ideal of the moral order of the universe is contained in the principle of justice ; and he believes that
he is forwarding this ideal by those arrangements. But
it is only in the growth of modern personality that we
find a far more beautiful ideal of the order of things.
This ideal is love. Compare the Promethean punishments, compare the inexorable marriage laws of Plato —
all in the interests of justice — with the principle under-

lying that adorable sonnet No. 116 of Shakspere's in which he really sets forth the doctrines of mercy, of charity, of love which must now forever supersede the reign of justice.

CXVI.

" Let me not to the marriage of true minds
  Admit impediments.   Love is not love
  Which alters when it alteration finds,
  Or bends with the remover to remove :
  O no; it is an ever-fixèd mark,
  That looks on tempests and is never shaken ;
  It is the star to every wandering bark,
  Whose worth's unknown although his height be taken.
  Love's not Time's fool, though rosy lips and cheeks
  Within his bending sickle's compass come ;
  Love alters not with his brief hours and weeks,
  But bears it out even to the edge of doom.
    If this be error, and upon me prov'd,
    I never writ nor no man ever lov'd."

Now this feeling of love towards man has become really possible as towards inanimate nature ; the modern personality can love nature directly as a man loves his friend ; when this love formulates itself in observing the facts of nature, classifying them, we have a Newton, a Darwin ; when it expresses itself in reproducing nature in beautiful forms we have the modern school of landscape-painting, the modern nature-poetry, the modern elaborate description of natural scenes in the novel and the like.

I should have been glad if the scope of this part of my inquiry had allowed me to give some sketch at least of the special workers in science who immediately preceded Newton, and some of whose lives were most pathetic and beautiful illustrations of this personal love for nature which I have tried to show as now coming

into being for the first time in the history of man.
Besides such spectacles as the lonesome researches of
Jeremiah Horrox, for example, I scarcely know anything
in history which yields such odd and instructive contrasts as those glimpses of the scientific work which went
on about the court of Charles II, and of what seems to
have been the genuine interest of the monarch himself,
in *Pepys's Diary*. For instance, under date of May 11th,
1663, I find the entry: "Went home after a little discourse with Mr. Pierce the surgeon who tells me that
. . . the other day Dr. Clarke and he did dissect
two bodies, a man and a woman, before the king, with
which the king was highly pleased." Again, February
1st of the next year: "Thence to Whitehall, where in
the Duke's chamber the King come and stayed an hour
or two, laughing at Sir W. Petty . . . and at Gresham
College in general: Gresham College he mightily
laughed at for spending time only in weighing of air
and doing nothing else since they sat." On the 4th he
was at St. Paul's school and "Dr. Wilkins" is one of
the "posers," Dr. Wilkins being John Wilkins, Bishop of
Chester, whose name was well-known in mathematics
and in physics. Under date of March 1st, same year,
the entry is: "To Gresham College where Mr. Hooke
read a second very curious lecture about the late comet;
among other things proving very probably that this is
the very same comet that appeared before in the year
1618, and that in such a time probably it will appear
again, which is a very new opinion; but all will be in
print." And again on the 8th of August, 1666, I find
an entry which is of considerable interest: "Discoursed
with Mr. Hooke about the nature of sounds, and he did
make me understand the nature of musical sounds made
by strings mighty prettily; and told me that having

come to a certain number of vibrations proper to make any tone, he is able to tell how many strokes a fly makes with her wings (those flies that hum in their flying) by the note that it answers to in music during their flying. That I suppose is a little too much refined ; but his discourse in general of sound was mighty fine."

On the other hand, I scarcely know how I could show the newness of this science thus entering the world more vividly than by recording two other entries which I find in the midst of these scientific notes.   One of these records a charm for a burn, which Pepys thought so useful as to preserve.   This is, in case one should be burned, to say immediately the following verse :

> " There came three angels out of the East ;
>   One brought fire, the other brought frost —
>   Out fire, in frost.
>   In the name of the Father, Son and Holy Ghost."

And the other is, under Sept. 29th, 1662, " To the King's Theatre where we saw ' Midsummer's Night's Dream,' which I had never seen before, nor shall ever again, for it is the most insipid, ridiculous play that ever I saw in my life."

Indeed, if you should wish to see how recently we are out of the range of Aristotle you have only to read the chapter on Human Anatomy which occurs in the early part of dear old Robert Burton's *Anatomy of Melancholy*. Here is an account of the body which makes curious reading for the modern biologist.   I give a line here and there.   The body is divided into parts containing or contained, and the parts contained are either humors or spirits.   Of these humors there are four : to wit, first, blood, next, phlegm, third, choler, and fourth, melancholy ; and this is part of the description of each.

"Blood is a hot, sweet, temperate, red humor, . . . made of the most temperate parts of the chylus in the liver. . . . And from it spirits are first begotten in the heart. Phlegm is a cold and moist humor, begotten of the colder part of the chylus in the liver. Choler is hot and dry, begotten of the hotter parts of the chylus. Melancholy, cold and dry, . . . is a bridle to the other two hot humors, blood and choler. These four humors have some analogy with the four elements and to the four ages in man." Having disposed thus of humors, we have this account of spirit or the other contained part of the body. "Spirit is a most subtle vapor which is expressed from the blood and the instrument of the soul to perform all his actions; a common tie or medium between the body and the soul, as some will have it; or as Paracelsus — a fourth soul of itself." Proceeding to other parts of the body, here are the lungs. "The lungs is a thin spongy part like an ox-hoof. . . . The instrument of voice; . . . and next to the heart to express their thoughts by voice. That it is the instrument of voice is manifest in that no creature can speak . . . which wanteth these lights. It is besides the instrument of breathing; and its office is to cool the heart by sending air into it by the venosal artery," &c., &c.

This anatomy of Burton's includes the soul, and here are some particulars of it. "According to Aristotle the soul is defined to be entelecheia, . . . the perfection or first act of an organical body having power of life. . . . But many doubts arise about the essence, subject, seat, distinction and subordinate faculties of it. . . . Some make one soul; . . . others, three. . . . The common division of the soul is into three principal faculties — vegetal, sensible and rational." The soul of man includes all three; for the "sensible includes vegetal and rational both; which are contained in it (saith Aristotle) *ut trigonus in tetragono*, as a triangle in a quadrangle. . . . Paracelsus will have four souls, adding to the three grand faculties a spiritual soul: which opinion of his Campanella in his book *De Sensu Rerum* much labors to demonstrate and prove, because carcases bleed at the sight of the murderer; with many such arguments." These are not the wanderings of ignorance; they represent the whole of human knowledge and are an epitome made up from Aristotle, Galen, Vesalius, Fallopius, Laurentius, Wecker, Melanchthon, Feruclius, Cicero, Pico Mirandola, Paracelsus, Campanella, Taurellus, Philip, Flavius, Macrobius, Alhazen the Arabian, Vittellio, Roger Bacon, Battista Porta, Cardan, Sambucus, Pliny, Avicenna, Lucretius, and such another list as makes one weary with the very names of authorities.

These details of antique science brought face to face with the weighing of air at Gresham College and with Sir Isaac Newton, represent with sufficient sharpness the change from the old reign of enmity between Nature and man, from the stern ideal of justice, to the later reign of love which embraces in one direction God, in another, fellow-man, in another, physical nature.

Now in these same sixteenth, seventeenth and eighteenth centuries in which we have seen science recovering itself after having been so long tongue-tied by authority, a remarkably similar process goes on in the art of music. If, as we did in considering the progress of science, we now place ourselves at a standpoint from which we can precisely estimate that extension of man's personal relation towards the unknown during these centuries, which resulted in modern music, we are met with a chain of strikingly similar facts and causes. The Greek music quite parallels Greek physical science.

We have seen how, in the latter, a Greek philosopher would start off with a well-sounding proposition that all things originated in moisture or in fire or in air; and we have seen how, instead of attacking moisture, fire and air, and of observing and classifying all the physical facts connected with them, the philosopher after awhile presents us with an amazing superstructure of pure speculation wholly disconnected from facts of any kind, physical or otherwise. Greek music offers us precisely the same net outcome. It was enthusiastically studied, there were multitudes of performers upon the lyre, the flute, and so on, it was a part of common education, and the loftiest souls exerted their loftiest powers in theorizing upon it. Thus, in Plato's *Republic* Socrates earnestly condemns every innovation upon music. His words are: "For any musical innovation is full of danger to the State. . . . Damon tells me, and I can quite believe him . . . that when modes of music change, the fundamental laws of the State always change with them;" . . . (therefore) "our guardians must lay the foundations of their fortress in music." Again, in Book III, during a discussion as to the kind of music to be permitted in our Republic, we have this kind of talk. Socrates asks: "Which are the harmonies expressive of sorrow?" It is replied, they are "the mixed Lydian, and the full-toned or bass Lydian."

"These must be banished. . . . Which are the soft or drinking harmonies?"

"The Ionian and the Lydian."

These it appears must also be banished.

"Then the Dorian and the Phrygian appear to be the only ones which remain."

Socrates "answered: of the harmonies I know nothing, but I want to have one warlike which will sound the word or note which a brave man utters in the hour of danger or stern resolve, or when his cause is failing . . . (and he) meets fortune with calmness and endurance; and another to be used by him in times of peace and freedom of action. . . . These two harmonies I ask you to leave : the strain of necessity and the strain of freedom, the strain of the unfortunate and the strain of the fortunate, the strain of courage and the strain of temperance ; these, I say, leave."

Simmias draws a charming analogy in the *Phædo* between the relation of a beautiful and divine harmony to the lyre, and that of the soul to the body ; Pythagoras dreams upon the music of the spheres; everywhere the Greek is occupied with music, practical and theoretical. I find a lively picture of the times where in Book VII of the *Republic* Socrates describes the activity of the musical searchers : " By heaven," he says, " 'tis as good as a play to hear them talking about their condensed notes, as they call them ; they put their ears alongside of their neighbors . . . one set of them declaring that they catch an intermediate note and have found the least interval which should be the unit of measurement; the others maintaining the opposite theory, that the two sounds have passed into the same, each party setting their ears before their understanding."

And in this last clause we have a perfectly explicit statement of that lack of personal relation to facts which makes Greek music as meagre as Greek science. We found it the common fault of Greek scientific thought that it took more satisfaction in an ingenious argument upon a pseudo-fact than in a solid conclusion based upon plain observation and reasoning. So here, Socrates is satirizing even the poor attempt at observation made by these people, and sardonically accuses them of what is the very pride of modern science — namely, of setting their ears before their understanding, — that is, of rigorously observing the facts before reasoning upon them.

At any rate, in spite of all this beautiful and comprehensive talk of harmony and the like, the fact is clear that the Greek had no harmony worth the name; he knew nothing but the crude concords of the octave, the fourth and the fifth; moreover, his melody was equally meagre; and altogether his ultimate flight in music was where voices of men and women sang, accompanied in unison or octave by the lyre, the flute and the like.

And if we consider the state of music after the passing away of the Greek cultus up to the fifteenth century we have much the same story to tell as was just now told of mediæval science. For a time the world's stock of tunes is practically comprised in the melodies collected by Gregory, known as the Gregorian Chant. Presently the system of polyphonic music arises in which several voices sing different melodies so arranged as not to jar with each other. But when we now come down to the sixteenth century we find a wonderful new activity in music accompanying that in science. Luther in Germany, Gondimel in France, push forward the song: in Spain, Salinas of Salamanca studies ancient music for thirty years, and finally arrives at the conclusion that the Greek had no instrumental music and that all their melody was originally derived from the order of syllables in verse. In Italy, Monteverde announces what were called his "new discords," and the beautiful *maestro* Palestrina writes compositions in several parts, which are at once noble, simple and devout. England at this time is filled with music, and by the end of the sixteenth century the whole land is a-warble with the madrigals and part-compositions of Weelkes, Wilbye, John Milton

Sr., and the famous Dr. John Bull, together with those of Tye, Tallis, Morley, Orlando Gibbons, and hundreds more. But as yet modern music is not. There is no orchestra; Queen Elizabeth's dinner-music is mainly drums and trumpets. It is not until the middle of the seventeenth century that Jenkins and Purcell begin to write sonatas for a small number of violins with organ accompaniment.

A curious note of the tendency towards instrumental music at this time, however, is found in the fact that people begin to care so little for the words of songs as to prefer them in a foreign language. Henry Lawes, one of the most famous musicians of the middle of the seventeenth century, he who suggested Milton's *Comus* and set it to music, endeavored to rebuke this affectation, as he supposed it, by a cruel joke: he wrote a song, of which the words were nothing more than the index of an old volume of musical compositions, and had it sung amidst great applause. It must have been in the same course of feeling that Waller — several of whose poems had been set to music by Lawes — addressed to him the following stanza:

> "Let those who only warble long
> And gargle in their throats a song
> Content themselves with do, re, mi;
> Let words of sense be set by thee."

And so through Allegri, Stradella, the Scarlattis and a thousand singers, players and composers we come to the year 1685 in which both Bach and Handel were born. Here we are fairly in the face of modern music. What then is modern music? Music at this time bounds forward in the joy of an infinitely developable principle. What is this principle? In its last analysis it is what has now come to be called Harmony, or more specially

Tonality. According to the modern musical feeling
when any tone is heard it is heard in its relation to some
other tone which from one circumstance or another may
have been taken as a basis of such relations. By a long
course of putting our ears before our understanding —
a course carried on by all those early musicians whose
names I have mentioned, each contributing some new
relation between tones which his ear had discovered —
we have finally been able to generalize these relations in
such a way as to make a complete system of tonality, .
in which every possible tone brings to our ear an impression dependent on the tone or tones in connection
with which it is heard. As the Pupil at Sais ere long
began to see nothing alone, so we hear nothing alone.
You have only to remember that the singer nowadays
must always have the piano accompaniment in order to
satisfy our demand for harmony, that we never hear any
unmixed melody in set music, in order to see how completely harmony reigns in our music instead of bare
melody. We may then broadly differentiate the modern
music which begins at the same time with modern science
from all precedent music as Harmony contrasted with
Melody. To this we must add the idea of instrumental
harmony, — of that vast extension of harmonies rendered
possible by the great development of orchestral instruments whose compass greatly exceeds that of the human
voice, which formerly limited all musical energy.

It is tempting, here, to push the theory of personality
into fanciful extremes. You have seen how the long
development of melody — melody being here the individual — receives a great extension in the polyphonic music,
where individual melodies move along side by side
without jostling : and how at length the whole suddenly
bursts into the highest type of social development, where
the melody is at once united with the harmony in the

most intimate way, yet never loses its individuality; where the melody would seem to maintain towards the harmony almost the ideal relation of our finite personality to the Infinite personality, at once autonomous as finite, and yet contained in, and rapturously united with the infinite.

But without pressing the matter, it now seems clear from our sketch that just as in the seventeenth century the spirit of man has opened up for the first time a perfectly clear and personal relation with physical nature, and has thus achieved modern science with Sir Isaac Newton, so in this same century, the spirit of man opens up a new relation to the infinite, to the unknown, and achieves modern music, in John Sebastian Bach. Nor need I waste time in defending this category in which I placed music, as a relation to the Unknown. If you collect all the expressions of poets and philosophers upon music, you will find them converging upon this idea. No one will think Thomas Carlyle sentimental: yet it is he who says "music which leads us to the verge of the infinite, and lets us gaze on that."

And so finally, with the first English novel of Richardson in 1739–40, we have completed our glance at the simultaneous birth of modern science, modern music, and the modern novel.

And we are now prepared to carry forward our third and fourth lines of thought together: which were to show the development of the novel from the Greek Drama, and to illustrate the whole of the principles now advanced with some special studies of the modern novel. These two lines will mutually support each other, and will emerge concurrently, as we now go on to study the life and works of that George Eliot who has so recently solved the scientific problem which made her life one of the most pathetic and instructive in human history.

VII

OUR custom, in these studies, of passing at the earliest possible moment from the abstract to the concrete, and of verifying theory by actual experiment, arrives at a sort of beautiful climax and apotheosis as we proceed from the abstract principles formulated in the last six lectures to their exquisite concrete and verification in George Eliot.

At our last meeting we saw that during a period of time which we fix to a point by sweeping the mind from the sixteenth century to the middle of the eighteenth, the growing personality of man sent out three new processes which have remarkably changed and enlarged the whole form of our individual and social structure.

I have found it highly useful in more than one connection to acquire a clear notion of these three processes by referring them all to a common physical concept of direction. For instance : we may with profit construct a diagram in which it shall appear that at the Renaissance period mentioned the three great and distinctive new personal relations which man established for himself were (1) a relation upward,

$$\begin{array}{c}
\text{Unknown (Music)} \\
\uparrow \\
\text{Personality} \longrightarrow \text{Fellow-man.} \quad \text{(The Novel)} \\
\downarrow \\
\text{Nature.} \quad \text{(Physical Science.)}
\end{array}$$

towards the Unknown, (2) a relation on our own level, a

relation towards our equal,—that is, towards our fellow-man, and (3) a relation towards our inferior,—in the sense that the world is for man's use, is made for man,—that is, towards physical nature. We have seen how from the beginning of man's history these three relations did not acquire the vividness and energy of personal relations, nor any fixed or developable existence at all, until the period mentioned.

I cannot help expressing earnest regret that the limits of my present subject have not allowed me to give any development whatever to this conception of the actual significance of the Renaissance as a significance which, crystallizing into Music, the Novel and Science, has left us those as the solid residuum of that movement; and it is not a mere sentimental generalization but a hard, scientific and unifiable fact that music is the distinctive form in which man's new relation to what is above him has expressed itself, the novel is the distinctive form in which man's new personal relation to his fellow-man has expressed itself, and science is the distinctive form in which man's new personal relation to nature has expressed itself.

I am perfectly well aware that when one thinks of the Italian Opera with its banalities and fleshly frenzies; or when one thinks of the small, low, unmanly, sensual lives which so many musicians have led under our eyes: one.may well feel inclined to dispute this category to which I have assigned music, and to question whether music does belong to this wholly religious sphere. I long to be able to remind such questioners of the historic fact that music has been brought into the church as the mouthpiece of our worship not by the sentimental people but by the sternest reformers and the most untheoretical and hard-handed workers: I long to

remind them how it is the same Luther who would meet
his accusers though ten thousand devils backed them,
that cares most assiduously for the hymns of the church,
makes them, sings them : how it is the same Puritan who
fights winter and hunger and the savage, that is noted
for his sweet songs and must have his periodic opening
of the musical avenue up towards the great God : or,
passing far back to the times before music was music,
and so making the case stronger, I long to remind them
of a single line in a letter from Pliny the younger to
Trajan in the year 110, which puts before me a dewy
morning-picture of music and Christian devotion that
haunts my imagination — a line in which Pliny mentions
some people who were in the habit of " meeting on a
certain day before daylight and singing a hymn to Christ
as to a God " : or how in the fourth century the very
Ambrosian chant which preceded the Gregorian chant is
due to the fact that the good Ambrose, Bishop of Milan,
casting about for solace, collects a number of psalm tunes
and hymns and appoints them to be sung for the express
purpose of consoling his people in their afflictions ; and
coming down to the birth of modern music, I long to
remind these questioners of the noble and simple devout-
ness which Palestrina brings into the church worship
with his music, of the perfect calm creative life of John
Sebastian Bach whose music is so compact of devotion
as to have inspired the well-known declaration that
wherever it is played, it makes that place a church ; and
finally, I long to remind them how essential a part of
every modern church the organ-loft and the choir have
come to be, and in full view of the terrible mistakes which
these often make, of the screechy Italian opera music
which one hears floating from this or that church on a
Sunday, of the wholly undevout organ music with which

the unfortunate flippant-minded organist often sends us
forth, — to declare that music is yet, as we have seen, a
new art, that we have not really learned the uses of it,
much less the scope of it, that indeed not all of us have
even yet acquired the physical capacity or ear for it, —
and that, finally, we are at the very threshold of those
sweet applications we may hereafter make of that awful
and mysterious power in music to take up our yearnings
towards the infinite, at the point where words and all
articulate utterance fail, and bear them onward often to
something like a satisfactory nearness to their divine
object.

But all this must be left aside, and we must now pass
on to consider that remarkable writer who for something
more than twenty years past has been chaining the attention of our English world purely by virtue of her extraordinary endowment as to all three of these relations
which I have here sketched in diagram — these relations
of the growing personality of man to that which is above
him, or the unknown, — to that which is on his level, or
his fellow-man, — and to that which is beneath him, or
nature, — which have resulted respectively in music, the
novel, and science.

If I could be allowed to construct a final text and
sweet summary of all the principles which have been
announced in the preceding lectures, I could make none
more . complete than is furnished me by two English
women who have recently been among us, and who, in
the quietest way have each made an epoch, not only in
literature, but in life.   These two women are Elizabeth
Barrett Browning and George Eliot; and although our
studies now lie more immediately with the latter, I shall
find a frequent delight as we go on in comparing her
printed words with those of Mrs. Browning, and in show-

ing through what diverse forms of personality — so diverse
as to be often really complementary to each other —
these two have illustrated the doctrines I have hitherto
expounded.

In beginning to get some clear view of the actual living
personality which I have hitherto designated as George
Eliot, one is immediately struck with the fact that it has
enjoyed more of what Jack Falstaff would call a com-
modity of good names than falls to the lot of most mortals.   As one rehearses these names it is curious also to
reflect what a different train of associations each one
suggests.   It is hard to believe that Marian Evans, Amos
Barton (for when the editor of *Blackwood's* was corresponding with her about her first unsigned manuscript,
which was entitled *The Sad Fortunes of the Rev. Amos
Barton,* I find him addressing her as " My dear Amos "),
George Eliot, Mrs. Lewes, and Mrs. Cross are one and
the same person.   Amid all these appellations I find
myself most strongly attracted towards that of George
Eliot.   This was the name which she chose for herself, it
was under this name that she made her great successes,
it was by this name that she endeared herself to all who
love great and faithful work; and surely — if one may
paraphrase Poe — the angels call her George Eliot.
Since therefore we are mainly interested in Marian
Evans, or Mrs. Lewes, or Mrs. Cross, just in so far as
they bear intimate relations to George Eliot, I find myself drawn, in placing before you such sketch as I have
been able to make of this remarkable personage, to begin
with some account of the birth of the specific George
Eliot, and having acquired a view of the circumstances
attending that event, to look backward and forward from
that as a central point at the origin and life of Marian
Evans on the one hand, and of Mrs. Lewes and Mrs.
Cross on the other.

On a certain night in the autumn of 1856 the editor of *Blackwood's Magazine* was seated in an apartment of his own house reading a manuscript which he had lately received from London, called *The Sad Fortunes of the Rev. Amos Barton.* About 11 o'clock in the evening Thackeray, who had been staying with him and had been out to dinner, entered the room, and the editor remarked, " Do you know I think I have lighted upon a new author who is uncommonly like a first-class passenger? "

Hereupon he read to Thackeray a passage from the manuscript which he held in his hand. We are able to identify this passage, and it seems interesting to repro-duce it here, not only as a specimen of the kind of matter which was particularly striking to the editor of a great magazine twenty-five years ago, but as about the first tangible utterance of the real George Eliot. The passage occurs early in the second chapter of the story. In the first chapter we have had some description of the old church and the existing society in Shepperton " twenty-five years ago," which dating from 1856 would show us that village about the year 1830–31. In the second chapter we are immediately introduced to the Rev. Amos Barton, and the page or two which our editor read to Thackeray was this :

Look at him as he winds through the little churchyard ! The silver light that falls aslant on church and tomb, enables you to see his slim black figure, made all the slimmer by tight pantaloons. He walks with a quick step, and is now rapping with sharp decision at the vicarage door. It is opened with-out delay by the nurse, cook, and housemaid, all at once, — that is to say, by the robust maid-of-all work, Nanny ; and as Mr. Barton hangs up his hat in the passage, you see that a narrow face of no particular complexion, — even the small-pox that has attacked it seems to have been of a mongrel, indefinite kind, — with features of no particular shape, and

an eye of no particular expression, is surmounted by a slope
of baldness gently rising from brow to crown. You judge
him, rightly, to be about forty. The house is quiet, for it is
half-past ten, and the children have long been gone to bed.
He opens the sitting-room door; but instead of seeing his
wife, as he expected, stitching with the nimblest of fingers
by the light of one candle, he finds her dispensing with the
light of a candle altogether. She is softly pacing up and
down by the red fire-light, holding in her arms little Walter,
the year-old baby, who looks over her shoulder with large
wide-open eyes, while the patient mother pats his back with
her soft hand, and glances with a sigh at the heap of large
and small stockings lying unmended on the table.

She was a lovely woman, — Mrs. Amos Barton; a large,
fair, gentle Madonna, with thick, close chestnut curls beside
her well rounded cheeks, and with large, tender, short-sighted
eyes. The flowing lines of her tall figure made the limpest
dress look graceful, and her old frayed black silk seemed to
repose on her bust and limbs with a placid elegance and
sense of distinction, in strong contrast with the uneasy sense
of being no fit, that seemed to express itself in the rustling
of Mrs. Farquhar's *gros de Naples*. The caps she wore
would have been pronounced, when off her head, utterly
heavy and hideous, — for in those days even fashionable
caps were large and floppy; but surmounting her long,
arched neck, and mingling their borders of cheap lace and
ribbon with her chestnut curls, they seemed miracles of successful millinery. Among strangers she was shy and tremu-
lous as a girl of fifteen; she blushed crimson if any one
appealed to her opinion; yet that tall, graceful, substantial
presence was so imposing in its mildness that men spoke to
her with an agreeable sensation of timidity. . . . I venture to
say, Mrs. Barton would never have grown half so angelic if
she had married the man you would perhaps have had in
your eye for her, — a man with sufficient income and abundant personal éclat. Besides, Amos was an affectionate
husband, and, in his way valued his wife as his best
treasure.

.   .   .   .

" I wish we could do without borrowing money, and yet I don't see how we can. Poor Fred must have some new shoes; I couldn't let him go to Mrs. Bond's yesterday because his toes were peeping out, dear child! and I can't let him walk anywhere except in the garden. He must have a pair before Sunday. Really, boots and shoes are the greatest trouble of my life. Everything else one can turn and turn about, and make old look like new; but there's no coaxing boots and shoes to look better than they are."

Mrs. Barton was playfully undervaluing her skill in meta-morphosing boots and shoes. She had at that moment on her feet a pair of slippers which had long ago lived through the prunella phase of their existence, and were now running a respectable career as black silk slippers, having been neatly covered with that material by Mrs. Barton's own neat fingers. Wonderful fingers those! they were never empty; for if she went to spend a few hours with a friendly parishioner, out came her thimble and a piece of calico or muslin, which before she left, had become a mysterious little garment with all sorts of hemmed ins and outs. She was even trying to persuade her husband to leave off tight pantaloons, because if he would wear the ordinary gun-cases, she knew she could make them so well that no one would suspect the tailor.

But by this time Mr. Barton has finished his pipe, the candle begins to burn low, and Mrs. Barton goes to see if Nanny has succeeding in lulling Walter to sleep. Nanny is that moment putting him in the little cot by his mother's bedside; the head with its thin wavelets of brown hair, in-dents the little pillow; and a tiny, waxen, dimpled fist hides the rosy lips, for baby is given to the infantine peccadillo of thumb-sucking.

So Nanny could now join in the short evening prayer, and all go to bed.

Mrs. Barton carried up stairs the remainder of her heap of stockings, and laid them on a table close to her bedside, where also she placed a warm shawl, removing her candle, before she put it out, to a tin socket fixed at the head of her bed. Her body was very weary, but her heart was not heavy, in spite of Mr. Woods the butcher, and the transitory nature of shoe-leather; for her heart so overflowed with love, she felt sure she was near a fountain of love that would care for her husband and babes better than she could foresee; so she was soon asleep. But about half-past five o'clock in the morning, if there were any angels watching round her bed, — and angels might be glad of such an office, — they saw Mrs. Barton rise up quietly, careful not to disturb the slumbering Amos, who was snoring the snore of the just; light her candle, prop herself upright with the pillows, throw the warm shawl round her shoulders, and renew her attack on the heap of undarned stockings. She darned away until she heard Nanny stirring, and then drowsiness came with the dawn; the candle was put out, and she sank into a doze. But at nine o'clock she was at the breakfast-table busy cutting bread-and-butter for five hungry mouths, while Nanny, baby on one arm, in rosy cheeks, fat neck, and night-gown, brought in a jug of hot milk-and-water.

Although Thackeray was not enthusiastic, the editor maintained his opinion and wrote the author that the manuscript was " worthy the honors of print and pay," addressing the author as " My dear Amos." Considerable correspondence followed in which the editor was free in venturing criticisms. The author had offered this as the first of a series to be called *Scenes of Clerical Life;* but no others of the series were yet written and the editor was naturally desirous to see more of them before printing the first. This appears to have made the author extremely timid, and for a time there was doubt whether it was worth while to write the remaining stories. For the author's encouragement, therefore, it was determined to print the first story without waiting to see the others; and accordingly in *Blackwood's Magazine* for January, 1857, the story of *Amos Barton* was printed. This stimulus appears to have had its effect; and after the January number, each succeeding issue of

Blackwood's Magazine contained an instalment of the series known as *Scenes of Clerical Life* until it was concluded in the number for November, 1857, the whole series embracing the three stories of *Amos Barton, Mr. Gilfil's Love-Story* and *Janet's Repentance*. It was only while the second of these — *Mr. Gilfil's Love-Story* — was appearing in the Magazine that our George Eliot was born; for it was at this time that the editor of the Magazine was instructed to call the author by that name.

The hold which these three stories immediately took upon all thinking people was most remarkable. In January, 1858 — that is, two months after the last instalment of *Janet's Repentance* — I find Charles Dickens writing this letter :

" My dear Longford,—

" Will you — by such roundabout ways and methods as may present themselves — convey this note of thanks to the author of ' Scenes of Clerical Life,' whose two first stories I can never say enough of, I think them so truly admirable. But, if those two volumes, or a part of them, were not written by a woman — then should I begin to believe that I am a woman myself.

" Faithfully yours always,

"Charles Dickens."

It is especially notable to find that the editor of the Magazine himself completely abandoned all those conservative habits of the prudent editor which have arisen from a thousand experiences of the vapid failures of this and that new contributor who seemed at first sure to sweep the world, and which always teach every conductor of a great magazine at an early stage of his career to be extremely guarded in his expressions to new writers however promising they may appear. This traditional guardedness seems to have been completely swept away by these stories ; Mr. Blackwood writes letter after letter to George Eliot, full of expressions that the hackneyed editor would ordinarily consider extravagant : and finally in a letter concerning the publication in bookform of the magazine-stories : " You will recollect . . . my impression was that the series had not lasted long enough in the Magazine to give you a hold on the general public, although long enough to make your literary reputation. Unless in exceptional cases, a very long time often elapses between the two stages of reputation — the literary and the public. Your progress will be *sure*, if not so quick as we could wish."

Before examining these stories, it seems a pleasant method of pursuing our account of the George Eliot thus introduced to go forward a little to the time when a curious and amusing circumstance resulted in revealing her actual name and sex. Thus we seem to be making this lovely star rise before us historically as it rose before the world. I have just spoken of the literary interest which the stories excited in Mr. Blackwood : the personal interest appears to have been as great, and he was at first very anxious to make the acquaintance of his new contributor in the flesh. He was given to understand, however, that the contributor wished to remain obscure, for the present, and he forbore further inquiries with scrupulous delicacy. It happened, however, that presently the authorship of *Scenes of Clerical Life* was claimed for another person, and the claim soon assumed considerable proportions. Certain residents about Nuneaton, in Warwickshire — where in point of fact George Eliot had been born and brought up — felt sure they recognized in the stories of Amos Barton and Mr. Gilfil portraits of people who had actually lived in that country, and began to inquire what member of their community could have painted these portraits.   Presently, while the stories were running in the magazine, a newspaper published in the Isle of Man boldly announced that a certain Mr. Liggins of Nuneaton was their author.   The only claim to literary power Mr. Liggins had, it seems, lay in the circumstance that he had run through a fortune at Cambridge : and in fact he himself denied the charge at first. But immediately upon the heels of *Scenes of Clerical Life* appeared *Adam Bede,* and the honor of that great work was so seductive that for some reason or other — whether because the reiteration of his friends had persuaded him that he actually did write the works, in some such way as it is said that a man may tell a lie so often and long that he will finally come to believe it himself, or for whatever other reason — it seems that Mr. Liggins so far compromised himself that, without active denial by him, a friendly clergyman down in Warwickshire sent a letter to the *Times* formally announcing Liggins as the author of *Scenes of Clerical Life* and of *Adam Bede.* Hereupon appeared a challenge from the still mythical George Eliot, inviting Mr. Liggins to make a fair test of his capacity by writing a chapter or two in the style of the disputed works.   The Blackwoods were thickly besieged with letters from various persons earnestly assuring them that Liggins was the author.   To add to the complications, it was given out that Liggins was poor, so that many earnest persons wrote to the Blackwoods declaring that so great a genius ought not to be hampered by want, and liberally offering their purses to place him in such condition that he might write without being handicapped by care.   It seems to have been particularly troublesome to the Blackwoods to prevent money from being misapplied in this way, — for they were satisfied that Liggins was not the author ; and they were made all the more careful by some previous experiences of a similar kind; in one of Blackwood's letters to George Eliot he comically exclaims that " some years ago a rascal nearly succeeded in marrying a girl with money on the strength of being the author of a series of articles in the Magazine."

Thus what with the public controversy between the Liggins and anti-Liggins parties — for many persons appear to have remained firmly persuaded that Liggins was the true author — and what with the more legitimate stimulus excited by the confirmatory excellence of *Adam Bede*, the public curiosity was thoroughly aroused, so that even before *The Mill on the Floss* appeared in 1860 it had become pretty generally known who " George Eliot " was.

Here, then, would seem to be a fitting point for us to pause a moment and endeavor to construct for ourselves some definite figure of the real flesh-and-blood creature who, up to this time, had remained the mere literary abstraction called George Eliot.

It appeared that her real name was Marian Evans and that she was the daughter of a respectable land surveyor who had married and settled at Nuneaton in Warwickshire. Here she was born in November, 1820; and it seems pleasant to reflect that but a few miles off in the same county of Warwick was the birthplace of Shakspere, whose place among male writers seems more nearly filled by Marian Evans or George Eliot among female writers than by any other woman, so that we have the greatest English man and the greatest English woman born, though two centuries and a half apart in time, but a few miles apart in space.

Here among the same thick hedges and green fields of the fair English Midlands with which Shakspere was

familiar Marian Evans lived for the first large part of
her life.   Perhaps a more quiet, uneventful existence as
to external happenings could hardly be imagined; and
that Marian Evans was among the quietest of the quiet
residents there seems cunningly enough indicated if we
remember that when the good people of Nuneaton first
began to suspect that some resident of that region had
been taking their portraits in *Scenes of Clerical Life*
none seemed to think for a moment of a certain Marian
Evans as possibly connected with the matter, and popular suspicion, after canvassing the whole ground, was
able to find only one person — to wit, the Mr. Liggins
just referred to — who seemed at all competent to such
work.

Of these demure, reserved, uneventful years of country
existence it is of course impossible to lay before you
any record : no life of George Eliot has yet been given
to the public.   Sometime ago, however, I happened
upon a letter of Marian Evans's published in an English
paper, in which she refers with so much particularity to
this portion of her life, that I do not know how we
could gain a more vivid and authentic view thereof than
by quoting it here.   Specifically, the letter relates to a
controversy that had sprung up as to who was the
original of the character of Dinah Morris, — that beautiful Dinah Morris you will remember in *Adam Bede,*
— solemn, fragile, strong Dinah Morris, the woman-
preacher whom I find haunting my imagination in
strange but entrancing unions of the most diverse forms,
as if, for instance, a snow-drop could also be St. Paul,
as if a kiss could be a gospel, as if a lovely phrase of
Chopin's most inward music should become suddenly
an Apocalypse revealing us Christ in the flesh, — that
rare, pure and marvelous Dinah Morris who would

alone consecrate English literature if it had yielded no other gift to man. It would seem that possibly a dim suggestion of such a character may have been due to a certain aunt of hers, Elizabeth Evans, whom Marian had met in her girlhood; but this suggestion was all; and the letter shows us clearly that the character of Dinah Morris was almost an entire creation. The letter is as follows :

HOLLY LODGE, Oct. 7, 1859.

DEAR SARA, — I should like, while the subject is vividly present with me, to tell you more exactly than I have ever yet done, what I knew of my aunt, Elizabeth Evans. My father, you know, lived in Warwickshire all my life with him, having finally left Staffordshire first, and then Derbyshire, six or seven years before he married my mother. There was hardly any intercourse between my father's family, resident in Derbyshire and Staffordshire, and our family — few and far-between visits of (to my childish feelings) strange uncles and aunts and cousins from my father's far-off native county, and once a journey of my own, as a little child, with my father and mother, to see my uncle William, a rich builder in Staffordshire — but not my uncle and aunt Samuel, so far as I can recall the dim outline of things — are what I remember of northerly relations in my childhood.

But when I was seventeen or more — after my sister was married and I was mistress of the house — my father took a journey into Derbyshire, in which, visiting my uncle and aunt Samuel, who were very poor, and lived in a humble cottage at Wirksworth, he found my aunt in a very delicate state of health after a serious illness, and, to do her bodily good, he persuaded her to return with him, telling her that I should be very, very happy to have her with me for a few weeks. I was then strongly under the influence of Evangelical belief, and earnestly endeavoring to shape this anomalous English-Christian life of ours into some consistency with the spirit and simple verbal tenor of the New Testament. I was delighted to see my aunt. Although I had

only heard her spoken of as a strange person, given to a
fanatical vehemence of exhortation in private as well as
public, I believed that we should find sympathy between us.
She was then an old woman — above sixty — and, I believe,
had for a good many years given up preaching. A tiny
little woman, with bright, small dark eyes, and hair that
had been black, I imagine, but was now gray — a pretty
woman in her youth, but of a totally different physical type
from Dinah. The difference — as you will believe — was
not simply physical; no difference is. She was a woman of
strong natural excitability, which, I know from the description
I have heard my father and half-sister give, prevented her
from the exercise of discretion under the promptings of her
zeal. But this vehemence was now subdued by age and
sickness; she was very gentle and quiet in her manners —
very loving — and (what she must have been from the very
first) a truly religious soul, in whom the love of God and
love of man were fused together. There was nothing
highly distinctive in her religious conversation. I had had
much intercourse with pious Dissenters before. The only
freshness I found in our talk came from the fact that she had
been the greater part of her life a Wesleyan, and though she
left the society when women were no longer allowed to
preach, and joined the new Wesleyans, she retained the
character of thought that belongs to the genuine old Wesleyan. I had never talked with a Wesleyan before, and we
used to have little debates about predestination, for I was
then a strong Calvinist. Here her superiority came out,
and I remember now, with loving admiration, one thing
which at the time I disapproved. It was not strictly a consequence of her Arminian belief, and at first sight might
seem opposed to it, — yet it came from the spirit of love
which clings to the bad logic of Arminianism. When my
uncle came to fetch her, after she had been with us a fort-
night or three weeks, he was speaking of a deceased minister, once greatly respected, who from the action of trouble
upon him had taken to small tippling, though otherwise not
culpable. " But I hope the good man's in heaven for all
that," said my uncle. " Oh, yes," said my aunt, with a deep

inward groan of joyful conviction, " Mr. A.'s in heaven —
that's sure." This was at the time an offence to my stern,
ascetic, hard views — how beautiful it is to me now!

As to my aunt's conversation, it is a fact that the only two
things of any interest I remember in our lonely sittings and
walks are her telling me one sunny afternoon how she had,
with another pious woman, visited an unhappy girl in prison,
stayed with her all night, and gone with her to execution;
and one or two accounts of supposed miracles in which she
believed — among the rest, the face with the crown of thorns
seen in the glass. In her account of the prison scenes, I
remember no word she uttered — I only remember her tone
and manner, and the deep feeling I had under the recital.
Of the girl she knew nothing, I believe — or told me nothing
— but that she was a common coarse girl, convicted of child-
murder. The incident lay in my mind for years on years, as
a dead germ, apparently — till time had made my mind a
nidus in which it could fructify; it then turned out to be the
germ of " Adam Bede."

I saw my aunt twice after this. Once I spent a day and
night with my father in the Wirksworth cottage, sleeping
with my aunt, I remember. Our interview was less interesting than in the former time : I think I was less simply devoted
to religious ideas. And once again she came with my uncle
to see me — when father and I were living at Foleshill; then
there was some pain, for I had given up the form of Christian
belief, and was in a crude state of free-thinking. She stayed
about three or four days, I think. This is all I remember
distinctly, as matter I could write down, of my dear aunt,
whom I really loved. You see how she suggested Dinah;
but it is not possible you should see as I do how entirely
her individuality differed from Dinah's. How curious it
seemed to me that people should think Dinah's sermon,
prayers and speeches were copied — when they were written
with hot tears, as they surged up in my own mind!

As to my indebtedness to facts of local and personal history of a small kind, connected with Staffordshire and Derbyshire — you may imagine of what kind that is when I tell you
that I never remained in either of those counties more than

a few days together, and of only two such visits have I more than a shadowy, interrupted recollection.   The details which I knew as facts, and have made use of for my picture, were gathered from such imperfect allusion and narrative as I heard from my father in his occasional talk about old times.

As to my aunt's children or grandchildren saying, if they did say, that Dinah is a good portrait of my aunt — that is the vague, easily satisfied notion imperfectly instructed people always have of portraits.   It is not surprising that simple men and women without pretension to enlightened discrimination should think a generic resemblance constitutes a portrait, when we see the great public so accustomed to be delighted with misrepresentations of life and character, which they accept as representations, that they are scandalized when art makes a nearer approach to truth.

Perhaps I am doing a superfluous thing in writing all this to you — but I am prompted to do it by the feeling that in future years " Adam Bede " and all that concerns it may have become a dim portion of the past, and I may not be able to recall so much of the truth as I have now told you.

Once more, thanks, dear Sara.

Ever your loving
MARIAN.

It is easy to gather from this letter that whilst the existence of Marian Evans was calm enough externally her inner life was full of stirring events — of the most stirring events, in fact, which can agitate the human soul : for it is evident that she had passed along some quite opposite phases of religious belief.   In 1851, after a visit to the Continent, she goes — where all English writers seem to drift by some natural magic — to London and fixes her residence there.   It is curious enough that with all her clearness of judgment she works here for five years, apparently without having perceived the vocation for which her whole natural and acquired outfit had so remarkably prepared her.   We find her translating

Spinoza's *Ethics;* not only translating but publishing
Feuerbach's *Essence of Christianity* and Strauss's *Life of
Jesus.* She contributes learned essays to *The Westminster
Review;* it is not until the year 1856, when she is thirty-
six years old, that her first slight magazine story is sent
to Blackwood; and even after his first commendations
her timidity and uncertainty as to whether she could
succeed in story-writing are so great that she almost
resolved to give it up.   I should regard it as mournful, if
I could think it religious to regard anything as mournful
which has happened and is not revocable, that upon
coming to London Marian Evans fell among a group of
persons represented by George Henry Lewes.   If one
could have been her spiritual physician at this time one
certainly would have prescribed for her some of those
warm influences which dissipate doubt by exposing it to
. the fierce elemental heats of love, of active charity.
One would have prescribed for her the very remedy she
herself has so wisely commended in *Janet's Repentance.*

" No wonder the sick room and the lazaretto have so often
been a refuge from the tossings of intellectual doubt, — a
place of repose for the worn and wounded spirit.   Here is a
duty about which all creeds and philosophers are at one;
here, at least, the conscience will not be dogged by doubt, the
benign impulse will not be checked by adverse theory; here
you may begin to act without settling one preliminary question.   To moisten the sufferer's parched lips through the
long night-watches, to bear up the drooping head, to lift the
helpless limbs, to divine the want that can find no utterance
beyond the feeble motion of the hand or beseeching glance
of the eye, — these are offices that demand no self-question-
ings, no casuistry, no assent to propositions, no weighing of
consequences.   Within the four walls where the stare and
glare of the world are shut out, and every voice is subdued, —
where a human being lies prostrate, thrown on the tender

mercies of his fellow, the moral relation of man to man is
reduced to its utmost clearness and simplicity; bigotry cannot confuse it; theory cannot pervert it; passion, awed into
quiescence, can neither pollute nor perturb it."

Or one might have prescribed for her America, where
the knottiest social and moral problems disappear unac-
countably before a certain new energy of individual
growth which is continually conquering new points of
view from which to regard the world.

At the time to which we have now brought her history
Marian Evans would seem to have been a singularly
engaging person.   She was small in stature and her face
was what would be called homely, here ; but she was widely
read, master of several languages, a good talker and lis-
tener ; and beyond all, every current of testimony runs
towards a certain intensity and loving fire which pervaded
her and which endowed her with irresistible magnetic
attraction for all sensitive souls that came near her.   Her
love for home matters, and for the spot of earth where
she had been born ; her gentle affection for animals ; how
the Bible and Thomas à Kempis were her favorite books :
these and a thousand womanly traits I hope to bring out
as we study some of her greater works, — for with all her
reputed reserve I find scarcely any writer so sincerely
communicative and so frankly desirous of sympathy on
the part of her reader as George Eliot.   In the next
lecture I shall ask leave to present you with some pictures
of the stage at which English novel-writing has arrived
under the recent hands of Scott, Thackeray and Dickens
when George Eliot is timidly offering her first manuscript
to *Blackwood's;* and I shall then offer some quotations
from these first three stories — particularly from *Janet's
Repentance* which seems altogether the most important
of the three — and shall attempt to show distinctly what

were the main new features of wit, of humor, of doctrine and of method which were thus introduced into our literature, especially in connection with similar features which about this same time were being imparted by Mrs. Browning.

Meantime let me conclude by asking you to fix your attention for a moment on this figure of Milly, sweet wife of Amos Barton, going to bed with her unmended basket of stockings in great fatigue yet in great love and trust, and contrast it with that figure of Prometheus, nailed to the Caucasian rock in pain and hate, which formed the first object of these studies. What a prodigious spiritual distance we have swept over from the Titan lying down to unrest, thundering defiance against Jove's thunder as if clashing shield against shield, and the tender-limbed woman whom the simple narrative puts before us in these words: "Her body was very weary, but her heart was not heavy . . .; for her heart so overflowed with love, she felt sure she was near a fountain of love that would care for her husband and babes better than she could foresee." Fixing your attention upon this word "love," and reminding you how, at the close of the last lecture, we found that the whole movement of the human spirit which we have traced here as the growth of personality towards the unknown, towards fellow-man, towards nature, — resulting in music, in the novel, in science — that this whole movement becomes a unity when we arrive at the fact that it really imports a complete change in man's most ultimate conception of things: a change, namely, from the conception of Justice as the organic idea of moral order, (a conception which we have seen Æschylus and Plato vainly working out to the outrageous conclusions of *Prometheus*, of the *Republic*,) to the conception of

Love as the organic idea of moral order, a conception which we are just now to see George Eliot working out to the divinely-satisfactory conclusion of Milly Barton, who conquers with gentle love a world which proved refractory alike to the justice of Jove and the defiance of Prometheus; reminding you, I say, of this concurrent change from feeble personality and justice to strong personality and love, what an amazing arc of progress we have traversed in coming from Æschylus to George Eliot!

And it is, finally, most interesting to find this change receiving clear expression for the first time in English literature in the works of the two women I have mentioned, Mrs. Browning and George Eliot. In this very autumn when we have seen the editor of *Blackwood's Magazine* reading the MS. of George Eliot's first story to Thackeray, Mrs. Browning is sending *Aurora Leigh* to print; and, as I shall have frequent occasion to point out, the burden of *Aurora Leigh* as well as of George Eliot's whole cyclus of characters is love, love, love.

There is a charming scene in the first act of Bayard Taylor's *Prince Deukalion* which, though not extending to the height we have reached, yet very dramatically sums up a great number of ideas that converge towards it. In this scene Gæa, the Earth, mother of men, is represented as tenderly meditating upon her son, man. Near her stands a rose-tree, from one bud of which Love is presently to emerge. She says:

> " I change with man,
> Mother, not more than partner, of his fate.
> Ere he was born I dreamed that he might be
> And through long ages of imperfect life
> Waited for him. Then, vexed with monstrous shapes
> That spawned and wallowed in primeval ooze,
> I lay supine and slept, or seemed to sleep;
> And dreamed, or waking felt as in a dream,

Some touch of hands, some soft delivering help.
And he was there!   His faint new voice I heard;
His eye that met the sun, his upright tread,
Thenceforth were mine!   And with him came the palm,
The oak, the rose, the swan, the nightingale:
The barren bough hung apples to the sun,
Dry stalks made harvest: breezes in the woods
Then first found music, and the turbid sea
First rolled a crystal breaker to the shore.
His foot was on the mountains, and the wave
Upheld him: over all things huge and coarse
There came the breathing of a regal sway,
Which bent them into beauty.   Order new
Followed the march of new necessity,
And what was useless, or unclaimed before,
Took value from the seizure of his hands."

In the midst of like thoughts a bud on a rose-tree which stands by Gæa bursts open, and Eros, the antique god of young love, appears from it.

GÆA.

"Lithe, tricksome spirit! art thou left alone
Of gods and all their intermediate kin
The sweet survivor?   Yet a single seed,
When soil and seasons lend their alchemy,
May clothe a barren continent in green."

EROS.

"Was I born, that I should die?
Stars that fringe the outer sky
Know me: yonder sun were dim
Save my torch enkindle him.
Then, when first the primal pair
Found me in the twilight air,
I was older than their day,
Yet to them as young as they.
All decrees of fate I spurn;
Banishment is my return;
Hate and force purvey for me,
Death is shining victory."

VIII

IF you should be wandering meditatively along the bank of some tiny brook, a brook so narrow that you can leap across it without effort, so quiet in its singing that its loudest tinkle cannot be heard in the next field, carrying upon its bosom no craft that would draw more water than the curving leaf of a wild-rose floating down stream, too small in volume to dream of a mill-wheel and turning nothing more practical than maybe a piece of violet-petal in a little eddy off somewhere, — if, I say, you should be strolling alongside such a brook and should see it suddenly expand, without the least intermediate stage, into a mighty river, turning a thousand great wheels for man's profit as it swept on to the sea, and offering broad highway and favorable currents to a thousand craft freighted with the most precious cargoes of human aspiration: you would behold the aptest physical semblance of that spiritual phenomenon which we witnessed at our last meeting, when in tracing the quiet and mentally-wayward course of demure Marian Evans among the suave pastorals of her native Warwickshire, we came suddenly upon the year 1857 when her first venture in fiction — *The Scenes of Clerical Life* — appeared in *Blackwood's Magazine* and magically enlarged the stream of her influence from the diameter of a small circle of literary people in London to the width of all England.

At this point it seems interesting now to pause a moment, to look about and see exactly what network

English fiction had done since its beginning, only about
a century before, to note more particularly what were
the precise gains to humanity which Thackeray and
Dickens had poured in just at this time of 1857, and
thus to differentiate a clear view of the actual contribution which George Eliot was now beginning to make to
English life and thought.

It is not a pleasant task, however instructive, to leave
off looking at a rose and cast one's contemplation down
to the unsavory muck in which its roots are imbedded.
This, however, is what one must do when one passes from
the many-petalled rose of George Eliot's fiction to the
beginning of the English novel.

This beginning was as curious as it was unlooked-for
by the people engaged in it.   In the year 1740 a book
in two volumes called *Pamela : or Virtue Rewarded*,
was printed, in which Samuel Richardson took what
seems to have been the first revolutionary departure from
the wild and complex romances — such as Sir Philip
Sidney's *Arcadia* — which had formed the nearest
approach to the modern novel until then.   At this time
Richardson was fifty years old, and probably the last
man in England who would have been selected as likely
to write an epoch-making book of any description.   He
had worked most of his life as a printer, but by the
time referred to had gotten so far towards the literary
life as to be employed by booksellers to arrange indexes
and to write prefaces and dedications.   It so happened
that on a certain occasion he was asked by two booksellers to write a volume of letters on different subjects
which might serve as models to uneducated persons — a
sort of Every Man His Own Letter Writer, or the like.

The letters, in order to be more useful, were to be upon
such subjects as the rustic world might likely desire to

correspond about.   Richardson thinks it over; and presently writes to inquire, "Will it be any harm, in a piece you want to be written so low, if we should instruct them how they should think and act in common cases, as well as indite?" This seemed a capital idea and in the course of time, after some experiments and after recalling an actual story he had once heard which gave him a sort of basis, he takes for his heroine a simple servant-girl, daughter of Goodman Andrews, a humbly born English farmer, rather sardonically names her Pamela after the Lady Pamela in Sir Philip Sidney's *Arcadia*, carries her pure through a series of incredibly villainous plots against her by the master of the house where she is at service, who has taken advantage of the recent death of his wife, Pamela's mistress, to carry these on, and finally makes the master marry her in a fit of highly spasmodic goodness, after a long course of the most infamous but unsuccessful villainy, calls the book *Pamela: or Virtue Rewarded*, prints it, and in a very short time wins a great host of admiring readers, insomuch that since the first two volumes ended with the marriage, he adds two more showing the married life of Pamela and her squire.

The whole novel, like all of Richardson's, is written in the form of letters passing between the characters. It is related, apropos of his genius in letter-writing, that in his boyhood he was the love-letter-writer-in-chief for three of the young ladies of his town, and that he maintained this embarrassing position for a long time without suspicion from either of the three.   Richardson himself announces the moral purpose of his book, saying that he thinks it might "introduce a new species of writing that might possibly turn young people into a course of reading different from the pomp and parade of romance-writing, and . . . promote the cause of religion and virtue ; " and in the preface to the continuation before-mentioned he remarks as follows : " The two former volumes of *Pamela* met with a success greatly exceeding the most sanguine expectations ; and the editor hopes " (Richardson calls himself the editor of the letters) " that the letters which compose these will be found equally written to nature ; avoiding all romantic flights, improbable surprises, and irrational machinery ; and that the passions are touched where requisite ; and rules equally new and practicable inculcated throughout the whole for the general conduct of life." I have given these somewhat tedious quotations from Richardson's own words to show first that the English novel starts out with a perfectly clear and conscious moral mission, and secondly to contrast this pleasing moral announcement of Richardson's with what I can only call the silly and hideous realization of it which meets us when we come actually to read this wonderful first English novel — *Pamela.*

I have already given the substance of the first two volumes in which the rich squire, Mr. B. (as he is called throughout the novel) finally marries and takes home the girl who had been the servant of his wife and against whom, ever since that lady's death, he had been plotting with an elaborate baseness which has never before been, and I sincerely hope will never hereafter be described. By this action Mr. B. has in the opinion of Richardson, of his wife, the servant-girl and the whole contemporary world, saturated himself with such a flame of saintliness as to have burnt out every particle of any little misdemeanor he may have been guilty of in his previous existence ; and I need only read you an occasional line from the first four letters of the third volume

in order to show the marvelous sentimentality, the un-
truth towards nature, and the purely commercial view of
virtue and of religion which make up this intolerable
book.   At the opening of Volume III we find that
Goodman Andrews, the father of the bride, and his wife
have been provided with a comfortable farm on the estate
of Mr. B., and the second letter is from Andrews to his
daughter, the happy bride, Pamela.   After rhapsodizing
for several pages Andrews reaches this climax — and it
is worth while observing that though only a rude farmer
of the eighteenth century, whose daughter was a servant
maid, he writes in the most approved epistolary style of
the period :

" When here in this happy dwelling and this well-stocked
farm, in these rich meadows and well-cropped acres, we look
around us and whichever way we turn our heads see blessings upon blessings and plenty upon plenty : see barns well
stored, poultry increasing, the kine lowing and crowding
about us, and all fruitful; and are bid to call all these our
own.   And then think that all is the reward of our child's
virtue!   O, my dear daughter, who can bear these things!
Excuse me!   I must break off a little!   For my eyes are as
full as my heart; and I will retire to bless God, and your
honored husband."

Here there is a break in the page, by which the honest
farmer is supposed to represent the period of time occupied by him in retiring, and dividing his blessing, as one
hopes, impartially, between the Creator and Pamela's
honored husband, — and the farmer resumes his writing :

"So — my dear child — I now again take up my pen.   But
reading what I had written, in order to carry on the thread,
I can hardly forbear again being in like sort affected. — "

And here we have a full stop and a dash, during which
it is only fair to suppose that the honest Andrews

manages to weep and bless up to something like a state of repose.

Presently Pamela writes :

"My dear father and mother; I have shown your letter to my beloved. . . . 'Dear good souls,' said he, ' how does every-thing they say and everything they write manifest the worthi-ness of their hearts! Tell them . . . let them find out another couple as worthy as themselves and I will do as much for them. Indeed I would not place them,' continued the dear obliger, ' in the same county, because I would wish two counties to be blessed for their sakes.' . . . I could only fly to his generous bosom . . . and with my eyes swimming in tears of grateful joy . . . bless God and bless him with my whole heart ; for speak I could not ! but almost choaked with my joy, sobbed to him my grateful acknowl-edgements. . . . ''Tis too much, too much,' said I, in broken accents : ' O, sir, bless me more gradually and more cautiously — for I cannot bear it ! ' And indeed my heart went flutter, flutter, flutter, at his dear breast as if it wanted to break its too narrow prison to mingle still more inti-mately with his own."

And a few lines further on we have this purely com-mercial view of religion :

"And if our prayers shall be heard," continues Pamela, " and we shall have the pleasure to think that his " (her hus-band's) "advances in piety are owing not a little to them ; . . . then indeed may we take the pride to think we have repaid his goodness to us and that we have satisfied the debt which nothing less can discharge."

Or again, in the same letter she exclaims anew :

"See, O see, my excellent parents, how we are crowned with blessings upon blessings until we are the talk of all who know us; you for your honesty, I for my humility and vir-tue ; " so that now I have " nothing to do but to reap all the rewards which this life can afford ; and if I walk humbly and improve my blessèd opportunities, will heighten and perfect all, in a still more joyful futurity."

Perhaps a more downright creed, not only of worldliness, but of "other-worldliness," was never more explicitly avowed.

Now — to put the whole moral effect of this book into a nutshell — Richardson had gravely announced it as a warning to young servant-girls : but why might he not as well have announced it as an encouragement to old villains? The virtue of Pamela, it is true, is duly rewarded : but Mr. B., with all his villainy, certainly fares better than Pamela : for he not only receives to himself a paragon of a wife, but the sole operation of his previous villainy towards her is to make his neighbors extol him to the skies as a saint, when he turns from it ; so that, considering the enormous surplus of Mr. B.'s rewards as against Pamela's, instead of the title *Pamela : or Virtue Rewarded*, ought not the book to have been called *Mr. B.: or Villainy Rewarded?*

It was expressly to ridicule some points of Richardson's *Pamela* that the second English novel was written. This was Henry Fielding's *Joseph Andrews*, which appeared in 1742. It may be that the high birth of Fielding — his father was great-grandson of the Earl of Denbigh, and a lieutenant-general in the army — had something to do with his opposition to Richardson, who was the son of a joiner ; at any rate, he puts forth a set of exactly opposite characters to those in Pamela, takes a footman for his virtuous hero, and the footman's mistress for his villainous heroine, names the footman Joseph Andrews, (explaining that he was the brother of Richardson's Pamela who you remember was the daughter of

Goodman Andrews) makes principal figures of two parsons (Parson Adams and Parson Trulliber, the former of whom is set up as a model of clerical behavior, and the latter the reverse) and with these main materials, together with an important pedler, he gives us the book still called by many the greatest English novel, originally entitled *The Adventures of Joseph Andrews and His Friend Abraham Adams*.

I will not, because I cannot, here cite any of the vital portions of *Joseph Andrews* which produce the real moral effect of the book upon a reader. I can only say that it is not different in essence from the moral effect of Richardson's book just described, though the tone is more clownish.   But for particular purposes of comparison with Dickens and George Eliot hereafter let me recall to you in the briefest way two of the funny scenes. To show that these are fair samples of the humorous atmosphere of the book I may mention that they are both among the number which were selected by Thackeray, who was a keen lover of Fielding generally, and of his *Joseph Andrews* particularly, for his own illustrations upon his own copy of this book.

In the first scene Joseph Andrews is riding along the road upon a very unreliable horse who has already given him a lame leg by a fall, attended by his friend Parson Adams.   They arrive at an inn, dismount, and ask for lodging; the landlord is surly and presently behaves uncivilly to Joseph Andrews; whereupon Parson Adams, in defence of his lame friend, knocks the landlord sprawling upon the floor of his own inn; the landlord, however, quickly receives reinforcements and his wife, seizing a pan of hog's blood which stands on the dresser, discharges it with powerful effect into the good parson's face.   While the parson is in this condition, enters Mrs. Slipshod — a veritable Grendel's mother —

"Terrible termagant, mindful of mischief,"

and attacks the landlady, with fearsome results of up-rooted hair and defaced feature.   In scene second, Parson Adams being in need of a trifling loan goes to see his counter-parson Trulliber, who was noted, among other things, for his fat hogs.   Unfortunately Parson Adams meets Mrs. Trulliber first, and is mistakenly introduced by her to her husband as "a man come for some of his hogs."   Trulliber immediately begins to brag of the fat-ness of his swine and drags Parson Adams to his sty insisting upon examination in proof of his praise.   Par-son Adams complies; they reach the sty and by way of beginning his examination Parson Adams lays hold of the tail of a very high-fed, capricious hog; the beast suddenly springs forward and throws Parson Adams headlong into the deep mire.   Trulliber bursts into laughter and contemptuously cries: "Why, dost not know how to handle a hog?"

It is impossible for lack of space to linger over further characteristics of these writers.   In 1748 appears Rich-ardson's *Clarissa Harlowe* in eight volumes, which from your present lecturer's point of view is quite sufficiently described as a patient analysis of the most intolerable crime in all history or fiction, watered with an amount of tears and sensibility as much greater than that in Pamela as the cube of eight volumes is greater than the cube of four volumes.

In 1753 Richardson's third and last novel, *Sir Charles Grandison*, appeared; a work differing in motive, but not in moral tone, from the other two, though certainly less hideous than *Clarissa Harlowe*.

Returning to bring up Fielding's novels, in 1743 appeared his *History of the Life of the late Mr. Jonathan Wild the Great*, in which the hero Jonathan Wild was a taker of thieves, or detective, who ended his own career by being hanged; the book being written professedly as "an exposition of the motives that actuate the unprincipled great, in every walk and sphere of life, and which are common alike to the thief or murderer on the small scale and to the mighty villain and reckless conqueror who invades the rights or destroys the liberties of nations." In 1749 Fielding prints his *Tom Jones*, which some consider his greatest book. The glory of *Tom Jones* is Squire Allworthy, whom we are invited to regard as the most miraculous product of the divine creation so far in the shape of man; but to your present lecturer's way of thinking the kind of virtue represented by Squire Allworthy is completely summed in the following sentence of the work introducing him in the midst of nature. It is a May morning, and Squire Allworthy is pacing the terrace in front of his mansion before sunrise; "when," says Fielding, "in the full blaze of his majesty up rose the sun, than which one object alone in this lower creation could be more glorious, and that Mr. Allworthy himself presented — a human being replete with benevolence meditating in what manner he might render himself most acceptable to his Creator by doing most good to his creatures:" that is, in plain commercial terms, how he might obtain the largest possible amount upon the letter of credit which he found himself forced to buy against the inevitable journey into those foreign parts lying beyond the waters of death.

Out of Fielding's numerous other writings, dramatic and periodical, it is perhaps necessary to mention farther only his *Amelia*, belonging to the year 1751, in which he praised his first wife and satirized the jails of his time.

We must now hastily pass to the third so-called classic writer in English fiction, Tobias Smollett, who, after being educated as a surgeon, and having experiences of life as surgeon's mate on a ship of the line in the expedition to Carthagena, spent some time in the West Indies, returned to London, wrote some satires, an opera, &c., and presently when he was still only twenty-seven years old captivated England with his first novel, *Roderick Random*, which appeared in 1748, the same year with *Clarissa Harlowe*. In 1751 came Smollett's *Peregrine Pickle*, famous for its bright fun and the caricature it contains of Akenside — *Pleasures of Imagination* Akenside — who is represented as the host in a very absurd entertainment after the ancient fashion. In 1752 Smollett's *Adventures of Ferdinand Count Fathom* gave the world a new and very complete study in human depravity. In 1769, appeared his *Adventures of an Atom*: a theme which one might suppose it difficult to make indecorous and which was really a political satire; but the unfortunate liberty of locating his atom as an organic particle in various parts of various successive human bodies gave Smollett a field for indecency which he cultivated to its utmost yield. A few months before his death in 1771 appeared his *Expedition of Humphrey Clinker*, certainly his best novel. It is worth while noticing that in *Humphrey Clinker* the veritable British poorly-educated and poor-spelling woman begins to express herself in the actual dialect of the species, and in the letters of Mrs. Winifred Jenkins to her fellow maid-servant Mrs. Mary Jones at Brambleton Hall, during a journey made by the family to the North, we have some very worthy and strongly-marked originals not only of Mrs. Malaprop and Mrs. Partington, but of the immortal Sairey Gamp and of scores of other descendants in Thackeray and Dickens, here and there.

I can quote but a few lines from the last letter of Mrs. Winifred Jenkins concluding the *Expedition of Humphrey Clinker*, which by the way is told entirely through letters from one character to another, like Richardson's.

" To Mrs. Mary Jones at Brambleton Hall.
     "Mrs. Jones, —
               " Providence has bin pleased to make great halteration in the pasture of our affairs. We were yesterday three kiple chined by the grease of God in the holy bands of matter-money."

(The novel winds up with a general marriage of pretty much all parties concerned, mistress, maid, master and man); "and I now subscribe myself Loyd, at your sarvice." Here she of course describes the wedding. "As for Madam Lashmiheygo, you nose her picklearities — her head to be sure was fantastical; and her spouse had wrapped her with a long . . . clock from the land of the selvedges. . . . Your humble servant had on a plain pea-green tabby sack, with my runnela cap, ruff toupee, and side-curls. They said I was the very moral of Lady Rickmanstone but not so pale — that may well be, for her ladyship is my elder by seven good years or more. Now, Mrs. Mary, our satiety is to suppurate; and we are coming home " — which irresistibly reminds us of the later Mrs. Malaprop's famous explanation in *The Rivals :* — " I was putrefied with astonishment." — " Present my compliments to Mrs. Gwillim, and I hope she and I will live upon dissent terms of civility. Being by God's blessing removed to a higher spear you'll excuse my being familiar with the lower sarvints of the family, but as I trust you will behave respectful and keep a proper distance you may always depend on the good will and protection of
               "Yours,
                         "W. Loyd."

To these three — Richardson, Fielding and Smollett — I have now only to add the name of Laurence Sterne, whose *Tristram Shandy* appeared in 1759, in order to complete a group of novel writers whose moral outcome is much the same and who are still reputed in all current manuals as the classic founders of English fiction. I need give no characterization of Sterne's book, which is probably the best known of all.   Every one recalls the Chinese puzzle of humor in *Tristram Shandy*, which pops something grotesque or indecent at us in every crook.   As to its morality, I know good people who love the book; but to me, when you sum it all up, its teaching is that a man may spend his life in low, brutish, inane pursuits and may have a good many little private sins on his conscience, — but will nevertheless be perfectly sure of heaven if he can have retained the ability to weep a maudlin tear over a tale of distress; or, in short, that a somewhat irritable state of the lachrymal glands will be cheerfully accepted by the Deity as a substitute for saving grace or a life of self-sacrifice.   As I have said, these four writers still maintain their position as the classic novelists and their moral influence is still copiously extolled; but I cannot help believing that much of this praise is simply well-meaning ignorance. I protest that I can read none of these books without feeling as if my soul had been in the rain, draggled, muddy, miserable.   In other words, they play upon life as upon a violin without a bridge, in the deliberate endeavor to get the most depressing tones possible from the instrument.   This is done under pretext of showing us vice.

In fine, and this is the characterization I shall use in contrasting this group with that much sweeter group led by George Eliot, the distinctive feature of these first novelists is to show men with microscopic detail how bad men may be.   I shall presently illustrate with the George Eliot group how much larger the mission of the

novel is than this : meantime, I cannot leave this matter
without recording in the plainest terms that — for far
deeper reasons than those which Roger Bacon gave for
sweeping away the works of Aristotle — if I had my way
with these classic books I would blot them from the face
of the earth.   One who studies the tortuous behaviors
of men in history soon ceases to wonder at any human
inconsistency ; but, so far as I can marvel, I do daily
that we regulate by law the sale of gunpowder, the
storage of nitro-glycerine, the administration of poison —
all of which can hurt but our bodies — but are absolutely
careless of these things — so-called classic books, which
wind their infinite insidiousnesses about the souls of
our young children and either strangle them or cover
them with unremovable slime under our very eyes,
working in a security of fame and so-called classicism
that is more effectual for this purpose than the security
of the dark.   Of this terror it is the sweetest souls who
know most.

In the beginning of *Aurora Leigh*, Mrs. Browning
speaks this matter so well that I must clinch my opinion
with her words.   Aurora Leigh says, recalling her own
youthful experience :

> " Sublimest danger, over which none weeps,
>   When any young wayfaring soul goes forth
>   Alone, unconscious of the perilous road,
>   The day-sun dazzling in his limpid eyes,
>   To thrust his own way, he an alien, through
>   The world of books ! Ah, you ! — you think it fine,
>   You clap hands — ' A fair day ! ' — you cheer him on
>   As if the worst, could happen, were to rest
>   Too long beside a fountain.   Yet behold,
>   Behold ! — the world of books is still the world ;
>   And worldlings in it are less merciful
>   And more puissant.   For the wicked there
>   Are winged like angels.   Every knife that strikes

Is edged from elemental fire to assail
A spiritual life; the beautiful seems right
By force of beauty, and the feeble wrong
Because of weakness.   .   .   .   .
                    . . . In the book-world, true,
There's no lack, neither, of God's saints and kings,
.   .   .   .
True, many a prophet teaches in the roads;   .
.   .   .   .
But stay — who judges?   .   .   .   .
                    . . . The child there?   Would you leave
That child to wander in a battle-field
And push his innocent smile against the guns;
Or even in a catacomb — his torch
Grown ragged in the fluttering air, and all
The dark a-mutter round him? not a child."

But to return to our sketch of English fiction, it is
now delightful to find a snowdrop springing from this
muck of the classics.   In the year 1766 appeared Gold-
smith's *Vicar of Wakefield.*

One likes to recall the impression which the purity of
this charming book made upon the German Goethe.
Fifty years after Goethe had read it — or rather after
Herder read to him a translation of the *Vicar of Wakefield* while he was a law-student at Strasburg — the old
poet mentions in one of his letters to Zelter the strong
and healthy influence of this story upon him, just at the
critical point of his mental development; and yesterday
while reading the just published *Reminiscences of Thomas
Carlyle* I found a pleasant pendant to this testimony of
Goethe's in favor of Goldsmith's novel in an entry of
the rugged old man in which he describes the far out-
look and new wisdom which he managed to conquer
from Goethe's *Wilhelm Meister*, after many repulsions.

" Schiller done, I began *Wilhelm Meister*, a task I liked
perhaps rather better, too scanty as my knowledge of the
element, and even of the language, still was.   Two years

before I had at length, after some repulsion, got into the heart of *Wilhelm Meister*, and eagerly read it through; my sally out, after finishing, along the vacant streets of Edinburgh, a windless, Scotch-misty morning, is still vivid to me. ' Grand, serenely, harmoniously built together, far-seeing, wise and true. Where, for many years, or in my whole life before, have I read such a book?' Which I was now, really in part as a kind of duty, conscientiously trans-lating for my countrymen, if they would read it — as a select few of them have ever since kept doing."

Of the difference between the moral effect of Gold-smith's *Vicar of Wakefield* and the classical works just mentioned I need not waste your time in speaking. No great work in the English novel appears until we reach Scott whose *Waverley* astonished the world in 1814; and during the intervening period from this book to the *Vicar of Wakefield* perhaps there are no works notable enough to be mentioned in so rapid a sketch as this unless it be the society novels of Miss Burney, *Evelina* and *Cecilia*, the dark and romantic stories of Mrs. Radcliffe, the *Caleb Williams* of William Godwin — with which he believed he was making an epoch because it was a novel without love as a motive — Miss Edge-worth's moral tales and the quiet and elegant narratives of Jane Austen.

But I cannot help mentioning here a book which occurs during this period, and which attaches itself by the oddest imaginable ties to what was said, in a pre-vious lecture, of the novel as the true meeting-ground where the poetic imagination and the scientific imagina-tion come together and incorporate themselves. Now, to make the true novel — the work which takes all the miscellaneous products of scientific observation and carries them up into a higher plane and incarnates them into the characters (as we call them) of a book, and makes them living flesh and blood like ourselves — to effect this, there must be a true incorporation and merger of the scientific and poetic faculties in one : it is not sufficient if they work side by side like two horses abreast, they must work like a man and wife with one soul ; or, to change the figure, their union must not be mechanical, it must be chemical, producing a thing better than either alone ; or, to change the figure again, the union must be like that which Browning has noticed as existing among the ingredients of a musical chord, when, as he says, out of three tones, one makes not a fourth, but a star.

Now the book I mean shows us the scientific faculty and the poetic faculty — and no weak faculties either — working along together, not merged, not chemically united, not lighting up matters like a star, — with the result, as seems to me, of producing the very funniest earnest book in our language. It is *The Loves of the Plants*, by Dr. Erasmus Darwin, grandfather, I believe, to our own grave and patient Charles Darwin. *The Loves of the Plants* is practically a series of little novels in which the heroes and heroines belong to the vegetable world. Linnæus had announced the sexuality of plants, and had made this idea a principle of classification, the one-stamen class, *Monandria*, two-stamen class, *Diandria*, etc., etc. All this the diligent and truly loving Doctor framed into poetry, and poetry which so far as technical execution goes is quite as good as the very best of the Pope school which it follows. Here are a few specimens of the poem :

" Descend, ye hovering Sylphs! aërial Quires ;
And sweep with little hands your silver lyres ;
With fairy footsteps print your grassy rings,
Ye Gnomes! accordant to the tinkling strings :

While in soft notes I tune to oaten reed
Gay hopes, and amorous sorrows of the mead ; —
From giant Oaks, that wave their branches dark,
To the dwarf Moss that clings upon their bark,
What Beaux and Beauties crowd the gaudy groves,
And woo and win their vegetable Loves."

.   .   .   .

" First the tall Canna lifts his curled brow
Erect to heaven, and plights his nuptial vow;
The virtuous pair, in milder regions born,
Dread the rude blast of Autumn's icy morn ;
Round the chill fair he folds his crimson vest,
And clasps the timorous beauty to his breast."

Here, however, a serious case presents itself ; in *Canna*
there was one stamen to one pistil, and this was comfortable ; but in the next flower he happened to reach —
the *Genista* or Wild Broom — there were ten stamens to
one pistil, that is, ten lovers to one lady ; but the intrepid
Doctor carries it through, all the same, managing the
whole point simply by airy swiftness of treatment :

" Sweet blooms Genista [1] in the myrtle shade,
And ten fond brothers woo the haughty maid."

But sometimes our botanist comes within a mere ace
of beautiful poetry, as for example :

" When o'er the cultured lawns and dreary wastes,
Retiring Autumn flings her howling blasts,
Bends in tumultuous waves the struggling woods,
And showers their leafy honors on the floods ;
In withering heaps collects the flowery spoil ;
And each chill insect sinks beneath the soil :
Quick flies fair Tulipa the loud alarms,
And folds her infant closer in her arms ;
In some lone cave, secure pavilion, lies,
And waits the courtship of serener skies."

[1] Genista, or *Planta Genista*, origin of " Plantagenet," from the
original name-giver's habit of wearing a tuft of his native heath or
broom in his bonnet.

This book has what it calls Interludes between the
parts, in which the Bookseller and the Poet discuss
various points arising in it ; and its oddity is all the
more increased when one finds here a number of the
most just, incisive, right-minded and large views not
only upon the mechanism of poetry, but upon its
essence and its relations to other arts.[1]

Nor need I dwell upon Scott's novels which stretch
from 1814 to 1831, which we have all known from our
childhood as among the most hale and strengthening
waters in which the young soul ever bathed. They
discuss no moral problems, they place us in no relation
towards our fellow that can be called moral at all, they
belong to that part of us which is youthful, undebating,
wholly unmoral — though not immoral,— they are simply
always young, always healthy, always miraculous. And
I can only give now a hasty additional flavor of these

---

[1] Carlyle's opinion of the book is given with a comical grimness
in his Reminiscences à propos of the younger Erasmus Darwin,
who used much to visit the Carlyles after they settled in London :

"Erasmus Darwin, a most diverse kind of mortal, came to seek
us out very soon ('had heard of Carlyle in Germany,' etc.), and
continues ever since to be a quiet house-friend, honestly attached ;
though his visits latterly have been rarer and rarer, health so poor,
I so occupied, etc., etc. He had something of original and sarcas-
tically ingenious in him ; one of the sincerest, naturally truest, and
most modest of men ; elder brother of Charles Darwin (the famed
Darwin on Species of these days), to whom I rather prefer him
for intellect, had not his health quite doomed him to silence and
patient idleness — grandsons, both, of the first famed Erasmus
('Botanic Garden,' etc.), who also seems to have gone upon
'species' questions, 'omnia ex conchis' (all from oysters) being a
dictum of his (even a stamp he sealed with still extant), as this
present Erasmus once told me, many long years before this of
Darwin on Species came up among us ! Wonderful to me, as
indicating the capricious stupidity of mankind : never could read
a page of it, or waste the least thought upon it."

Scott days by reminding you of the bare names of
Thomas Hope, Lockhart, Theodore Hook, Mrs. Trol-
lope, Mrs. Gore and Miss Mitford. It seems always
comfortable in a confusion of this kind to have some
easily-remembered formula which may present us a
considerable number of important facts in portable
shape. Now the special group of writers which I wish
to contrast with the classic group, consisting of Dickens,
Thackeray, Tennyson, Mrs. Browning, Charlotte Brontë
and George Eliot, are at work between 1837 and 1857,
and for the purpose of giving you a convenient skeleton
or set of vertebræ containing some main facts affecting
the English novel of the nineteenth century I have
arranged this simple table which proceeds by steps of
ten years up to the period mentioned.

For example : since these all end in seven ; beginning
with the year 1807 it seems easy to remember that that
is the date of Charles and Mary Lamb's *Tales from
Shakspere ;* skipping ten years to 1817, in this year
Blackwood's Magazine is established, a momentous event
in fiction generally and particularly as to George Eliot's ;
advancing ten years, in 1827 Bulwer's *Pelham* appears
and also the very stimulating *Specimens of German
Romance* which Thomas Carlyle edited ; in 1837 the
adorable *Pickwick* strolls into fiction ; in 1847 Thackeray prints *Vanity Fair*, Charlotte Brontë gives us *Jane
Eyre*, and Tennyson *The Princess ;* and finally in 1857,
as we have seen, George Eliot's *Scenes of Clerical Life*
are printed, while so closely upon it in the previous year
as to be fairly considered contemporary comes Mrs.
Browning's *Aurora Leigh.*

I do not know any more vivid way of bringing before
you the precise work which English fiction is doing at
the time George Eliot sets in than by asking you to run

your eye along the last four dates here given, 1827, 1837, 1847, 1857. Here, in 1827, advances a well-dressed man, bows a fine bow, and falls to preaching his gospel: " My friends, under whatever circumstances a man may be placed, he has it always in his power to be a gentleman ; " and Bulwer's gentleman is always given as a very manful and Christian being. I am well aware of the modern tendency to belittle Bulwer, as a slight creature ; but with the fresh recollection of his books as they fell upon my own boyhood, I cannot recall a single one which did not leave as a last residuum the picture in some sort of the chivalrous gentleman impressed upon my heart. I cheerfully admit that he sometimes came dangerously near snobbery, and that he was uncivil and undignified and many other bad things in the *New Timon* and the Tennyson quarrel ; and I concede that it must be difficult for us — you and me, who are so superior and who have no faults of our own — to look upon these failings with patience ; and yet I cannot help remembering that every novel of Bulwer's is skillfully written and entertaining, and that there is not an ignoble thought or impure stimulus in the whole range of his works.

But, advancing, here in 1837 comes on a preacher who takes up the slums and raggedest miseries of London and plumps them boldly down in the parlors of high life and, like the boy in the fairy tale whose fiddle compelled every hearer to dance in spite of himself, presently has a great train of people following him, ready to do his bidding in earnestly reforming the prisons, the schools, the workhouses, and the like, what time the entire train are roaring with the genialest of laughter at the comical and grotesque figures which this preacher Dickens has fished up out of the London mud.

But again : here in 1847 we have Thackeray exposing
shame and high vulgarity and minute wickedness, while
Charlotte Brontë and Tennyson, with the widest difference
in method, are for the first time expounding the doctrine
of co-equal sovereignty as between man and woman,
and bringing up the historic conception of the personality of woman to a plane in all respects level with,
though properly differentiated from, that of man.   It is
curious to see the depth of Charlotte Brontë's adoration
for Thackeray, the intense, high-pitched woman for the
somewhat slack and, as I always think, somewhat low-
pitched satirist ; and perhaps the essential utterance of
Thackeray, as well as the fervent tone which I beg you
to observe is now being acquired by the English novel,
the awful consciousness of its power and its mission, may
be very sufficiently gathered from some of Charlotte
Brontë's words about Thackeray which occur in the
Preface to the second edition of her *Jane Eyre.*

"There is a man in our own days whose words are not
framed to tickle delicate ears ; who, to my thinking, comes
before the great ones of society much as the son of Imlah
came before the throned kings of Judah and Israel; and who
speaks truth as deep, with a power as prophet-like and as
vital — a mien as dauntless and as daring.   Is the satirist of
Vanity Fair admired in high places ?   I cannot tell; but I
think if some of those amongst whom he hurls the Greek-
fire of his sarcasm, and over whom he flashes the levin-brand
of his denunciation, were to take his warnings in time, they
or their seed might yet escape a fatal Ramoth-Gilead.

"Why have I alluded to this man ?   I have alluded to him,
reader, because I think I see in him an intellect profounder
and more unique than his contemporaries have yet recognized ; because I regard him as the first social regenerator
of the day — as the very master of that working corps who
would restore to rectitude the warped system of things."

Into this field of beneficent activity which the novel has created, comes in 1857 George Eliot : comes with no more noise than that of a snow-flake falling on snow, yet — as I have said and as I wish now to show with some detail — comes as an epoch-maker, both by virtue of the peculiar mission she undertakes and of the method in which she carries it out.

What then is that peculiar mission?

In the very first of these stories, *Amos Barton*, she announces it quite explicitly, though it cannot be supposed at all consciously. Before quoting the passage, in order that you may at once take the full significance of it, let me remind you of a certain old and grievous situation as between genius and the commonplace person. For a long time every most pious thinker must have found immediately in his path a certain obstructive odium upon the Supreme Being (I speak with the greatest reverence) in the matter of the huge and apparently unjustifiable partiality of His spiritual gifts as between man and man.

We have a genius (say) once in a hundred years : but this hundred years represents three generations of the whole world ; that is to say, here are three thousand million commonplace people to one genius.

At once, with all the force of this really inconceivable numerical majority, the cry arises, How monstrous ! Here are three thousand millions of people to eat, sleep, die, and rot into oblivion, and but one man is to have such faculty as may conquer death, win fame, and live beyond the worms !

No one feels this inequality so keenly as the great genius himself. I find in Shakspere, in Beethoven, in others, often an outcrop of feeling which shows that the genius cringes under this load of favoritism, as if he should cry in his lonesome moments, *Dear Lord, why hast thou provided so much for me, and so little for yonder multitude ?* In plain fact, it seems as if there was never such a problem as this : what shall we do about these three thousand millions of common men as against the one uncommon man, to save the goodness of God from seeming like the blind caprice of a Roman Emperor?

It is precisely here that George Eliot comes to the rescue, and though she does not solve the problem — no one expects to do that — at any rate she seems to me to make it tolerable, and to take it out of that class of questions which one shuts back for fear of nightmare and insanity. Emerson has treated this matter, partially, and from a sort of side-light. "But," he exclaims in the end of his essay on *The Uses of Great Men,* "*great men :* — the word is injurious. Is there caste ? Is there fate ? What becomes of the promise to virtue ? . . . Why are the masses, from the dawn of history down, food for knives and powder? The idea dignifies a few leaders, . . . and they make war and death sacred ; but what for the wretches whom they hire and kill? The cheapness of man is everyday's tragedy." And more to this purport. But nothing could be more unsatisfactory than Emerson's solution of the problem. He unhesitatingly announces on one page that the wrong is to be righted by giving every man a chance in the future, in (say) different worlds ; every man is to have his turn at being a genius : until "there are no common men." But two pages farther on this elaborate scheme of redress is completely swept away by the announcement that after all the individual is nothing, the quality is what abides, and so falls away in that most marvelous delusion of his — the strange wise man ! — that personality is to die away into the first cause.

On the other hand, if you will permit me to quote a few pathetic words which I find in Carlyle's *Reminiscences*, in the nature of a sigh and aspiration and breathed blessing all in one upon his wife and her ministrations to him during that singular period of his life when he suddenly left London and buried himself in his wild Scotch farm of Craigenputtoch, I shall be able to show you how Carlyle, most unconsciously, dreams toward a far more satisfactory end of this matter than Emerson's, and then how George Eliot actually brings Carlyle's dream to definite form and at least partial fulfilment in the very beginning of her work. Carlyle is speaking of the rugged trials and apparent impossibilities of living at Craigenputtoch when he and his Jeanie went there, and how bravely and quietly she faced and overcame the poverty, the ugliness, the almost squalor, which was their condition for a long time. " Poverty and mean obstruction continued," he says, " to preside over it, but were transformed by human valor of various sorts into a kind of victory and royalty. Something of high and great dwelt in it, though nothing could be smaller and lower than many of the details. How blessed might poor mortals be in the straitest circumstances, if only their wisdom and fidelity to Heaven and to one another were *adequately* great ! It looks to me now like a kind of humble russet-coated *epic*, that seven years' settlement at Craigenputtoch, very poor in this world's goods, but not without an intrinsic dignity greater and more important than then appeared ; thanks very mainly to her, and her faculties and magnanimities, without whom it had not been possible."

And now, let us hear the words in which George Eliot begins to preach the " russet-coated epic " of everyday life and of commonplace people.

" The Rev. Amos Barton, whose sad fortunes I have under-taken to relate, was, you perceive, in no respect an ideal or exceptional character; and perhaps I am doing a bold thing to bespeak your sympathy on behalf of a man who was so very far from remarkable, — a man whose virtues were not heroic, and who had no undetected crime within his breast; who had not the slightest mystery hanging about him, but was palpably and unmistakably commonplace; who was not even in love, but had had that complaint favourably many years ago. ' An utterly uninteresting character ! ' I think I hear a lady reader exclaim — Mrs. Farthingale, for example, who prefers the ideal in fiction; to whom tragedy means ermine tippets, adultery, and murder; and comedy, the adventures of some personage who is quite a ' character.'

" But, my dear madam, it is so very large a majority of your fellow-countrymen that are of this insignificant stamp. At least eighty out of a hundred of your adult male fellow-Britons returned in the last census are neither extraordinarily silly, nor extraordinarily wicked, nor extraordinarily wise; their eyes are neither deep and liquid with sentiment, nor sparkling with suppressed witticisms; they have probably had no hair-breadth escapes or thrilling adventures; their brains are certainly not pregnant with genius, and their pas-sions have not manifested themselves at all after the fashion of a volcano. They are simply men of complexions more or less muddy, whose conversation is more or less bald and disjointed. Yet these commonplace people — many of them —'bear a conscience, and have felt the sublime prompting to do the painful right; they have their unspoken sorrows and their sacred joys; their hearts have perhaps gone out towards their first-born, and they have mourned over the irreclaimable dead. Nay, is there not a pathos in their very insignificance, — in our comparison of their dim and narrow existence with the glorious possibilities of that human nature which they share?

" Depend upon it, you would gain unspeakably if you would learn with me to see some of the poetry and the pathos, the tragedy and the comedy, lying in the experience of a human soul that looks out through dull gray eyes, and that speaks in a voice of quite ordinary tone. In that case, I should have no fear of your not caring to know what farther befell the Rev. Amos Barton, or of your thinking the homely details I have to tell at all beneath your attention. As it is, you can, if you please, decline to pursue my story farther; and you will easily find reading more to your taste, since I learn from the newspapers that many remarkable novels, full of striking situations, thrilling incidents, and eloquent writing, have appeared only within the last season."

Passing on to *Adam Bede*, *The Mill on the Floss*, and the rest of George Eliot's works in historic order, let us see with what delicious fun, what play of wit, what ever-abiding and depth-illuminating humor, what creative genius, what manifold forms of living flesh and blood, George Eliot preached the possibility of such moral greatness on the part of every most commonplace man and woman as completely reduces to a level the apparent inequality in the matter of genius, and so illustrated the universal "russet-coated epic."

IX

BEFORE *Scenes of Clerical Life* had ceased to run, in the latter part of the year 1857, George Eliot had already begun a novel more complete in form than any of the three tales which composed that series. Early in 1858 she made a visit to the Continent, and it was from Munich that a considerable portion of the MS. of her new book was sent to her publisher, Mr. Blackwood. This was *Adam Bede*, which she completed by the end of October, 1858.

It was brought out immediately in book form; George Eliot seemed desirous of putting her public to a speedier test than could be secured by running the story through successive numbers of the magazine, as usual; although the enthusiastic editor declared himself very willing to enrich the pages of *Blackwood's* with it. It was therefore printed in January, 1859.

I have already cited a letter from Marian Evans to Miss Henschel in which she mentions the only two matters of fact connected in the most shadowy way as originals with the plot of *Adam Bede*. One of these is that in her girlhood she had met an aunt of hers, about sixty years old, who had in early life been herself a preacher. To this extent, and this only, is there any original for our beautiful snowdrop — Dinah Morris, in *Adam Bede*. Again, in the same letter, George Eliot mentions that this same aunt had told her of once spending a night in prison to comfort a poor girl who had murdered her own child, and that this incident lay in her mind for many years until it became the germ of *Adam Bede*.

These are certainly but shadowy connections; yet probably the greatest works are built upon quite as filmy a relation to any actual precedent facts.   A rather pretty story is told of Mrs. Carlyle, which perhaps very well illustrates this filmy relation.   It is told that one evening she gave to Dickens a subject for a novel which she had indeed worked out up to the second volume, the whole subject consisting of a weaving together of such insignificant observations as any one must make of what goes on at houses across the street.   Thus, Mrs. Carlyle observed of a house nearly opposite them that one day the blinds or curtains would be up or down; the next day a figure in a given costume would appear at the window, or a cab would drive — hastily or otherwise — to the door, a visitor would be admitted or rejected, etc.; such bits of circumstances she had managed to connect with human characters in a subtle way which is said to have given Dickens great delight.   She never lived, however, to finish her novel thus begun.

This publication of *Adam Bede* placed George Eliot decisively at the head of English novel-writers, with only Dickens for second, even; and thus enables us at this point fairly to do what the ages always do in order to get that notoriously clear view of things which comes with time, and time only: that is, to brush away all small circumstances and cloudy non-essentials of time so as to bring before our minds the whole course of English fiction, from its beginning to the stage at which it is now pending with *Adam Bede,* as if it concerned but four names and two periods, to wit:

RICHARDSON, FIELDING. } middle 18th century

and

DICKENS, GEORGE ELIOT. } middle 19th century.

It was shown in the last lecture how distinctly the
moral purpose of the English fiction represented by this
upper group was announced, though we were obliged to
record a mournful failure in realizing that announcement.
Adam Bede gives us the firmest support for a first and
most notable difference between these two periods of
English fiction : that while the former professes morality
yet fails beyond description, the latter executes its
moral purpose to a practical degree of beneficence
beyond its wildest hopes.   Without now specifying the
subtle revolutions which lie in *Adam Bede,* a single more
tangible example will be sufficient to bring this entire
difference before you.   If I ask you to recall how it is
less than fifty years ago that Charles Dickens was writing
of the debtors' prisons with all the terrible earnest of
one who had lived with his own father and mother in
those unspeakable dens ; if I recall to you what marvelous haste for proverbially slow England the reform thus
initiated took upon itself, how it flew from this to that
prison, from this to that statute, from this to that country, until now not only is no such thing as imprisonment
for debt known to any of Dickens's readers, but, with
the customary momentum of such generous impulses in
society, the whole movement in favor of debtors is
clearly going too far and is beginning to oppress the
creditor with part of the injustice it formerly meted out
to the debtor ; if, I say, I thus briefly recall to you this
single instance of moral purpose carried into perfect
practice, I typify a great and characteristic distinction
between these two schools.   For in point of fact what
one may call an organic impracticability lay at the core
of the moral scheme of Richardson and Fielding.   I
think all reasoning and experience show that if you con-
front a man day by day with nothing but a picture of

his own unworthiness the final effect is, not to stimulate, but to paralyze his moral energy. The picture of the man becomes the head of a Gorgon. And this was precisely what this early English fiction professed to do. It professed to show man exactly as he is; but although this profession included the good man as well as the bad man, and although there was some endeavor to relieve the picture with tints of goodness here and there, the final result was — and I fearlessly point any doubter to the net outcome from *Pamela* and *Clarissa Harlowe* down to *Humphrey Clinker* — the final result was such a portrayal as must make any man sit down before the picture in a miserable deep of contempt for himself and his fellow out of which many spirits cannot climb at all, and none can climb clean.

On the other hand, the work of Dickens I have just referred to is a fair specimen of the way in which the later school of English fiction — while glozing no evil — showed man, not how bad he might be, but how good he might be; and thus, instead of paralyzing the moral energy, stimulated it to the most beneficent practical reform. I think it is Robert Browning who has declared that a man is as good as his best; and there is the subtlest connection between the right to measure a man's moral stature by the highest thing that he has done, rather than the lowest, on the one hand, and that new and beautiful inspiration which comes into one's life as one contemplates more and more instances of the best in human behavior, as these are given by a literature which thus lifts one up, from day to day, with the declaration that however commonplace a man may be he yet has within himself the highest capabilities of what we have agreed to call the russet-coated epic. The George Eliot and Dickens school, in fact, do but expand the text of the Master when He urges His disciples: "Be ye perfect as I am perfect."

Let me here suggest a second difference between the two schools which involves an interesting coincidence and specially concerns us at this point. As between Richardson and Fielding: it has been well said (by whom I cannot now remember) that Fielding tells you the time of day, whilst Richardson shows you how the watch is made. As indicating Fielding's method of conducting the action rather by concrete dialogue and event, than by those long analytic discussions of character in which Richardson would fill whole pages with minute descriptions of the changing emotions of Clarissa upon reading a certain letter from Lovelace, pursuing the emotion as it were tear by tear, *lachrymatim*, — this characterization happily enough contrasts the analytic strength of Richardson with the synthetic strength of Fielding.

A strikingly similar contrast obtains as between George Eliot and Charles Dickens. Every one will recognize as soon as it is mentioned the microscopic analysis of character throughout George Eliot as compared with the rapid cartoon-strokes by which Dickens brings out his figures. But the antithesis cannot be left here as between George Eliot and Dickens: for it is the marvel of the former's art that, though so cool and analytic, it nevertheless sets before us perfect living flesh-and-blood people by fusing the whole analytic process with a synthetic fire of the true poet's human sympathy.

And here we come upon a further difference between George Eliot and Dickens of which we shall have many and beautiful examples in the works we have to study. This is a large, poetic tolerance of times and things which, though worthy of condemnation, nevertheless appeal to our sympathy because they once were closely bound with our fellow-men's daily life. For example, George Eliot writes often and lovingly about the England of the days before the Reform Bill, the careless, pictur-esque, country-squire England ; not because she likes it, or thinks it better than the England of the present, but with much the same feeling with which a woman looks at the ragged, hob-nailed shoes of her boy who is gone, — a boy who doubtless was often rude and diso-bedient and exasperating to the last degree, but who was her boy.

A keen insight into this remarkable combination of the poetic tolerance with the sternness of scientific accuracy possessed by this remarkable woman — the most remarkable of all writers in this respect, we should say, except Shakspere — is offered us in the opening lines of the first chapter of her first story, *Amos Barton*.   (I love to look at this wonderful faculty in its germ.)   The chap-ter begins : " Shepperton Church was a very different looking building five-and-twenty years ago. . . . Now there is a wide span of slated roof flanking the old steeple ; the windows are tall and symmetrical ; the outer doors are resplendent with oak graining, the inner doors reverentially noiseless with a garment of red baize ; " and we have a minute description of the church as it is. Then we have this turn in the next paragraph, altogether wonderful for a George Eliot who has been translating Strauss and Feuerbach, studying physics, Comtism and the like among the London agnostics, a fervent disciple of progress, a frequent contributor to the *Westminster Review :* " Immense improvement ! says the well-regu-lated mind, which unintermittingly rejoices in the new police . . . the penny-post, and all guarantees of human advancement, and has no moments when conservative reforming intellect takes a nap, while imagination does a

little Toryism by the sly, revelling in regret that dear old
brown, crumbling, picturesque inefficiency is everywhere
giving place to spick-and-span, new-painted, new-var-
nished efficiency, which will yield endless diagrams,
plans, elevations and sections, but alas! no picture.
Mine, I fear, is not a well-regulated mind: it has an
occasional tenderness for old abuses; it lingers with a
certain fondness over the days of nasal clerks and top-
booted parsons, and has a sigh for the departed shades
of vulgar errors." And it is worth while, if even for an
aside, to notice in the same passage how this immense
projection of herself out of herself into what we may
fairly call her antipodes is not only a matter of no
strain, but from the very beginning is accompanied by
that eye-twinkle between the lines which makes much
of the very ruggedest writing of George Eliot's like a
Virginia fence from between whose rails peep wild roses
and morning-glories.

This is in the next paragraph where after thus recalling the outside of Shepperton church she exclaims:
"Then inside what dear old quaintnesses! which I
began to look at with delight even when I was so crude
a member of the congregation that my nurse found it
necessary to provide for the reinforcement of my devo-
tional patience by smuggling bread and butter into the
sacred edifice." Or, a few lines before, a still more
characteristic twinkle of the eye which in a flash carries
our thoughts all the way from evolution to pure fun, when
she describes the organ-player of the new Shepperton
church as a rent-collector " differentiated by force of circumstances into an organist." Apropos of this use of
the current scientific term "differentiation," it is worth
while noting, as we pass, an instance of the extreme
vagueness and caprice of current modern criticism.

When George Eliot's *Daniel Deronda* was printed in 1876, one of the most complacent English reviews criticised her expression " dynamic power of" a woman's glance, which occurs in her first picture of Gwendolen Harleth, as an inappropriate use of scientific phraseology; and was immediately followed by a chorus of small voices discussing the matter with much minute learning, rather as evidence of George Eliot's decline from proper artistic style. But here, as you have just seen, in the very first chapter of her first story, written twenty years before, scientific " differentiation " is made to work very effectively; and a few pages further on we have an even more striking instance in this passage : " This allusion to brandy-and-water suggested to Miss Gibbs the introduction of the liquor decanters now that the tea was cleared away; for in bucolic society five-and-twenty years ago the human animal of the male sex was understood to be perpetually athirst, and ' something to drink ' was as necessary a ' condition of thought ' as Time and Space." Other such happy uses of scientific phrases occur indeed throughout the whole of these first three stories and form an integral part of that ever-brooding humor which fills with a quiet light all the darkest stories of George Eliot.

On the other hand, it is in strong contrast that we find her co-laborer, Dickens, always growing furious (as his biographer describes), when the ante-reform days are mentioned, those days of rotten boroughs, when, as Lord John Russell said, "a ruined mound sent two representatives to Parliament, three niches in a stone wall sent three representatives to Parliament, and a park where no houses were to be seen sent two representatives to Parliament." While George Eliot is indulging in the tender recollections of picturesqueness etc.,

just given, Dickens is writing savage versions of the old
ballad, *The Fine Old English Gentleman,* in which he
fiercely satirizes the old, Tory England.

"I'll sing you a new ballad" (he cries), "and I'll warrant it first-
    rate,
Of the days of that old gentleman who had that old estate;

.   .   .   .

"The good old laws were garnished well with gibbets, whips, and
    chains,
With fine old English penalties and fine old English pains,
With rebel heads and seas of blood once hot in rebel veins:
For all these things were requisite to guard the rich old gains
Of the fine old English Tory times;
Soon may they come again!

.   .   .   .

"The good old times for cutting throats that cried out in their need,
The good old times for hunting men who held their father's creed,
The good old times when William Pitt, as all good men agreed,
Came down direct from Paradise at more than railroad speed. . . .
Oh, the fine old English Tory times;
When will they come again!

"In those rare days the press was seldom known to snarl or bark,
But sweetly sang of men in pow'r like any tuneful lark;
Grave judges, too, to all their evil deeds were in the dark;
And not a man in twenty score knew how to make his mark.
Oh, the fine old English Tory times,
Soon may they come again! . . ."

.   .   .   .

In a word, the difference between Dickens's and George
Eliot's powers is here typified: Dickens tends toward
the satiric or destructive view of the old times; George
Eliot, with an even more burning intolerance of the
essential evil, takes on the other hand the loving or
constructive view. It is for this reason that George
Eliot's work, as a whole, is so much finer than some of
Dickens's. The great artist never can work in haste,

never in malice, never in even the sub-acid, satiric mood of Thackeray: in love, and love only, can great work, work that not only pulls down but builds up, be done; it is love, and love only, that is truly constructive in art.

And here it seems profitable to contrast George Eliot's peculiar endowment as shown in these first stories with that of Thackeray. Thackeray was accustomed to lament that "since the author of *Tom Jones* was buried no writer of fiction among us has been permitted to depict to his utmost powers a man. . . . Society will not tolerate the natural in art." Under this yearning of Thackeray's after the supposed freedom of Fielding's time lie at once a short-coming of love, a limitation of view and an actual fallacy of logic which always kept Thackeray's work below the highest, and which formed the chief reason why I have been unable to place him here, along with Dickens and George Eliot. This short-coming and limitation still exist in our literature and criticism to such an extent that I can do no better service than by asking you to examine them. And I think I can illustrate the whole in the shortest manner by some considerations drawn from that familiar wonder of our times, the daily newspaper. Consider the printed matter which is brought daily to your breakfast table. The theory of the daily paper is that it is the history of the world for one day: and let me here at once connect this illustration with the general argument by saying that Thackeray and his school, when they speak of drawing a man as he is — of the natural, etc., in art — would mean drawing a man as he appears in such a history as the daily newspaper gives us. But let us test this history: let us examine, for instance, the telegraphic column in the morning journal. I have made a faithful transcript on the morning of this writing of every item

in the news summary involving the moral relation of
man to man ; the result is as follows : one item concerning the assassination of the Czar; the recent war with
the Boers in Africa; the quarrel between Turkey and
Greece ; the rebellion in Armenia ; the trouble about
Candahar; of a workman in a lumber-camp in Michigan,
who shot and killed his wife, twenty-two years old, yesterday; of the confession of a man just taken from the
West Virginia penitentiary to having murdered an old
man in Michigan, three years ago ; of the suicide of
Mrs. Scott at Williamstown, Mississippi; of the killing
of King by Clark in a fight in Logan county, Kentucky,
on Sunday; of how, about 10 o'clock last night, a certain John Cram was called to the door of his house
near Chicago and shot dead by William Seymour;
of how young Mohr, thirteen years of age, died at the
Charity Hospital in Jersey City yesterday, from the
effects of a beating by his father ; of how young Clasby
was arrested at Richmond, Virginia, for stealing letters
out of the mail bag ; of how the miners of the Connells-
ville, Pennsylvania coke regions, the journeyman bakers
of Montreal, Canada, the rubber-workers of New Bruns-
wick, New Jersey, and the Journeyman Tailors' Union
in Cincinnati, are all about to strike ; and finally, of how
James Tolen, an insane wife-murderer, committed suicide
in Minnesota yesterday, by choking himself with a
twisted sheet. These are all the items involving the
moral relations of man to man contained in the history
of the world for Tuesday, March 22d, 1881, as given by
a journal noted for the extent and accuracy of its daily
collection.

Let us suppose a picture were drawn of the moral condition of the United States from these data : how nearly
would it represent the facts? This so-called " history of

the world for one day," if you closely examine it, turns out to be, you observe, only a history of the world's crimes for one day. The world's virtues do not appear. It is true that Patrick Kelly murdered his wife yesterday : but then how many Kellys who came home tired from work and found the wife drunk and the children crying for bread, instead of murdering the whole family, with a rugged sigh drew the beastly woman's form into one corner, fumbled about the poor, dirty cupboard in another for crusts of bread, fed the crying youngsters after some rude fashion and finally lay down with dumb heaviness to sleep off the evil of that day. It is true that Jones, the bank clerk, was yesterday exposed in a series of defalcations : but how many thousands of bank clerks on that same day resisted the strongest temptations to false entries and the allurements of private stock speculations. It is true that yesterday Mrs. Lighthead eloped with the music-teacher, leaving six children and a desolate husband : but how many thousands of Mrs. Heavyhearts spent the same day in nursing some drunken husband, who had long ago forfeited all love ; how many Milly Bartons were darning six children's stockings at five o'clock of that morning ; nay, what untold millions of faithful women made this same day a sort of paradise for husband and children. And finally you have but to consider a moment that if it lay within the power of the diligent collector of items for the Associated Press despatches to gather together the virtuous, rather than the criminal, actions of mankind, the virtuous would so far exceed the criminal as that no journal would find columns enough to print them in, so as to put a wholly different complexion upon matters. The use of this newspaper illustration in my present argument is this : I complain that Thackeray, and the Fielding school, in professing to paint men as they are, really paint men only as they appear in some such necessarily one-sided representations as the newspaper history just described. And it is perfectly characteristic of the inherent weakness of Thackeray that he should so utterly fail to see the true significance underlying society's repudiation of his proposed natural picture. The least that such a repudiation could mean, would be that even if the picture were good in Fielding's time, it is bad now. It is beautiful, therefore, remembering Thackeray's great influence at the time when *Scenes of Clerical Life* were written, to find a woman, George Eliot, departing utterly out of that mood of hate or even of acidulous satire in which Thackeray so often worked — and in which, one may add, the world is seldom benefited, however skillful the work may be — departing from all that, deftly painting for us these pathetic Milly Bartons, and Mr. Gilfils, and Janet Dempsters, and Rev. Tryans, and arranging the whole into a picture which becomes epic because it is filled with the reverend struggles of human personalities, dressed in whatever russet garb, of clothing or of circumstances.

Those who were at my first lecture on George Eliot will remember that we found the editor of *Blackwood's Magazine*, on a certain autumn night in 1856, reading part of the MS. of *Amos Barton* in his drawing-room to Thackeray, and remarking to Thackeray, who had just come in late from dinner, that he had come upon a new author who seemed uncommonly like a first-class passenger; it is significantly related that Thackeray said nothing, and evinced no further interest in it than civilly to say, sometime afterward, that he would have liked to hear more of it. In the light of the contrast I have just drawn Thackeray's failure to be impressed seems natural enough, and becomes indeed all the more impressive when we compare it with the enthusiastic praise which Charles Dickens lavished upon this same work in the letter which you will remember I read from him.

And here I come upon a further contrast between George Eliot and Dickens which I should be glad now to bring out as clearly appearing in these first three *Scenes of Clerical Life* before *Adam Bede* was written.

This is her exquisite modernness in that intense feeling for personality which I developed with so much care in my first six lectures, and her exquisite scientific precision in placing the personalities or characters of her works before the reader.

All the world knows how Dickens puts a personality on his canvas: he always gives us a vividly descriptive line of facial curve, of dress, of form, of gesture and the like, which distinguishes a given character. Whenever we see this line we know the character so well that we are perfectly content that two rings for the eyes, a spot for the nose and a blur for the body may represent the rest; and we accept always with joy the rich mirthfulness or pathetic matter with which Dickens's large soul manages to invest such hastily drawn figures. George Eliot's principle and method are completely opposite; at the time of her first stories which we are now considering they were unique; and the quietness with which she made a real epoch in all character-description is simply characteristic of the quietness of all her work. She showed for the first time that without approaching dangerously near to caricature, as Dickens was often obliged to do, a lovable creature of actual flesh and blood could be drawn in a novel with all the advantage of completeness derivable from microscopic analysis, scientific precision, and moral intent; and with abso-

lutely none of the disadvantages, such as coldness, dead-
ness and the like, which had caused all sorts of mere-
tricious arts to be adopted by novelists in order to save
the naturalness of a character.

A couple of brief expressions from *Janet's Repentance*, the third of *Scenes of Clerical Life*, show how
intensely George Eliot felt upon this matter. At the
end of Chapter X of that remarkable story she says:
" Our subtlest analysis of schools and sects must miss
the essential truth unless it be lit up by the love that
sees in all forms of human thought and work the life-
and-death struggles of separate human beings." And
again in Chapter XXII: " Emotion, I fear, is obstinately
irrational: it insists on caring for individuals; it absolutely refuses to adopt the quantitative view of human
anguish, and to admit that thirteen happy lives are
a set-off against twelve miserable lives," leaving " a
clear balance on the side of satisfaction. . . . One must
be a great philosopher," she adds, sardonically, " to
have emerged into the serene air of pure intellect in
which it is evident that individuals really exist for no
other purpose than that abstractions may be drawn from
them: " (which is dangerously near, by the way, to a
complete formula of the Emersonian doctrine which
I had occasion to quote in my last lecture). She continues: " And so it comes to pass that for the man who
knows sympathy because he has known sorrow, that old,
old saying, about the joy of angels over the repentant
sinner out-weighing their joy over the ninety-nine just,
has a meaning that does not jar with the language of
his own heart. It only tells him that for angels too
there is a transcendent value in human pain which refuses
to be settled by equations; . . . that for angels too the
misery of one casts so tremendous a shadow as to eclipse

the bliss of ninety-nine." The beautiful personality who suggests this remark is Janet Dempster, the heroine of *Janet's Repentance*: a tall, grand, beautiful girl who has married the witty Lawyer Dempster and who, after a bitter married life of some years in which Dempster finally begins amusing himself by beating her, has come to share the customary wine decanter at table, and thus by insensible degrees to acquire the habit of taking wine against trouble. Presently a terrible catastrophe occurs; she is thrust out of doors barefooted at midnight, half clad, by her brutal husband, and told never to return. Finding lodgment with a friend next day a whirlwind of necessity for complete spiritual re-adjustment shakes her. "She was sick," says George Eliot, "of that barren exhortation, 'Do right and keep a clear conscience and God will reward you, etc.' She wanted strength to do right;" and at this point the thought of Tryan, an unorthodox clergyman who had made a great stir in the village and whom she had been taught to despise, occurs to her. "She had often heard Mr. Tryan laughed at for being fond of great sinners; she began to see a new meaning in those words; he would perhaps understand her helplessness. If she could pour out her heart to him!" Then here we have this keen glimpse into some curious relations of personality. "The impulse to confession almost always requires the presence of a fresh ear and a fresh heart; and in our moments of spiritual need the man to whom we have no tie but our common nature seems nearer to us than mother, brother or friend. Our daily, familiar life is but a hiding of ourselves from each other behind a screen of trivial words and deeds, and those who sit with us at the same hearth are often the farthest off from the deep human soul within us, full of unspoken evil and unacted good." Nor can I ever read the pathetic scene in which Janet secures peace for her spirit and a practicable working-theory for the rest of her active life, without somehow being reminded of the second scene in Mrs. Browning's *Drama of Exile*, prodigiously different as that is from this in all external setting : — the scene where the figures of Adam and Eve are discovered at the extremity of the sword-glare, flying from Eden, and Adam begins :

> " Pausing a moment on the outer edge,
>   Where the supernal sword-glare cuts in light
> The dark exterior desert, — hast thou strength,
> Beloved, to look behind us to the gate ?
> *Eve.* Have I not strength to look up to thy face ? "

This story of *Janet's Repentance* offers us, by the way, a strong note of modernness as between George Eliot and Shakspere. Shakspere has never drawn, so far as I know, a repentance of any sort. Surely, in the whole range of our life no phenomenon can take more powerful hold upon the attention of the thinker than that of a human spirit suddenly, of its own free-will, turning the whole current of its love and desire from a certain direction into a direction entirely opposite : so that from a small spiteful creature, enamored with all ugliness, we have a large, generous spirit, filled with the love of true love. In looking upon such a sight one seems to be startlingly near to the essential mystery of personality — to that hidden fountain of power not preceded, power not conditioned, which probably gives man his only real conception of Divine power, or power acting for itself. It would be wonderful that the subtleties of human passion comprehended in the situation of repentance had not attracted Shakspere's imagination if one did not remember that the developing personality of man was then only coming into literature. The only apparent change

of character of this sort in Shakspere which I recall is
that of the young king Henry V leaving Falstaff and
his other gross companions for the steadier matters of
war and government; but the soliloquy of Prince Hal
in the very first act of *King Henry IV* precludes all
idea of repentance here, by showing that at the outset
his heart is not in the jolly pranks, but that he is calcu-
latingly ambitious from the beginning; and his whole
apparent dissipation is but a scheme to enhance his
future glory.   In the first act of *Henry IV* (first part),
when the plot is made to rob the carriers, at the end of
Scene II, *exeunt* all but Prince Hal, who soliloquizes
thus :

> " I know you all, and will awhile uphold
> The unyoked humor of your idleness :
> Yet herein will I imitate the sun,
> Who doth permit the base contagious clouds
> To smother up his beauty from the world
> That, when he please again to be himself,
> Being wanted, he may be more wondered at
> By breaking through the foul and ugly mists
> Of vapors that did seem to strangle him.
> . . . So when this loose behaviour I throw off
> And pay the debt I never promisèd,
> By how much better than my word I am
> By so much shall I falsify men's hopes ;
> And, like bright metal on a sullen ground,
> My reformation, glittering o'er my fault,
> Shall show more goodly and attract more eyes
> Than that which had no foil to set it off.
> I'll so offend to make offense a skill,
> Redeeming time when men think least I will."

Here the stream of his love is from the beginning and
always towards ambition ; there is never any turn at all ;
and Prince Hal's assumption of the grace *reformation*,
as applied to such a career of deliberate acting, is merely
a piece of naive complacency.

Let us now go further and say that with this reverence for personality as to the ultimate important fact of human existence George Eliot wonderfully escapes certain complexities due to the difference between what a man is, really, and what he seems to be to his fellows.   Perhaps I may most easily specify these complexities by asking you to recall the scene in one of Dr. Holmes's *Breakfast-Table* series, where the Professor laboriously expounds to the young man called John that there are really three of him, to wit: John as he appears to his neighbors, John as he appears to himself, and John as he really is.

In George Eliot's *Theophrastus Such* one finds explicit mention of the trouble that had been caused to her by two of these: " With all possible study of myself," she says in the first chapter . . . " I am obliged to recognize that while there are secrets in me unguessed by others these others have certain items of knowledge about the extent of my powers and the figure I make with them which, in turn, are secrets unguessed by me. . . . Thus . . . O fellow-men ! if I trace with curious interest your labyrinthine self-delusions . . . it is not that I feel myself aloof from you : the more intimately I seem to discern your weaknesses the stronger to me is the proof I share them. . . . No man can know his brother simply as a spectator.   Dear blunderers, I am one of you."

Perhaps nothing less than this underlying reverence for all manner of personality could have produced this first chapter of *Adam Bede*. " With this drop of ink," she says at starting, " I will show you the roomy workshop of Mr. Jonathan Burge, carpenter and builder in the village of Hayslope, as it appeared on the 18th of June, in the year of our Lord 1799."   I can never read this opening of the famous carpenter's shop without indulging myself for a moment in the wish that this same marvelous eye might have dwelt upon a certain carpenter's shop I wot of, on some 18th of June, in the year of our Lord 25. What would we not give for such a picture of the work-shop of that master-builder and of the central figure in it as is here given us of the old English room ringing with the song of Adam Bede. Perhaps we could come upon no clearer proof of that modernness of personality which I have been advocating than this very fact of our complete ignorance as to the physical person of Christ. One asks one's self, how comes it never to have occurred to St. Matthew, nor St. Mark, nor St. Luke, nor St. John to tell us what manner of man this was, — what stature, what complexion, what color of eye and hair, what shape of hand and foot. A natural instinct arising at the very outset of the descriptive effort would have caused a modern to acquaint us with these and many like particulars.

It is advancing upon the same line of thought to note that here, in this opening of *Adam Bede*, not only are the men marked off and differentiated for our physical eye but the very first personality described is that of a dog, and this is subtly done. "On a heap of soft shavings a rough gray shepherd-dog had made himself a pleasant bed, and was lying with his nose between his fore-paws, occasionally wrinkling his brows to cast a glance at the tallest of the five workmen, who was carving a shield in the centre of a wooden mantel-piece." This dog is our friend Gyp, who emerges on several occasions through *Adam Bede*. Gyp is only one of a number of genuine creations in animal character which show the modernness of George Eliot and Charles Dickens, and make them especially dear. How, indeed, could society get along without that famous cock in

Adam Bede, who, as George Eliot records, was accustomed to crow as if the sun was rising on purpose to hear him ! And I wish here to place upon the roll of fame, also, a certain cock who entered literature about this time in a series of delicious papers called *Shy Neighborhoods*. In these Charles Dickens gave some account, among many other notable but unnoted things, of several families of fowls in which he had become — as it were — intimate during his walks about outlying London. One of these was a reduced family of Bantams whom he was accustomed to find crowding together in the side entry of a pawnbroker's shop. Another was a family of Dorkings who regularly spent their evenings in somewhat riotous company at a certain tavern near the Haymarket, and seldom went to bed before two in the morning.

My particular immortal, however, was a member of the following family : I quote from Dickens, here : — " But the family I am best acquainted with reside in the densest parts of Bethnal-Green. Their abstraction from the objects amongst which they live, or rather their conviction that those objects have all come into existence in express subservience to fowls has so enchanted me that I have made them the subject of many journeys at divers hours. . . . ' The leading lady ' is an aged personage afflicted with a paucity of feather and visibility of quill that give her the appearance of a bundle of officepens. When a railway goods-van that would crush an elephant comes round the corner, tearing over these fowls, they emerge unharmed from under the horses perfectly satisfied that the whole rush was a passing property in the air which may have left something to eat behind it. They look upon old shoes, wrecks of kettles and saucepans, and fragments of bonnets as a kind of

meteoric discharge for fowls to peck at. . . . Gaslight comes
quite as natural to them as any other light; and I have
more than a suspicion that in the minds of the two lords,
the early public-house at the corner has superseded the
sun.   They always begin to crow when the public-house
shutters begin to be taken down; and they salute the
Pot-boy when he appears to perform that duty as
if he were Phœbus in person."   And alongside these
two cocks I must place a hen whom I find teaching a
wise and beautiful lesson to the last man in the world
you would suspect as accessible to influences from any
such direction.   This was Thomas Carlyle.   Among his
just-published *Reminiscences* I find the following entry
from the earlier dyspeptic times, which seems impossible
when we remember the well-known story — true, as I
know — how, after Thomas Carlyle and his wife had settled at Chelsea, London, and the crowing of the neigh-
borhood cocks had long kept him in martyrdom, Mrs.
Carlyle planned and carried out the most brilliant cam-
paign of her life, in the course of which she succeeded
in purchasing or otherwise suppressing every cock within
hearing distance.   But this entry is long before:

"Another morning, what was wholesomer and better,
happening to notice, as I stood looking out on the bit
of green under my bedroom window, a trim and rather
pretty hen actively paddling about and picking up what
food might be discoverable, 'See,' I said to myself;
'look, thou fool!   Here is a two-legged creature with
scarcely half a thimbleful of poor brains; thou call'st
thyself a man with nobody knows how much brain, and
reason dwelling in it; and behold how the one *life* is
regulated and how the other!   In God's name concentrate, collect whatever of reason thou hast, and direct it on
the one thing needful.'   Irving, when we did get into

intimate dialogue, was affectionate to me as ever, and had always to the end a great deal of sense and insight into things about him, but he could not much help me; how could anybody but myself? By degrees I was doing so, taking counsel of that *symbolic* HEN."

In George Eliot all the domestic animals are true neighbors and are brought within the Master's exhortation: " Thou shalt love thy neighbor as thyself," by the tenderness and deep humor with which she treats them. This same Gyp, who is honored with first place among the characters described in the carpenter's shop, is continually doing something charming throughout *Adam Bede.* In *Janet's Repentance* dear old Mr. Jerome comes down the road on his roan mare, " shaking the bridle and tickling her flank with the whip as usual, though there was a perfect mutual understanding that she was not to quicken her pace; " and everywhere I find those touches of true sympathy with the dumb brutes, such as only earnest souls or great geniuses are capable of.

Somehow — I cannot now remember how — a picture was fastened upon my mind in childhood which I always recall with pleasure: it is the figure of man emerging from the dark of barbarism attended by his friends the horse, the cow, the chicken and the dog. George Eliot's animal painting brings always this picture before me.

In April, 1860, appeared George Eliot's second great novel, *The Mill on the Floss.* This book, in some respects otherwise her greatest work, possesses a quite extraordinary interest for us now in the circumstance that a large number of traits in the description of the heroine, Maggie Tulliver, are unquestionably traits of George Eliot herself, and the autobiographic character of the book has been avowed by her best friends. I propose therefore in the next lecture to read some pas-

sages from *The Mill on the Floss* in which I may
have the pleasure of letting this great soul speak for
herself with little comment from me, except that I wish
to compare the figure of Maggie Tulliver, specially, with
that of Aurora Leigh, in the light of the remarkable
development of womanhood, both in real life and in fiction, which arrays itself before us when we think only of
what we may call the Victorian women : that is, of the
Queen herself, Sister Dora, Florence Nightingale, Ida, in
Tennyson's *Princess*, Jane Eyre, Charlotte Brontë and
her sisters, Mrs. Browning, with her Eve and Catarina
and Aurora Leigh, and George Eliot, with her creations.
I shall thus make a much more extensive study of *The
Mill on the Floss* than of either of the four works which
preceded it.   It is hard to leave Adam Bede, and Dinah
Morris and Bartle Massey, and Mrs. Poyser, but I must
select ; and I have thought this particularly profitable
because no criticism that I have yet seen of George Eliot
does the least justice to the enormous, the simply unique
equipment with which she comes into English fiction, or
in the least prepares the reader for those extraordinary
revolutions which she has wrought with such demure
quietness that unless pointed out by some diligent pro-
fessional student no ordinary observer would be apt to
notice them.   Above all have I done this because it is
my deep conviction that we can find more religion in
George Eliot's works than she herself dreamed she was
putting there, and a clearer faith for us than she ever
formulated for herself : a strange and solemn result, but
one not without parallel : for Mrs. Browning's words of
Lucretius, in *The Vision of Poets*, partly apply here :

> "Lucretius, nobler than his mood !
> Who dropped his plummet down the broad
> Deep Universe, and said ' No God,'

Finding no bottom! He denied
Divinely the divine, and died
Chief-poet on the Tiber-side,
By grace of God! His face is stern,
As one compelled, in spite of scorn,
To teach a truth he could not learn."

X

Wʜɪʟᴇ it is true that the publication of *Adam Bede* enables us — as stated in the last lecture — to fix George Eliot as already at the head of English novel writers in 1859, I should add that the effect of the book was not so well defined upon the public of that day. The work was not an immediate popular success; and even some of the authoritative critics, instead of recognizing its greatness with generosity, went pottering about to find what existing authors this new one had most likely drawn her inspiration from.

But *The Mill on the Floss*, which appeared in April, 1860, together with some strong and generous reviews of *Adam Bede* which had meantime appeared in *Blackwood's Magazine* and in the *London Times*, quickly carried away the last vestige of this suspense, and *The Mill on the Floss* presently won for itself a popular audience and loving appreciation which appear to have been very gratifying to George Eliot herself. This circumstance alone would make the book an interesting one for our present special study; but the interest is greatly heightened by the fact — a fact which I find most positively stated by those who most intimately knew her — that the picture of girlhood which occupies so large a portion of the first part of the book is, in many particulars, autobiographic. The title originally chosen for this work by George Eliot was *Sister Maggie :* from which we may judge the prominence she intended to give to the character of Maggie Tulliver. After the book was finished, however, this title was felt to be for several reasons insufficient. It was a happy thought of Mr. Blackwood's to call the book *The Mill on the Floss ;* and George Eliot immediately adopted his suggestion to that effect. There is too a third reason why this particular work offers some peculiar contributions to the main lines of thought upon which these lectures have been built. As I go on to read a page here and there, merely by way of recalling the book and the actual style to you, you will presently find that the interest of the whole has for the time concentrated itself upon the single figure of a little wayward English girl some nine years old, — perhaps alone in a garret in some fit of childish passion accusing the Divine order of things as to its justice or mercy, crudely and inarticulately enough, yet quite as keenly after all as our Prometheus, either according to Æschylus or Shelley. As I pass along rapidly bringing back to you these pictures of Maggie's girlish despairs, I beg you to recall the first scenes which were set before you from the Prometheus, to bear those in mind along with these, to note how Æschylus — whom we have agreed to consider as a literary prototype, occupying much the same relation to his age as George Eliot does to ours — in stretching Prometheus upon the bare Caucasian rock and lacerating him with the just lightnings of outraged Fate is at bottom only studying with a ruder apparatus the same phenomena which George Eliot is here unfolding before us in the microscopic struggles of the little English girl ; and I ask you particularly to observe how here, as we have so many times found before, the enormous advance from Prometheus to Maggie Tulliver — from Æschylus to George Eliot — is summed up in the fact that while personality in Æschylus' time had got no further than the conception of a universe in which justice is the organic idea, in George Eliot's time it has arrived at the conception of a universe in which love is the organic idea; and that it is precisely upon the stimulus of this new growth of individualism that George Eliot's readers crowd up with interest to share the tiny woes of insignificant Maggie Tulliver, while Æschylus, in order to assemble an interested audience, must have his Jove, his Titans, his earthquakes, his mysticism, and the blackness of inconclusive Fate withal.

Everyone remembers a sense of mightiness in this opening chapter of *The Mill on the Floss* where the great river Floss, thick with heavy-laden ships, sweeps down to the sea by the red-roofed town of St. Ogg's. Remembering how we found that the first personality described in *Adam Bede* was that of a shepherd-dog, here too we find that the first prominent figures in our landscape are those of animals. The author is indulging in a sort of dreamy prelude of reminiscences, and in describing Dorlcote Mill, Maggie's home, says:

" The rush of the water and the booming of the mill bring a dreamy deafness which seems to heighten the peacefulness of the scene. They are like a great curtain of sound, shutting one out from the world beyond. And now there is the thunder of the huge covered wagon coming home with sacks of grain. That honest wagoner is thinking of his dinner, getting sadly dry in the oven at this late hour; but he will not touch it until he has fed his horses, — the strong, submissive, meek-eyed beasts, who, I fancy, are looking mild reproach at him from between their blinkers, that he should crack his whip at them in that awful manner, as if they needed that hint! See how they stretch their shoulders up the slope to the bridge, with all the more energy because they are so near home. Look at their grand, shaggy feet, that seem to grasp the firm earth, at the patient strength of their necks bowed under the heavy collar, at the mighty muscles of their struggling haunches! I should like well to hear them neigh over their hardly earned feed of corn, and see them, with their moist necks freed from the harness, dipping their eager nostrils into the muddy pond. Now they are on the bridge, and down they go again at a swifter pace, and the arch of the covered wagon disappears at a turning behind the trees."

Remembering how we have agreed that the author's comments in the modern novel, acquainting us with such parts of the action as could not be naturally or conveniently brought upon the stage, might be profitably regarded as a development of certain well-known functions of the Chorus in the Greek drama — we have here a quite palpable instance of the necessity for such development; how otherwise, could we be let into the inner emotions of farm-horses so genially as in this charming passage?

In Chapter II we are introduced to Mr. and Mrs. Tulliver talking by the fire in the left-hand corner of their cosy English home, and I must read a page or two of their conversation before bringing Maggie on the stage if only to show the intense individualism of the latter by making the reader wonder how such an individualism could ever have been evolved from any such precedent conditions as those of Mr. and Mrs. Tulliver. "What I want, you know," said Mr. Tulliver, —

"'What I want is to give Tom a good eddication — an eddication as'll be bread to him. That was what I was thinking of when I gave notice for him to leave th' academy at Ladyday. I mean to put him to a downright good school at Midsummer. The two years at th' academy 'ud ha' done well enough, if I'd meant to make a miller and farmer of him, for he's had a fine sight more schoolin' nor *I* ever got: all the learnin' *my* father ever paid for was a bit o' birch at one end and the alphabet at th' other. But I should like Tom to be a bit of a scholard, so as he might be up to the tricks o' these fellows as talk fine and write with a flourish. It 'ud be a help to me wi' these lawsuits, and arbitrations, and things. I wouldn't make a downright lawyer o' the lad, — I should be sorry for him to be a raskill, — but a sort o' engineer, or a surveyor, or an auctioneer and vallyer, like Riley, or one o' them smartish businesses as are all profits and no out-lay, only for a big watch-chain and a high stool. They're putty nigh all one, and they're not far off being even wi' the law, *I* believe; for Riley looks Lawyer Wakem i' the face as hard as one cat looks another. *He's* none frightened at him.'

"Mr. Tulliver was speaking to his wife, a blond comely woman, in a fan-shaped cap (I am afraid to think how long it was since fan-shaped caps were worn, — they must be so near coming in again. At that time, when Mrs. Tulliver was nearly forty, they were new at St. Ogg's, and considered sweet things).

"'Well, Mr. Tulliver, you know best: *I've* no objections. But hadn't I better kill a couple o' fowl and have th' aunts and uncles to dinner next week, so as you may hear what sister Glegg and sister Pullet have got to say about it? There's a couple o' fowl *wants* killing!'

"'You may kill every fowl i' the yard, if you like, Bessy; but I shall ask neither aunt nor uncle what I'm to do wi' my own lad,' said Mr. Tulliver, defiantly.

"'Dear heart!' said Mrs. Tulliver, shocked at this sanguinary rhetoric, 'how can you talk so, Mr. Tulliver? But it's your way to speak disrespectful o' my family; and sister Glegg throws all the blame upo' me, though I'm sure I'm as innocent as the babe unborn. For nobody's ever heard *me* say as it wasn't lucky for my children to have aunts and uncles as can live independent. Howiver, if Tom's to go to a new school, I should like him to go where I can wash him and mend him; else he might as well have calico as linen, for they'd be one as yallor as th' other before they'd been washed half a dozen times. And then, when the box is goin' backards and forrards, I could send the lad a cake, or a pork-pie or an apple; for he can do with an extry bit, bless him, whether they stint him at the meals or no. My children can eat as much victuals as most, thank God.'

.   .   .   .

"Mr. Tulliver paused a minute or two, and dived with both hands into his breeches pockets as if he hoped to find some suggestion there. Apparently he was not disappointed, for he presently said, 'I know what I'll do, — I'll talk it over wi' Riley: he's coming to-morrow, t' arbitrate about the dam.'

"'Well, Mr. Tulliver, I've put the sheets out for the best bed, and Kezia's got 'em hanging at the fire. They are n't the best sheets, but they're good enough for anybody to sleep in, be he who he will; for as for them best Holland sheets, I should repent buying 'em, only they'll do to lay us out in. An' if you was to die to-morrow, Mr. Tulliver, they're mangled beautiful, an' all ready, an' smell o' lavender, as it 'ud be a pleasure to lay 'em out; an' they lie at the left-hand corner o' the big oaken chest at the back: not as I should trust anybody to look 'em out but myself.'"

In the next chapter Mr. Tulliver at night, over a cosy glass of brandy-and-water, is discussing with Riley the momentous question of a school for Tom. Mrs. Tulliver is out of the room upon household cares and Maggie is off on a low stool close by the fire, apparently buried in a large book that is open on her lap, but betraying her interest in the conversation by occasionally shaking back her heavy hair and looking up with gleaming eyes when Tom's name is mentioned. Presently Maggie in an agitated outburst on Tom's behalf drops the book she has been reading. Mr. Riley picks it up, and here we have a glimpse at the kind of food which nourished Maggie's infant mind. Mr. Riley calls out, "Come, come and tell me something about this book; here are some pictures — I want to know what they mean."

Maggie, with deepening color, went without hesitation to Mr. Riley's elbow and looked over the book, eagerly seizing one corner and tossing back her mane, while she said :

"'Oh, I'll tell you what that means. It's a dreadful picture, isn't it? But I can't help looking at it. That old woman in the water's a witch, — they've put her in to find out whether she's a witch or no, and if she swims she's a witch, and if she's drowned — and killed, you know — she's innocent, and not a witch, but only a poor silly old woman. But what good would it do her then, you know, when she was drowned ? Only, I suppose, she'd go to heaven, and God would make it up to her. And this dreadful blacksmith, with his arms akimbo, laughing — oh, isn't he ugly? — I'll tell you what he is. He's the devil *really*' (here Maggie's voice became louder and more emphatic), 'and not a right blacksmith; for the devil takes the shape of wicked men, and walks about and sets people doing wicked things, and he's oftener in the shape of a bad man than any other, because, you know, if people saw he was the devil, and he roared at 'em, they'd run away, and he couldn't make 'em do what he pleased.'

" Mr. Tulliver had listened to this exposition of Maggie's with petrifying wonder.

"'Why, what book is it the wench has got hold on?' he burst out, at last.

"'*The History of the Devil*, by Daniel Defoe ; not quite the right book for a little girl,' said Mr. Riley. 'How came it among your books, Tulliver ? '

" Maggie looked hurt and discouraged, while her father said, 'Why, it's one o' the books I bought at Partridge's sale. They was all bound alike, — it's a good binding, you see, — and I thought they'd be all good books. There's Jeremy Taylor's *Holy Living and Dying* among 'em ; I read in it often of a Sunday ' (Mr. Tulliver felt somehow a familiarity with that great writer because his name was Jeremy) ; ' and there's a lot more of 'em, sermons mostly, I think ; but they've all got the same covers, and I thought they were all o' one sample, as you may say. But it seems one mustn't judge by th' outside. This is a puzzlin' world.'

"'Well,' said Mr. Riley, in an admonitory patronizing tone, as he patted Maggie on the head, 'I advise you to put by the *History of the Devil*, and read some prettier book. Have you no prettier books?'

"'Oh, yes,' said Maggie, reviving a little in the desire to vindicate the variety of her reading; 'I know the reading in this book isn't pretty, but I like to look at the pictures, and I make stories to the pictures out of my own head, you know. But I've got *Æsop's Fables*, and a book about kangaroos and things, and the *Pilgrim's Progress*'—

"'Ah! a beautiful book,' said Mr. Riley; 'you can't read a better.'

"'Well, but there's a great deal about the devil in that,' said Maggie, triumphantly, 'and I'll show you the picture of him in his true shape, as he fought with Christian.'

"Maggie ran in an instant to the corner of the room, jumped on a chair, and reached down from the small bookcase a shabby old copy of Bunyan, which opened at once, without the least trouble of search, at the picture she wanted.

"'Here he is,' she said, running back to Mr. Riley, 'and Tom coloured him for me with his paints when he was at home last holidays—the body all black, you know, and the eyes red, like fire, because he's all fire inside, and it shines out at his eyes.'

"'Go, go!' said Mr. Tulliver, peremptorily, beginning to feel rather uncomfortable at these free remarks on the personal appearance of a being powerful enough to create lawyers; 'shut up the book, and let's hear no more o' such talk. It is as I thought,—the child 'ud learn more mischief nor good wi' the books. Go, go and see after your mother.'"

And here are further various hints of Maggie's ways, in which we find clues to many outbursts of her later life.

"It was a heavy disappointment to Maggie that she was not allowed to go with her father in the gig when he went to fetch Tom home from the academy; but the morning was too wet, Mrs. Tulliver said, for a little girl to go out in her best bonnet. Maggie took the opposite view very strongly, and it was a direct consequence of this difference of opinion that when her mother was in the act of brushing out the reluctant black crop, Maggie suddenly rushed from under her hands and dipped her head in a basin of water standing near, — in the vindictive determination that there should be no more chance of curls that day.

" ' Maggie, Maggie ! ' exclaimed Mrs. Tulliver, sitting stout and helpless with the brushes on her lap, ' what is to become of you if you're so naughty ? I'll tell your aunt Glegg and your aunt Pullet when they come next week, and they'll never love you any more. Oh dear, oh dear ! look at your clean pinafore, wet from top to bottom. Folks 'ull think it's a judgment on me as I've got such a child, — they'll think I've done summat wicked.'

" Before this remonstrance was finished, Maggie was already out of hearing, making her way toward the great attic that ran under the old high-pitched roof, shaking the water from her black locks as she ran, like a Skye terrier escaped from his bath. This attic was Maggie's favourite retreat on a wet day, when the weather was not too cold; here she fretted out all her ill-humours, and talked aloud to the worm-eaten floors and the worm-eaten shelves, and the dark rafters festooned with cobwebs; and here she kept a Fetish which she punished for all her misfortunes. This was the trunk of a large wooden doll, which once stared with the roundest of eyes above the reddest of cheeks, but was now entirely defaced by a long career of vicarious suffering. Three nails driven into the head commemorated as many crises in Maggie's nine years of earthly struggle; that luxury of vengeance having been suggested to her by the picture of Jael destroying Sisera in the old Bible. The last nail had been driven in with a fiercer stroke than usual, for the Fetish on that occasion represented aunt Glegg."

But a ray of sunshine on the window of the garret proves too much for her; she dances down stairs, and after a wild whirl in the sunshine with Yap the terrier goes up into the mill for a talk with Luke the miller.

" Maggie loved to linger in the great spaces of the mill, and often came out with her black hair powdered to a soft whiteness that made her dark eyes flash out with a new fire. The resolute din, the unresting motion of the great stones, giving her a dim delicious awe as at the presence of an uncontrollable force, — the meal forever pouring, pouring, — the fine white powder softening all surfaces, and making the very spider-nets look like a fancy lace-work, — the sweet, pure scent of the meal — all helped to make Maggie feel that the mill was a little world apart from her outside, everyday life. The spiders were especially a subject of speculation with her. She wondered if they had any relations outside the mill, for in that case there must be a painful difficulty in their family intercourse, — a flat and floury spider, accustomed to take his fly well dusted with meal, must suffer a little at a cousin's table where the fly was *au naturel;* and the lady-spiders must be mutually shocked at each other's appearance.   But the part of the mill she liked best was the topmost story, — the corn-hutch, where there were the great heaps of grain, which she could sit on and slide down continually.   She was in the habit of taking this recreation as she conversed with Luke, to whom she was very communicative, wishing him to think well of her understanding, as her father did.

" Perhaps she felt it necessary to recover her position with him on the present occasion, for, as she sat sliding on the heap of grain near which he was busying himself, she said, at that shrill pitch which was requisite in mill society, —

" ' I think you never read any book but the Bible, — did you Luke ? '

" ' Nay, miss, — an' not much o' that,' said Luke, with great frankness.   ' I'm no reader, I are n't.'

" ' But if I lent you one of my books, Luke ?   I've not got any *very* pretty books that would be easy for you to read, but there's *Pug's Tour of Europe,* — that would tell you all about the different sorts of people in the world, and if you didn't understand the reading, the pictures would help you — they show the looks and the ways of the people, and what they do.   There are the Dutchmen, very fat, and smoking, you know, — and one sitting on a barrel.'

"'Nay, miss, I've no opinion o' Dutchmen.   There ben't much good i' knowin' about *them*.'

"'But they're our fellow-creatures, Luke, — we ought to know about our fellow-creatures.'

"'Not much o' fellow-creatures, I think, miss; all I know, — my old master, as war a knowin' man, used to say, says he, "If e'er I sow my wheat wi'out brinin', I'm a Dutchman," says he; an' that war as much as to say as a Dutchman war a fool, or next door.   Nay, nay, I are n't goin' to bother mysen about Dutchmen.   There's fools enoo, — an' rogues enoo, — wi'out lookin' i' books for 'em.'

"'Oh, well,' said Maggie, rather foiled by Luke's unexpectedly decided views about Dutchmen, 'perhaps you would like *Animated Nature* better; that's not Dutchmen, you know, but elephants, and kangaroos, and the civet cat, and the sunfish, and a bird sitting on its tail, — I forget its name.   There are countries full of those creatures, instead of horses and cows, you know.   Shouldn't you like to know about them, Luke?'

"'Nay, miss, I'n got to keep count o' the flour an' corn, — I can't do wi' knowin' so many things besides my work.   That's what brings folks to the gallows, — knowin' every thing but what they'n got to get their bread by.   An' they're mostly lies, I think, what's printed i' the books; them printed sheets are, anyhow, as the men cry i' the streets.'"

But these are idyllic hours; presently the afternoon comes, Tom arrives, Maggie has an hour of rapturous happiness over him and a new fishing-line which he has brought her, to be hers all by herself; and then comes tragedy.   Tom learns from Maggie the death of certain rabbits which he had left in her charge and which, as might have been expected, she had forgotten to feed. Here follows a harrowing scene of reproaches from Tom, of pleadings for forgiveness from Maggie, until finally Tom appears to close the door of mercy.   He sternly insists: "Last holidays you licked the paint off my lozenge box, and the holidays before that you let the boat drag my fish-line down when I set you to watch it, and you pushed your head through my kite, all for nothing." "But I didn't mean," said Maggie; "I couldn't help it." "Yes, you could," said Tom, "if you'd minded what you were doing. . . . And you shan't go fishing with me to-morrow." With this terrible conclusion Tom runs off to the mill, while the heartbroken Maggie creeps up to her attic, lays her head against the worm-eaten shelf and abandons herself to misery.

In the scene which I now read, howbeit planned upon so small a scale, the absolute insufficiency of justice to give final satisfaction to human hearts as now constituted, and the inexorable necessity of love for such satisfaction appear quite as plainly as if the canvas were of Promethean dimensions.

"Maggie soon thought she had been hours in the attic, and it must be tea-time, and they were all having their tea, and not thinking of her. Well, then, she would stay up there and starve herself, — hide herself behind the tub, and stay there all night; and then they would all be frightened, and Tom would be sorry. Thus Maggie thought in the pride of her heart, as she crept behind the tub; but presently she began to cry again at the idea that they didn't mind her being there. If she went down again to Tom now, would he forgive her? Perhaps her father would be there, and he would take her part. But, then she wanted Tom to forgive her because he loved her, and not because his father told him. No, she would never go down if Tom didn't come to fetch her. This resolution lasted in great intensity for five dark minutes behind the tub; but then the need of being loved, the strongest need in poor Maggie's nature, began to wrestle with her pride, and soon threw it. She crept from behind her tub into the twilight of the long attic, but just then she heard a quick footstep on the stairs."

In point of fact Tom has been sent from the tea-table
for her and mounts the attic munching a great piece of
plum-cake.

. . . "He went out rather sullenly, carrying his piece of
plum-cake, and not intending to retrieve Maggie's punishment, which was no more than she deserved. Tom was
only thirteen, and had no decided views in grammar and
arithmetic, regarding them for the most part as open questions; but he was particularly clear and positive on one
point, — namely, that he would punish every body who deserved it: why, he wouldn't have minded being punished
himself, if he deserved ; but then he never *did* deserve it.

" It was Tom's step, then, that Maggie heard on the stairs
when her need of love had triumphed over her pride, and
she was going down with her swollen eyes and dishevelled hair
to beg for pity. At least her father would stroke her head
and say, ' Never mind, my wench.' It is a wonderful sub-
duer, this need of love, — this hunger of the heart, — as per-
emptory as that other hunger by which Nature forces us to
submit to the yoke, and change the face of the world.

" But she knew Tom's step, and her heart began to beat
violently with the sudden shock of hope. He only stood
still at the top of the stairs and said ' Maggie, you're to
come down.' But she rushed to him and clung round his
neck, sobbing, ' Oh, Tom, please forgive me — I can't bear
it — I will always be good — always remember things — do
love me — please, dear Tom ? '

" We learn to restrain ourselves as we get older. We keep
apart when we have quarrelled, express ourselves in well-bred
phrases, and in this way preserve a dignified alienation, showing much firmness on one side, and swallowing much grief
on the other. We no longer approximate in our behaviour to
the mere impulsiveness of the lower animals, but conduct
ourselves in every respect like members of a highly civilized
society. Maggie and Tom were still very much like young
animals, and so she could rub her cheek against his, and
kiss his ear in a random, sobbing way; and there were
tender fibres in the lad that had been used to answer to

Maggie's fondling; so that he behaved with a weakness quite inconsistent with his resolution to punish her as much as she deserved: he actually began to kiss her in return, and say,

"'Don't cry, then, Magsie — here, eat a bit o' cake.' Maggie's sobs began to subside, and she put out her mouth for the cake and bit a piece; and then Tom bit a piece, just for company, and they ate together and rubbed each other's cheeks, and brows, and noses together, while they ate, with a humiliating resemblance to two friendly ponies.

"'Come along, Magsie, and have tea,' said Tom at last, when there was no more cake except what was down stairs."

Various points of contrast lead me to cite some types of character which appear to offer instructive comparisons with this picture of the healthy English boy and girl. Take for example this portrait of the modern American boy given us by Mr. Henry James, Jr., in his *Daisy Miller* — which was, I believe, the work that first brought him into fame. The scene is in Europe. A gentleman is seated in the garden of a hotel at Geneva, smoking his cigarettes after breakfast.

" Presently a small boy came walking along the path — an urchin of nine or ten. The child, who was diminutive for his years, had an aged expression of countenance, a pale complexion, and sharp little features. He was dressed in Knickerbockers, with red stockings, which displayed his poor little spindleshanks; he also wore a brilliant red cravat. He carried in his hand a long alpenstock, the sharp point of which he thrust into everything that he approached — the flower-beds, the garden benches, the trains of the ladies' dresses. In front of Winterbourne he paused, looking at him with a pair of bright penetrating little eyes.

"'Will you give me a lump of sugar?' he asked in a sharp, hard little voice — a voice immature, and yet, somehow, not young.

"Winterbourne glanced at the small table near him on which his coffee-service rested, and saw that several morsels

of sugar remained. ' Yes, you may take one,' he answered,
' but I don't think sugar is good for little boys.'

" This little boy slipped forward and carefully selected three
of the coveted fragments, two of which he buried in the
pocket of his Knickerbockers, depositing the other as promptly
in another place. He poked his alpenstock lance-fashion
into Winterbourne's bench, and tried to crack the lump of
sugar with his teeth.

"'Oh, blazes; it's har-r-d!' he exclaimed, pronouncing
the adjective in a peculiar manner.

" Winterbourne had immediately perceived that he might
have the honor of claiming him as a fellow-countryman.
' Take care you don't hurt your teeth,' he said paternally.

"'I haven't got any teeth to hurt.   They have all come out.
I have only got seven teeth.   My mother counted them last
night, and one came out right afterwards.   She said she'd
slap me if any more came out.   I can't help it.   It's this
old Europe.   It's the climate that makes them come out.
In America they didn't come out.   It's these hotels.'

" Winterbourne was much amused.   ' If you eat three
lumps of sugar, your mother will certainly slap you,' he said.

"'She's got to give me some candy, then,' rejoined his
young interlocutor.   ' I can't git any candy here — any
American candy.   American candy's the best candy.'

"'And are American boys the best little boys?' asked
Winterbourne.

"'I don't know.   I'm an American boy,' said the child.

"'I see you are one of the best!' laughed Winterbourne.

"'Are you an American man?' pursued this vivacious
infant.   And then on Winterbourne's affirmative reply, —
' American men are the best,' he declared."

On the other hand compare this intense dark-eyed
Maggie in her garret and with her flaming ways, with
Mrs. Browning's Aurora Leigh.   Aurora Leigh, too, has
her garret, and doubtless her intensity, too, blossoms
in that congenial dark and lonesomeness.   I read a few
lines from Book 1st by way of reminder.

" Books, books, books !
    I had found the secret of a garret-room
    Piled high with cases in my father's name
    . . . Where, creeping in and out
    Among the giant fossils of my past
    Like some small nimble mouse between the ribs
    Of a mastodon, I nibbled here or there
    At this or that box, pulling through the gap
    In heats of terror, haste, victorious joy,
    The first book first.   And how I felt it beat
    Under my pillow in the morning's dark,
    An hour before the sun would let me read !
    My books !   At last, because the time was ripe,
    I chanced upon the poets."

And here, every reader of *The Mill on the Floss* will remember how, at a later period, Maggie chanced upon Thomas à Kempis at a tragic moment of her existence ; and it is fine to see how, in describing situations so alike, the purely elemental differences between the natures of Mrs. Browning and George Eliot project themselves upon each other.

The scene in George Eliot concerning Maggie and Thomas à Kempis is too long to repeat here, but everyone will recall the sober, analytic, yet altogether vital and thrilling picture of the trembling Maggie, as she absorbs wisdom from the sweet old mediæval soul.   But, on the other hand, Mrs. Browning sings it out, after this riotous melody :

" As the earth   .   .   .   .   .
    Plunges in fury when the internal fires
    Have reached and pricked her heart,
                and throwing flat
    The marts and temples, — the triumphal gates
    And towers of observation, — clears herself
    To elemental freedom — thus, my soul,
    At poetry's divine first finger-touch
    Let go conventions and sprang up surprised,

Convicted of the great eternities
Before two worlds   .   .   .

   .   .   .   .   .   .

            . . . "But the sun was high
When first I felt my pulses set themselves
For concord; when the rhythmic turbulence
Of blood and brain swept outward upon words,
As wind upon the alders, blanching them
By turning up their under-natures till
They trembled in dilation.   O delight
And triumph of the poet, who would say
A man's mere 'yes,' a woman's common 'no,'
A little human hope of that or this,
And says the word so that it burns you through
With special revelation, shakes the heart
Of all the men and women in the world
As if one came back from the dead and spoke,
With eyes too happy, a familiar thing
Become divine i' the utterance!"

I have taken special pleasure in the last sentence of this outburst because it restates with a precise felicity at once poetic and scientific, but from a curiously different point of view, that peculiar function of George Eliot which I pointed out as appearing in the very first of her stories : namely, the function of elevating the plane of all commonplace life into the plane of the heroic by keeping every man well in mind of the awful *ego* within him which includes all the possibilities of heroic action. Now this is what George Eliot does, in putting before us these humble forms of Tom and Maggie, and the like : she says these common "yes's" and "noes" in terms of Tom and Maggie; and yet says them so that this particular Tom and Maggie burn you through with a special revelation, — though one has known a hundred Maggies and Toms before. Thus we find the delight and triumph of the poetic and analytic novelist, George Eliot, precisely parallel to this delight and triumph of the more exclusively poetic Mrs. Browning, who says a man's mere " yes," a woman's common " no," so that it shakes the hearts of all the men and women in the world, etc. Aurora Leigh continues :

> "In those days, though, I never analysed
>   Myself even.　All analysis comes late.
>   You catch a sight of nature, earliest ;
>   In full front sun-face, and your eye-lids wink
>   And drop before the wonder of 't ; you miss
>   The form, through seeing the light.　I lived those days,
>   And wrote because I lived — unlicensed else ;
>   My heart beat in my brain.　Life's violent flood
>   Abolished bounds, — and, which my neighbor's field,
>   Which mine, what mattered ?　It is thus in youth !
>   We play at leap-frog over the god Term ;
>   The love within us and the love without
>   Are mixed, confounded ; if we are loved or love
>   We scarce distinguish　　.　　.　　.
>   In that first onrush of life's chariot wheels
>   We know not if the forests move, or we."

And now as showing the extreme range of George Eliot's genius, — in regions where perhaps Mrs. Browning never penetrated, — let me recall Sister Glegg and Sister Pullet, as types of women contrasting with Maggie and Aurora Leigh.　You will remember how Mrs. Tulliver has bidden her three sisters, Mrs. Glegg, Mrs. Pullet, and Mrs. Deane, with their respective husbands, to a great and typical Dodson dinner, in order to eat and drink upon the momentous changes impending in Tom's educational existence :

" The Dodsons were certainly a handsome family, and Mrs. Glegg was not the least handsome of the sisters.　As she sat in Mrs. Tulliver's arm-chair, no impartial observer could have denied that for a woman of fifty, she had a very comely face and figure, though Tom and Maggie considered their aunt Glegg as the type of ugliness.　It is true she despised the advantages of costume; for though, as she often observed, no woman had better clothes, it was not her way to wear her new things out before her old ones. Other women, if they liked, might have their best thread lace in every wash, but when Mrs. Glegg died it would be found that she had better lace laid by in the right-hand drawer of her wardrobe, in the Spotted Chamber, than ever Mrs. Wooll of St. Ogg's had bought in her life, although Mrs. Wooll wore her lace before it was paid for. So of her curled fronts. Mrs. Glegg had doubtless the glossiest and crispest brown curls in her drawers, as well as curls in various degrees of fuzzy laxness; but to look out on the week-day world from under a crisp and glossy front would be to introduce a most dream-like and unpleasant confusion between the sacred and the secular. . . .

"So if Mrs. Glegg's front to-day was more fuzzy and lax than usual, she had a design under it: she intended the most pointed and cutting allusion to Mrs. Tulliver's bunches of blond curls, separated from each other by a due wave of smoothness on each side of the parting. Mrs. Tulliver had shed tears several times at sister Glegg's unkindness on the subject of these unmatronly curls, but the consciousness of looking the handsomer for them naturally administered support. Mrs. Glegg chose to wear her bonnet in the house to-day, — untied and tilted slightly, of course, — a frequent practice of hers when she was on a visit, and happened to be in a severe humour; she didn't know what draughts there might be in strange houses. For the same reason she wore a small sable tippet, which reached just to her shoulders, and was very far from meeting across her well-formed chest, while her long neck was protected by a *chevaux-de-frise* of miscellaneous frilling. One would need to be learned in the fashions of those times to know how far in the rear of them Mrs. Glegg's slate-coloured silk gown must have been; but, from certain constellations of small yellow spots upon it, and a mouldy odour about it suggestive of a damp clothes-chest, it was probable that it belonged to a stratum of garments just old enough to have come recently into wear.

" Mrs. Glegg held her large gold watch in her hand with

the many-doubled chain round her fingers, and observed to Mrs. Tulliver, who had just returned from a visit to the kitchen, that whatever it might be by other people's clocks and watches, it was gone half-past twelve by hers.

"'I don't know what ails sister Pullet,' she continued. 'It used to be the way in our family for one to be as early as another, — I'm sure it was so in my poor father's time, — and not for one sister to sit half an hour before the others came. But if the ways o' the family are altered, it shan't be *my* fault, — I'll never be the one to come into a house when all the rest are going away. I wonder *at* sister Deane, — she used to be more like me. But if you'll take my advice, Bessy, you'll put the dinner forrard a bit, sooner than put it back, because folks are late as ought to ha' known better.' . . .

"The sound of wheels while Mrs. Glegg was speaking was an interruption highly welcome to Mrs. Tulliver, who hastened out to receive sister Pullet, — it must be sister Pullet, because the sound was that of a four-wheel.

"Mrs. Glegg tossed her head and looked rather sour about the mouth at the thought of the 'four-wheel.' She had a strong opinion on that subject.

"Sister Pullet was in tears when the one-horse chaise stopped before Mrs. Tulliver's door, and it was apparently requisite that she should shed a few more before getting out; for though her husband and Mrs. Tulliver stood ready to support her, she sat still and shook her head sadly, as she looked through her tears at the vague distance.

"'Why, whativer is the matter, sister?' said Mrs. Tulliver. She was not an imaginative woman, but it occurred to her that the large toilet-glass in sister Pullet's best bedroom was possibly broken for the second time.

"There was no reply but a further shake of the head, as Mrs. Pullet slowly rose and got down from the chaise, not without casting a glance at Mr. Pullet to see that he was guarding her handsome silk dress from injury. Mr. Pullet was a small man with a high nose, small twinkling eyes, and thin lips, in a fresh-looking suit of black and a white cravat, that seemed to have been tied very tight on some higher

principle than that of mere personal ease. He bore about
the same relation to his tall, good-looking wife, with her
balloon sleeves, abundant mantle, and large be-feathered and
be-ribboned bonnet, as a small fishing-smack bears to a brig
with all its sails spread.

.   .   .   .

" Mrs. Pullet brushed each door-post with great nicety
about the latitude of her shoulders (at that period a woman
was truly ridiculous to an instructed eye if she did not
measure a yard and a half across the shoulders), and having
done that, sent the muscles of her face in quest of fresh
tears as she advanced into the parlour where Mrs. Glegg was
seated.

" ' Well, sister, you're late ; what's the matter? ' said
Mrs. Glegg, rather sharply, as they shook hands.

" Mrs. Pullet sat down, lifting up her mantle carefully
behind before she answered, —

" ' She's gone,' unconsciously using an impressive figure of
rhetoric.

" ' It isn't the glass this time, then,' thought Mrs. Tulliver.

" ' Died the day before yesterday,' continued Mrs. Pullet ;
' an' her legs was as thick as my body,' she added with deep
sadness, after a pause. 'They'd tapped her no end o'
times, and the water — they say you might ha' swum in it, if
you'd liked.'

" ' Well, Sophy, it's a mercy she's gone, then, whoiver she
may be,' said Mrs. Glegg, with the promptitude and empha-
sis of a mind naturally clear and decided; 'but I can't
think who you're talking of, for my part.'

" ' But *I* know,' said Mrs. Pullet, sighing and shaking her
head ; 'and there isn't another such a dropsy in the parish.
I know as it's old Mrs. Sutton o' the Twentylands.'

" ' Well, she's no kin o' yours, nor much acquaintance as
I've ever heard of,' said Mrs. Glegg, who always cried just
as much as was proper when anything happened to her own
'kin,' but not on other occasions.

" ' She's so much acquaintance as I've seen her legs when
they were like bladders. . . . And an old lady as had
doubled her money over and over again, and kept it all

in her own management to the last, and had her pocket with her keys in under her pillow constant. There isn't many old *par*ish'ners like her, I doubt.'

"'And they say she'd took as much physic as 'ud fill a wagon,' observed Mr. Pullet.

"'Ah!' sighed Mrs. Pullet, 'she'd another complaint iver so many years before she had the dropsy, and the doctors couldn't make out what it was. And she said to me, when I went to see her last Christmas, she said, "Mrs. Pullet, if iver you have the dropsy, you'll think o' me." She *did* say so,' added Mrs. Pullet, beginning to cry bitterly again; 'those were her very words. And she's to be buried o' Saturday, and Pullet's bid to the funeral.'

"'Sophy,' said Mrs. Glegg, unable any longer to contain her spirit of rational remonstrance, — 'Sophy, I wonder *at* you, fretting and injuring your health about people as don't belong to you. Your poor father never did so, nor your aunt Frances neither, nor any o' the family, as I ever heared of. You couldn't fret no more than this if we'd heared as our cousin Abbott had died sudden without making his will.'

"Mrs. Pullet was silent, having to finish her crying, and rather flattered than indignant at being upbraided for crying too much. It was not every body who could afford to cry so much about their neighbours who had left them nothing; but Mrs. Pullet had married a gentleman farmer, and had leisure and money to carry her crying and every thing else to the highest pitch of respectability.

"'Mrs. Sutton didn't die without making her will, though,' said Mr. Pullet, with a confused sense that he was saying something to sanction his wife's tears; 'ours is a rich parish, but they say there's nobody else to leave as many thousands behind 'em as Mrs. Sutton. And she's left no leggicies, to speak on, — left it all in lump to her husband's nevvy.'

"'There wasn't much good i' being so rich, then,' said Mrs. Glegg, 'if she'd got none but husband's kin to leave it to. It's poor work when that's all you're got to pinch yourself for; — not as I'm one o' those as 'ud like to die without leaving more money out at interest than other folks had reckoned. But it's a poor tale when it must go out o' your own family.'

" ' I'm sure, sister,' said Mrs. Pullet, who had recovered sufficiently to take off her veil and fold it carefully, 'it's a nice sort o' man as Mrs. Sutton has left her money to, for he's troubled with the asthmy, and goes to bed every night at eight o'clock. He told me about it himself — as free as could be — one Sunday when he came to our church. He wears a hareskin on his chest, and has a trembling in his talk, — quite a gentleman sort o' man. I told him there wasn't many months in the year as I wasn't under the doctor's hands. And he said, " Mrs. Pullet, I can feel for you." That was what he said, — the very words. Ah ! ' sighed Mrs. Pullet, shaking her head at the idea that there were but few who could enter fully into her experiences in pink mixture and white mixture, strong stuff in small bottles, and weak stuff in large bottles, damp boluses at a shilling, and draughts at eighteen pence. ' Sister, I may as well go and take my bonnet off now. Did you see as the capbox was put out ? ' she added, turning to her husband.

" Mr. Pullet, by an unaccountable lapse of memory, had forgotten it, and hastened out, with a stricken conscience, to remedy the omission."

Next day Mrs. Tulliver and the children visit Aunt Pullet : and we have some further affecting details of that sensitive lady weeping at home instead of abroad.

" Aunt Pullet, too, appeared at the doorway, and as soon as her sister was within hearing said, ' Stop the children, for God's sake, Bessy, — don't let 'em come up the doorsteps : Sally's bringing the old mat and the duster to rub their shoes.'

" Mrs. Pullet's front door mats were by no means intended to wipe shoes on : the very scraper had a deputy to do its dirty work. Tom rebelled particularly against this shoe-wiping, which he always considered in the light of an indignity to his sex. He felt it as the beginning of the disagreeable incident to a visit at aunt Pullet's where he had once been compelled to sit with towels wrapped around his boots, — a fact which may serve to correct the too hasty conclusion that a visit to Garum Firs must have been a great treat to a young gentleman fond of animals, — fond, that is, of throwing stones at them.

" The next disagreeable was confined to his feminine companions: it was the mounting of the polished oak stairs, which had very handsome carpets rolled up and laid by in a spare bedroom, so that the ascent of these glossy steps might have served, in barbarous times, as a trial by ordeal from which none but the most spotless virtue could have come off with unbroken limbs. Sophy's weakness about these polished stairs was always a subject of bitter remonstrance on Mrs. Glegg's part; but Mrs. Tulliver ventured on no comment, only thinking to herself it was a mercy when she and the children were safe on the landing.

"' Mrs. Gray has sent home my new bonnet, Bessy,' said Mrs. Pullet, in a pathetic tone, as Mrs. Tulliver adjusted her cap.

"' Has she, sister?' said Mrs. Tulliver with an air of much interest. 'And how do you like it?'

"' It's apt to make a mess with clothes, taking 'em out and putting 'em in again,' said Mrs. Pullet, drawing a bunch of keys from her pocket and looking at them earnestly, ' but it 'ud be a pity for you to go away without seeing it. There's no knowing what may happen.'

" Mrs. Pullet shook her head slowly at this last serious consideration, which determined her to single out a particular key.

"' I'm afraid it'll be troublesome to you getting it out, sister,' said Mrs. Tulliver, ' but I *should* like to see what sort of a crown she's made you.'

" Mrs. Pullet rose with a melancholy air and unlocked one wing of a very bright wardrobe, where you may have hastily supposed she would find the new bonnet. Not at all. Such a supposition could only have arisen from a too superficial acquaintance with the habits of the Dodson family. In this wardrobe Mrs. Pullet was seeking something small enough to be hidden among layers of linen, — it was a door key.

" ' You must come with me into the best room,' said Mrs. Pullet.

" ' May the children come too, sister?' inquired Mrs. Tulliver, who saw that Maggie and Lucy were looking rather eager.

" ' Well,' said aunt Pullet, reflectively, ' it'll perhaps be safer for 'em to come, — they'll be touching something if we leave 'em behind.'

" So they went in procession along the bright and slippery corridor, dimly lighted by the semilunar top of the window which rose above the closed shutter: it was really quite solemn. Aunt Pullet paused and unlocked a door which opened on something still more solemn than the passage: a darkened room, in which the outer light, entering feebly, showed what looked like the corpses of furniture in white shrouds. Everything that was not shrouded stood with its legs upward. Lucy laid hold of Maggie's frock, and Maggie's heart beat rapidly.

" Aunt Pullet half opened the shutter, and then unlocked the wardrobe, with a melancholy deliberateness which was quite in keeping with the funereal solemnity of the scene. The delicious scent of rose leaves that issued from the wardrobe made the process of taking out sheet after sheet of silver paper quite pleasant to assist at, though the sight of the bonnet at last was an anticlimax to Maggie, who would have preferred something more strikingly preternatural. But few things could have been more impressive to Mrs. Tulliver. She looked all round it in silence for some moments, and then said emphatically, ' Well, sister, I'll never speak against the full crowns again!'

" It was a great concession, and Mrs. Pullet felt it: she felt something was due to it.

" ' You'd like to see it on, sister?' she said sadly. ' I'll open the shutter a bit farther.'

" ' Well, if you don't mind taking off your cap, sister,' said Mrs. Tulliver.

" Mrs. Pullet took off her cap, displaying the brown silk scalp with a jutting promontory of curls which was common to the more mature and judicious women of those times, and, placing the bonnet on her head, turned slowly round, like a draper's lay-figure, that Mrs. Tulliver might miss no point of view.

" ' I've sometimes thought there's a loop too much o' ribbon on this left side, sister; what do you think ? ' said Mrs. Pullet.

" Mrs. Tulliver looked earnestly at the point indicated, and turned her head on one side. ' Well, I think it's best as it is; if you meddled with it, sister, you might repent.'

" ' That's true,' said aunt Pullet, taking off the bonnet and looking at it contemplatively.

" ' How much might she charge you for that bonnet, sister ? ' said Mrs. Tulliver, whose mind was actively engaged on the possibility of getting a humble imitation of this *chef-d'œuvre* made from a piece of silk she had at home.

" Mrs. Pullet screwed up her mouth, and shook her head, and then whispered, ' Pullet pays for it; he said I was to have the best bonnet at Garum church, let the next best be whose it would.'

" She began slowly to adjust the trimmings, in preparation for returning it to its place in the wardrobe, and her thoughts seemed to have taken a melancholy turn, for she shook her head.

" ' Ah ! ' she said at last, ' I may never wear it twice, sister : who knows ? '

" ' Don't talk o' that, sister,' answered Mrs. Tulliver. ' I hope you'll have your health this summer.'

" ' Ah ! but there may come a death in the family, as there did soon after I had my green satin bonnet. Cousin Abbott may go, and we can't think o' wearing crape less than half a year for him.'

" ' That *would* be unlucky,' said Mrs. Tulliver, entering thoroughly into the possibility of an inopportune decease. ' There's never so much pleasure i' wearing a bonnet the second year, especially when the crowns are so chancy, — never two summers alike.'

" ' Ah ! it's the way i' this world,' said Mrs. Pullet, returning the bonnet to the wardrobe and locking it up. She maintained a silence characterized by head-shaking, until they had all issued from the solemn chamber and were in her own room again. Then, beginning to cry, she said, 'Sister, if you should never see that bonnet again till I'm dead and gone, you'll remember I showed it you this day.'"

I sincerely wish it were in my power to develop, alongside of the types of Maggie Tulliver and Aurora Leigh, a number of other female figures which belong to the same period of life and literature. I please myself with calling these the Victorian women. They would include the name-giving queen, herself, the Eve in Mrs. Browning's *Drama of Exile*, Princess Ida in Tennyson's *Princess*, Jane Eyre, Charlotte Brontë, (one of these figures, you observe, is just as real to us as the other; and I have lost all sense of difference between actual and literary existence), Mrs. Browning, Dinah Morris, Milly Barton, Janet Dempster, Florence Nightingale and Sister Dora, Romola, Dorothea Brooke, Myra, Charlotte Cushman, Mary Somerville and some others. If we are grateful to our sweet master Tennyson for his *Dream of Fair Women*, how grateful should we be to an age which has given us this realization of ideal women, of women who are so strong and so beautiful that they have subtly brought about that I can find no adjective so satisfactory for them as " womanly" women. They have redeemed the whole time. When I hear certain mournful people crying out that this is a gross and material age, I reply that gross and material are words that have no meaning as of the epoch of the Victorian women. When the pessimists accuse the time of small aims and over-selfishness, I plead the Victorian women. When the pre-Raphaelites clamor that railroad and telegraph have fatally scarred the whole face of the picturesque and the ideal among us, I reply that on the other hand the Victorian women are more beautiful than any product of times that they call picturesque and ideal.

And it is singularly fine that in some particulars the best expression of the corresponding attitude which man has assumed toward the Victorian women in the growth of the times has been poetically formulated by a woman. In Mrs. Browning's *Drama of Exile*, during those first insane moments when Eve is begging Adam to banish her for her transgression, or to do some act of retributive justice upon her, Adam continually comforts her and finally speaks these words :

> . . . "I am deepest in the guilt,
> If last in the transgression. . . . If God
> Who gave the right and joyance of the world
> Both unto thee and me, — gave thee to me,
> The best gift last, the last sin was the worst,
> Which sinned against more complement of gifts
> And grace of giving.   God! I render back
> Strong benediction and perpetual praise
> From mortal feeble lips (as incense smoke,
> Out of a little censer, may fill heaven),
> That Thou, in striking my benumbèd hands
> And forcing them to drop all other boons
> Of beauty and dominion and delight, —
> Hast left this well-beloved Eve, this life
> Within life, this best gift, between their palms,
> In gracious compensation !
>
> .   .   .   .   .
>
> "Oh my God!
> I, standing here between the glory and dark, —
> The glory of thy wrath projected forth
> From Eden's wall, the dark of our distress
> Which settles a step off in that drear world —
> Lift up to Thee the hands from whence hath fallen
> Only creation's sceptre, — thanking Thee
> That rather Thou hast cast me out with *her*
> Than left me lorn of her in Paradise,
> With angel looks and angel songs around

To show the absence of her eyes and voice,
And make society full desertness
Without her use in comfort!

.   .   .   .

          "Because with *her*, I stand
Upright, as far as can be in this fall,
And look away from heaven which doth accuse,
And look away from earth which doth convict,
Into her face, and crown my discrowned brow
Out of her love, and put the thought of her
Around me, for an Eden full of birds,
And with my lips upon her lips, — thus, thus, —
Do quicken and sublimate my mortal breath
Which cannot climb against the grave's steep sides
But overtops this grief!"

XI

THE fullness of George Eliot's mind at this time may be gathered from the rapidity with which one work followed another. A book from her pen had been appearing regularly each year: The *Scenes of Clerical Life* had appeared in book form in 1858, *Adam Bede* was printed in 1859, *The Mill on the Floss* came out in 1860, and now, in 1861, followed *Silas Marner, the Weaver of Raveloe*. It is with the greatest reluctance that I find myself obliged to pass this book without comment. In some particulars *Silas Marner* is the most remarkable novel in our language. On the one hand, when I read the immortal scene at the Rainbow Inn where the village functionaries, the butcher, the farrier, the parish clerk and so on are discussing ghosts, bullocks and other matters over their evening ale, my mind runs to Dogberry and Verges and the air feels as if Shakspere were sitting somewhere not far off. On the other hand, the downright ghastliness of the young Squire's punishment for stealing the long-hoarded gold of Silas Marner the weaver always carries me straight to that pitiless *Pardoner's Tale* of Chaucer in which gold is so cunningly identified with death. I am sure you will pardon me if I spend a single moment in recalling the plots of these two stories so far as concerns this point of contact. In Chaucer's *Pardoner's Tale* three riotous young men of Flanders are drinking one day at a tavern. In the midst of their merriment they hear the clink of a

bell before a dead body which is borne past the door on
its way to burial.   They learn that it is an old companion who is dead ; all three become suddenly inflamed
with mortal anger against Death ; and they rush forth
resolved to slay him wherever they may find him.   Presently they meet an old man.   " Why do you live so
long?" they mockingly inquire of him.   " Because,"
says he,

> " Deth, alas, ne will not han my lif ;
> Thus walke I like a resteles caitif,
> And on the ground, which is my modres gate,
> I knocke with my staf erlich and late
> And say to hire ' Leve moder, let me in.' "

" Where is this Death of whom you have spoken? "
furiously demand the three young men.   The old man
replied, " You will find him under an oak tree in yonder
grove."   The three rush forward ; and upon arriving at
the oak find three bags full of gold coin.   Overjoyed at
their good fortune they are afraid to carry the treasure
into town by day lest they be suspected of robbery.
They therefore resolve to wait until night and in the
meantime to make merry.   For the latter purpose one of
the three goes to town after food and drink.   As soon as
he is out of hearing the two who remain under the tree
resolve to murder their companion on his return so that
they may be the richer by his portion of the treasure :
he, on the other hand, whilst buying his victual in town,
shrewdly drops a great lump of poison into the bottle of
drink he is to carry back, so that his companions may
perish and he take all.

To make a long story short, the whole plot is carried
out.   As soon as he who was sent to town returns, his
companions fall upon him and murder him ; they then
proceed merrily to eat and drink what he has brought ;

the poison does its work; presently all three lie dead under the oak tree by the side of the gold, and the old man's direction has proved true : they have found death under that tree. In George Eliot's story the young English Squire also finds death in finding gold. You will all remember how Dunstan Cass in returning late at night from a fox-hunt on foot — for he had killed his horse in the chase — finds himself near the stone hut where Silas Marner the weaver has long plied his trade, and where he is known to have concealed a large sum in gold. The young man is extraordinarily pressed for money; he resolves to take Marner's gold; the night is dark and misty; he makes his way through the mud and darkness to the cottage and finds the door open, Marner being, by the rarest of accidents, away from the hut. The young man quickly discovers the spot in the floor where the weaver kept his gold; he seizes the two heavy leathern bags filled with guineas, and the chapter ends, "So he stepped forward into the darkness." All this occurs in Chapter IV. The story then proceeds; nothing more is heard of Dunstan Cass in the village for many years; the noise of the robbery has long ago died away; Silas Marner has one day found a golden head of hair lying on the very spot of his floor where he used to finger his own gold ; the little outcast who had fallen asleep with her head in this position, after having wandered into Marner's cottage, has been brought up by him to womanhood; when one day, at a critical period in Silas Marner's existence, it happens that in draining some lower grounds the pit of an old stone quarry, which had for years stood filled with rain-water near his house, becomes dry, and on the bottom is revealed a skeleton with a leathern bag of gold in each hand. The young man plunging out into the dark, laden with his treasure, had fallen in and lain for all these years to be afterwards brought to light as another phase of the frequent identity between death and gold.   Here, too, one is obliged to remember those doubly dreadful words in *Romeo and Juliet*, where Romeo having with difficulty bought poison from the apothecary, cries :

> " There is thy gold; worse poison to men's souls,
>   Doing more murder in this loathsome world
>   Than these poor compounds which thou mayst not sell :
>   I sell thee poison, thou hast sold me none.
>   Farewell ; buy food and get thyself in flesh."

I must also instance one little passing picture in *Silas Marner* which, though extremely fanciful, is yet a charming type of some of the greatest and most characteristic work that George Eliot has done.   Silas Marner had been a religious enthusiast of an obscure sect of a small manufacturing town of England ; suddenly a false accusation of theft in which the circumstantial evidence was strong against him brings him into disgrace among his fellow-disciples ; with his whole faith in God and man shattered he leaves his town, wanders over to the village of Raveloe, begins aimlessly to pursue his trade of weaving, presently is paid for some work in gold ; in handling the coin he is smit with the fascination of its yellow radiance, and presently we find him pouring out all the prodigious intensity of his nature, which had previously found a fitter field in religion, in the miser's passion.   Working day and night, while yet a young man he fills his two leathern bags with gold ; and George Eliot gives us some vivid pictures of how, when his day's work would be done, he would brighten up the fire in his stone hut which stood at the edge of the village, eagerly lift up the particular brick of the stone floor under which he kept his treasure concealed, pour out the bright yellow heaps of coin and run his long white fingers through them with all the miser's ecstasy. But after he is robbed the utter blank in his soul — and one can imagine such a blank in such a soul, for he was essentially religious — becomes strangely filled. One day a poor woman leading her little golden-haired child is making her way along the road past Marner's cottage; she is the wife, by private marriage, of the Squire's eldest son, and after having been cruelly treated by him for years has now desperately resolved to appear with her child at a great merry-making which goes on at the Squire's to-day, there to expose all and demand justice. It so happens however that in her troubles she has become an opium-taker; just as she is passing Marner's cottage the effect of an unusually large dose becomes overpowering; she lies down and falls off into a stupor which this time ends in death. Meantime the little golden-haired girl innocently totters into the open door of Marner's cottage during his absence, presently lies down, places her head with all its golden wealth upon the very brick which Marner used to lift up in order to bring his gold to light, and so falls asleep, while a ray of sunlight strikes through the window and illuminates the little one's head. Marner now returns; he is dazed at beholding what seems almost to be another pile of gold at the familiar spot on the floor. He takes this new treasure into his hungry heart and brings up the little girl who becomes a beautiful woman and faithful daughter to him. His whole character now changes and the hardness of his previous brutal misanthropy softens into something at least approaching humanity. Now it is fairly characteristic of George Eliot that she constantly places before us lives which change in a manner of which this is typical: that is to say, she is constantly showing us intense and hungry spirits first wasting their intensity and hunger upon that which is unworthy, often from pure ignorance of anything worthier, then finding where love *is* worthy, and thereafter loving larger loves, and living larger lives.

Is not this substantially the experience of Janet Dempster; of Adam Bede, replacing the love of Hetty with that of Dinah Morris; of Romola; of Dorothea; of Gwendolen Harleth?

This last name brings us directly to the work which we were specially to study to-day. George Eliot's novels have all striking relationships among themselves which cause them to fall into various groups according to various points of view. There is one point however from which her entire work divides itself into two groups, of which one includes the whole body of her writings up to 1876 : the other group consists solely of *Daniel Deronda*. This classification is based on the fact that all the works in the first group concern the life of a time which is past. It is only in *Daniel Deronda*, after she has been writing for more than twenty years, that George Eliot first ventures to deal with English society of the present day. To this important claim upon our interest may be added a further circumstance which will in the sequel develop into great significance. *Daniel Deronda* has had the singular fate of being completely misunderstood to such a degree that the greatest admirers of George Eliot have even ventured to call it a failure, while the Philistines have rioted in abusing Gwendolen Harleth as a weak and rather disagreeable personage, Mirah and Daniel as unmitigated prigs, and the plot as an absurd attempt to awaken interest in what is called the religious patriotism of the Jews. This comparative failure of *Daniel Deronda* to please current criticism, and even the ardent admirers of George Eliot, so clearly opens up what is to my view a singular and lamentable weakness in certain vital portions of the structure of our society that I have thought I could not render better service than by conducting our analysis of *Daniel Deronda* so as to make it embrace some of the most common of the objections urged against that work.   Let us recall in largest possible outline the movement of *Daniel Deronda*.   This can be done in a surprisingly brief statement.   The book really concerns two people ; one is Gwendolen Harleth, a beautiful English girl, brought up with all those delicate tastes and accomplishments which we understand when we think of the highest English refinement, — wayward — mainly because she has seen as yet no way that seemed better to follow than her own — and ambitious, but evidently with that sacred discontent which desires the best and which will only be small when its horizon contains but small objects.   The other main personage is Daniel Deronda, who has been brought up as an Englishman of rank, has a striking face and person, a natural love for all that is beautiful and noble, a good sense that enables him to see through the banalities of English political life and to shrink from involving his own existence in such littleness, and who, after some preliminary account of his youth in the earlier chapters, is placed before us early in the first book as a young man of twenty who is seriously asking himself whether life is worth living.

It so happens however that presently Gwendolen Harleth is found asking herself this same question.   Tempted by a sudden reverse of fortune, by the chance to take care of her mother, and one must add by her own desire — guilty enough in such a connection — for plenty of horses to ride and for all the other luxurious accompaniments which form so integral a portion of modern

English life ; driven, too, by what one must not hesitate to call the cowardliest shrinking from the name and position of a governess ; conciliated by a certain infinite appearance of lordliness which in Grandcourt is mainly nothing more than a blasé brutality which has exhausted desire, — Gwendolen accepts the hand of Grandcourt, quickly discovers him to be an unspeakable brute, suffers a thousand deaths from remorse and is soon found — as is just said — wringing her hands and asking if life is worth living.

Now the sole purpose and outcome of the book lie in its answers to the questions of these two young people. It does answer them, and answers them satisfactorily. On the one hand, Gwendolen Harleth, in the course of her married life, is several times thrown with Daniel Deronda ; his loftiness, his straightforwardness, his fervor, his frankness, his general passion for whatsoever things are large and fine, — in a word, his goodness — form a complete revelation to her.   She suddenly discovers that life is not only worth living but that the possibility of making one's life a good life invests it with a romantic interest whose depth is infinitely beyond that of all the society pleasures which had hitherto formed her horizon. On the other hand, Daniel Deronda discovers that he is a Jew by birth, and, fired by the visions of a fervent Hebrew friend, he resolves to devote his life and the wealth.that has fallen to him from various sources to the cause of reëstablishing his people in their former Eastern home.   Thus also for him, instead of presenting the dreary doubt whether it is worth living, life opens up a boundless and fascinating field for energies of the loftiest kind.

Place, then, clearly before your minds these two distinct strands of story.   One of these might be called *The*

Repentance of Gwendolen Harleth, and this occupies much the larger portion of the work. The other might be called *The Mission of Daniel Deronda*. These two strands are, as we have just seen, united into one artistic thread by the organic purpose of the book, which is to furnish a fair and satisfactory answer to the common question over which these two young protagonists struggle : " Is life worth living ? " The painting of this repentance of Gwendolen Harleth, the development of this beautiful young aristocrat Daniel Deronda into a great and strong man consecrated to a holy purpose : all this is done with such skillful reproduction of contemporary English life, with such a wealth of flesh-and-blood characters, with an art altogether so subtle, so analytic, yet so warm and so loving withal, that if I were asked for the most significant, the most tender, the most pious and altogether the most uplifting of modern books it seems to me I should specify *Daniel Deronda*.

It was remarked two lectures ago that Shakspere had never drawn a repentance ; and if we consider for a single moment what is required in order to paint such a long and intricate struggle as that through which our poor, beautiful Gwendolen passed we are helped towards a clear view of some reasons at least why this is so. For upon examining the instances of repentance alleged by those who disagree with me on this point — as mentioned in my last lecture — I find that the real difference of opinion between us is, not as to whether Shakspere ever drew a repentance, but as to what is a repentance. There certainly are in Shakspere pictures of regret for injuries done to loved ones under mistake or under passion, and sometimes this regret is long-drawn. But surely such reversal of feeling is only that which would be felt by any man of ordinarily manful make upon discovering that he had greatly wronged any one, particularly a loved one. It is to this complexion that all the alleged instances of repentances in Shakspere come at last. Nowhere do we find any special portrayal of a character engaged to its utmost depths in that complete subversion of the old by the new, — that total substitution of some higher motive for the whole existing body of emotions and desires, — that emergence out of the twilight world of selfishness into the large and sunlit plains of a love which does not turn upon self,

> "Which bends not with the remover to remove,"
> Nor "alters when it alteration finds."

For example, Leontes, in *Winter's Tale*, who is cited as a chief instance of Shakspere's repentances, quite clearly shows by word and act that his regret is mainly a sense of personal loss, not a change of character. He is sorrowful not so much because he has sinned as because he has hurt himself. In Act V, just before the catastrophe which restores him his wife and daughter, we find him exclaiming :

> "Good Paulina
> .   .   .   O that ever I
> Had squared me to thy counsel ! Then even now
> I might have looked upon my queen's full eyes,
> Have taken treasure from her lips — "   .   .   .

And again in the same scene, where Florizel and Perdita have been brought before him, he cries :

> "What might I have been,
> Might I a son and daughter now have look'd on,
> Such goodly things as you !"

In these it is clear that Leontes is speaking from personal regret ; there is no thought here of that total expansion of an *ego* into a burning love of all other *egos*,

implied in the term repentance, as I have used it. Similarly, King Lear, who has also been cited as an example
of Shakspere's repentances, is simply an example of
regret for the foulest of wrongs done in a moment of
silly passion. After the poor old man, upon regaining
his consciousness under Cordelia's tender ministrations,
is captured together with Cordelia, in Scene III of Act
V, Cordelia says, as if to comfort him :

> " We are not the first
> Who with best meaning have incurred the worst.
> For thee, oppressed king, am I cast down.
>
> .　　.　　.　　.　　.　　.
>
> Shall we not see these daughters and these sisters ? "
> *Lear.* — " No, no, no, no ! Come, let's away to prison ;
> We two alone will sing like birds i' the cage ;
> When thou dost ask me blessing I'll kneel down
> And ask of thee forgiveness."

Here, clearly enough, is regret for his injury to Cordelia, but, quite as clearly, no general state of repentance ;
and in the very few other words uttered by the old king
before the play ends surely nothing indicating such a
state appears. Of all the instances suggested only one
involves anything like the process of character-change
which I have called a repentance, such as Gwendolen
Harleth's, for example ; but this one, unfortunately, is
not drawn by Shakspere : it is only mentioned as having
occurred. This is the repentance of Duke Frederick
in *As you Like it.* Just at the end of that play, when
Orlando and Rosalind, Oliver and Celia and all the rest
have unravelled all their complications, and when everything that can be called plot in the play is finished, the
son of old Sir Rowland appears before the company in
the wood and calls out :

> " Let me have audience for a word or two.

" Duke Frederick hearing how that every day
    Men of great worth resorted to this forest
    Addressed a mighty power   .   .   .
    .   .   .   purposely to take
    His brother here and put him to the sword,
    And to the skirts of this wild wood he came
    Where, meeting with an old religious man,
    After some questions with him was converted
    Both from his enterprise and from the world ;
    His crown bequeathing to his banished brother,
    And all their lands restored to them again
    That were with him exiled."

Here we have indeed a true repentance, but this is all we have of it ; the passage I have read contains the whole picture.

If we now go on and ask ourselves why these fascinating phenomena of repentance which George Eliot has treated with such success never engaged Shakspere's energy, we come at the very first step upon a limitation of the drama as opposed to the novel which, in the strongest way, confirms the view I was at such pains to set forth in my earlier lectures, of that necessity for a freer form than the dramatic which arises from the more complete relations between modern personalities and which has really developed the novel out of the drama.

How, for instance, could Shakspere paint the yeas and nays, the twists, the turns, the intricacies of Gwendolen Harleth's thought during the long weeks while she was debating whether she should accept Grandcourt ? The whole action of this drama, you observe, is confined within the small round head of the girl herself. How could such action be brought before the audience of a play ? The only hope would be in a prolonged soliloquy, for these are thoughts which no young woman would naturally communicate to any one ; but what audience

could stand so prolonged a soliloquy, even if any
character could be found in whom it would be natural?
And sometimes, too, the situation is so subtly complex
that Gwendolen is soliloquizing in such a manner that
we, the audience, hear her while Grandcourt, who is
standing by, does not.

"'I used to think archery was a great bore,' Grandcourt
began. He spoke with a fine accent, but with a certain
broken drawl, as of a distinguished personage with a distinguished cold in his chest.

"'Are you converted to-day?' said Gwendolen.

"(Pause, during which she imagined various degrees and
modes of opinion about herself that might be entertained by
Grandcourt.)

"'Yes, since I saw you shooting. In things of this sort
one generally sees people missing and simpering.'

.   .   .   .

"'And do you care about the turf? or is that among the
things you have left off?'

"(Pause, during which Gwendolen thought that a man of
extremely calm cold manners might be less disagreeable as
a husband than other men, and not likely to interfere with
his wife's preferences.)

.   .   .   .

"'You would perhaps like tiger-hunting or pig-sticking. I
saw some of that for a season or two in the East. Everything here is poor stuff after that.'

"' *You* are fond of danger then?'

"(Pause, during which Gwendolen speculated on the prob-
ability that the men of coldest manners were the most ad-
venturous, and felt the strength of her own insight, supposing
the question had to be decided.)

"'One must have something or other. But one gets used
to it.'

"'I begin to think I am very fortunate, because everything
is new to me: it is only that I can't get enough of it. I am

not used to anything except being dull, which I should like
to leave off as you have left off shooting.'

"(Pause, during which it occurred to Gwendolen that a
man of cold and distinguished manners might possibly be a
dull companion; but on the other hand she thought that most
persons were dull, that she had not observed husbands to be
companions, and that after all she was not going to accept
Grandcourt.)

"' Why are you dull ? '

"' This is a dreadful neighbourhood, there is nothing to
be done in it.   That is why I practised my archery.'

"(Pause, during which Gwendolen reflected that the life of
an unmarried woman who could not go about and had no
command of anything, must necessarily be dull through all
the degrees of comparison as time went on.)

"' You have made yourself queen of it.   I imagine you will
carry the first prize.'

"' I don't know that.   I have great rivals.   Did you not
observe how well Miss Arrowpoint shot ? '

"(Pause, wherein Gwendolen was thinking that men had
been known to choose some one else than the woman they
most admired, and recalled several experiences of that kind
in novels.) "

At this point we come upon an element of difference
between the novel and the drama which has not hitherto
been fairly appreciated, so far as I know.   Consider for
a moment the wholly supernatural power which is necessarily involved in the *projet* of thus showing the most
secret workings of the mind and heart of this young
girl, Gwendolen Harleth!   In real life what power less
than God's can make me see the deepest thought and
feeling of a fellow-creature?   But since the novel is always a transcript of real, or at any rate of possible, life
you observe that wherever these workings of heart and
brain are thus laid bare the tacit supposition is, in plain
terms, that God is the writer, or that the writer is a god.

In the drama no supposition is necessary because here we become acquainted with only such matters as are shown us in the ordinary way, by scenery or by the speech or gesture of the actor. This consideration seems to me to lift the novel to the very highest and holiest plane of creative effort; he who takes up the pen of the novelist assumes, as to that novel, to take up along with it the omniscience of God. He proposes, in effect, to bring about the revelations of Judgment Day long before the trumpet has sounded. George Eliot shows us the play of Gwendolen Harleth's soul with the same uncompromising fullness with which the most literal believer expects to give account of the deeds done in the body at the last day.

In contemplating this vast ascent from the attitude of the dramatist to that of the novelist — the dramatist is a man; the novelist, as to that novel, is a god — we are contemplating simply another phase of the growth of man from Shakspere to George Eliot.

And we reach still another view of that growth when we reflect that even if Shakspere could have overcome the merely mechanical difficulty of presenting a repentance without overmuch soliloquy, he would probably have found but poorly-paying houses at the Globe Theatre to witness any drama so purely spiritual as that which George Eliot has shown us going on upon the little, ill-lighted stage of a young girl's consciousness. Just as we found that the prodigious advance in the nearness of man to his fellow from the time of Æschylus to that of George Eliot was implied in the fact that the latter could gather an interested audience about a couple of commonplace children (as in *The Mill on the Floss*), whilst the former required the larger stimulus of Titanic quarrel and angry Jove, so here we have reached an evidence of still more subtle advance as between the times of Shakespere and of George Eliot when we find the latter gathering a great audience about this little inward, actionless, complex drama of Gwendolen Harleth, while we reflect that Shakspere must have his stimulant passion, his crime, his patriotism, and the like, as the only attracting motives. In truth I find what seems to be a cunning indication that George Eliot herself did not feel quite sure of her audience for this same little play. At the end of Chapter XI she breaks off from a description of one of Gwendolen's capricious turns, and as if in apologetic defence says:

"Could there be a slenderer, more insignificant thread in human history than this consciousness of a girl, busy with her small inferences of the way in which she could make her life pleasant?—in a time, too, when ideas were with fresh vigour making armies of themselves and the universal kinship was declaring itself fiercely; . . a time when the soul of man was waking to pulses which had for centuries been beating in him unheard. . . . What, in the midst of that mighty drama, are girls and their blind visions? They are the Yea or Nay of that good for which men are enduring or fighting. In these delicate vessels is borne onward through the ages the treasure of human affections."

Thus it appears that for Shakspere to draw such repentances as Gwendolen Harleth's was not only difficult from the playwright's point of view but premature from the point of view of the world's growth. In truth I suspect if we had time to pursue this matter that we should find it leading us into some very instructive views of certain rugged breaking-off places in Shakspere. I suppose we must consider the limitations of his time, though it is just possible they may be limitations of his genius, also. We should presently find ourselves

asking further how it is that Shakspere not only never
drew a great reformation, but never painted a great
reformer?   It seems a natural question :   How is it that
it is Milton and not Shakspere who has treated the
subject of Paradise Lost and Regained ; how is it that
the first-class subject was left for the second-class genius?
We all know how Milton has failed in what he intended
with his poem, and how astonished he would be at finding that the only one of his characters which has taken
any real hold upon the world is his Satan.   It seems
irresistible to ask ourselves why might not our most
eloquent tongue have treated our most lofty theme?
Or, if we should find special reasons in the temper of
his time why Shakspere could not or should not have
treated this theme, we may still ask, why did he never
paint for us one of those men who seem too large to be
bounded in their affections merely by limits of country,
but who loved and worked for the whole world, Buddha,
Zoroaster, Mahomet, Socrates, Luther ; nay, why may
not the master have given us a master's picture of Chris-
topher Columbus or even of John Vannini, the scientific
martyr, or even of the fantastic Giordano Bruno who
against all warnings boldly wandered from town to town
defending his doctrines until he was burned, in 1600?
And if any of the academicians now in my audience
should incline to pursue this strange psychologico-literary
problem, I make no doubt that useful light would be
cast upon the search if you should consider along with
these questions the further inquiries why Shakspere never
mentions either of the two topics which must have been
foremost in the talk of his time : namely, America and
tobacco.   Among all the allusions to contemporary matter in his plays the nearest he ever comes to America
is the single instance in *The Tempest* where Ariel is

mentioned as "fetching dew from the still-vexed Ber-moothes" (Bermudas). As for tobacco : although pretty much all London must have been smoking vigorously about the time Shakspere was writing *Much Ado About Nothing*, and *The Merry Wives of Windsor ;* although certainly to a countryman not a great while out of the woods of Warwickshire it must have been the oddest of sights to see people sucking at hollow tubes and puffing smoke from their mouths and nostrils ; although, too, the comedies of his contemporary Ben Jonson are often cloudy with tobacco smoke : nevertheless there is not, so far as my recollection goes, the faintest allusion to the drinking of tobacco (as it was then called) in the whole body of his writings. Now all these omissions are significant because conspicuous ; always, in studying genius, we learn as much from what it has not done, as from what it has done ; and if research should succeed in arranging these neglects from any common point of view, it is possible that something new might still be said about Shakspere.

But, to return to *Daniel Deronda*. A day or two after George Eliot's death the *Saturday Review* contained an elaborate editorial summary of her work. For some special ends, permit me to read so much of it as relates to the book now under consideration. "*Daniel Deronda* is devoted to the whimsical object of glorifying real or imaginary Jewish aspirations. It cannot be doubted that so fantastic a form of enthusiasm was suggested by some personal predilection or association. A devotion to the Jewish cause unaccompanied by any kind of interest in the Jewish religion is not likely to command general sympathy ; but even if the purpose of the story had been as useful as it is chimerical and absurd, the inherent fault of didactic fiction would scarcely have been diminished.

. . . It is significant that when George Eliot deliberately preferred the function of teaching to her proper office of amusing she sacrificed her power of instruction as well as her creative faculty."

Of course, in general, no man in his senses thinks of taking in serious earnest every proposition in the *Saturday Review*. It is an odd character which long ago assumed the rôle of teasing English society by gravely advancing any monstrous assertion at random and laughing in its sleeve at the elaborate replies with which this assertion would be honored by weak and unsuspecting people. But its position upon this particular point of *Daniel Deronda* happens to be supported by similar views among her professed admirers.

Even *The Spectator* in its obituary notice completely mistakes the main purpose of *Daniel Deronda*, in declaring that " she takes religious patriotism for the subject; " although, as I have just indicated, surely the final aim of the book is to furnish to two young modern people a motive sufficient to make life not only worth living but fascinating; and of the two distinct plots in the book one — and the one to which most attention is paid — hinges upon Gwendolen Harleth's repentance, while it is only the other and slighter which is concerned with what these papers call religious patriotism; and here the phrase " religious patriotism " if we examine it is not only meaningless — what is religious patriotism? — but has the effect of dwarfing the two grand motives which are given to Daniel Deronda : namely, religion *and* patriotism.

Upon bringing together, however, all the objections which have been urged against *Daniel Deronda*, I think they may be classified and discussed under two main heads. First it is urged that Daniel Deronda and Mirah —and even Gwendolen Harleth, after her change of spirit — are all prigs ; secondly, it is urged that the moral purpose of the book has overweighted the art of it, that what should have been pure nature and beauty have been obscured by didacticism, thus raising the whole question of Art for Art's sake which has so mournfully divided the modern artistic world.   This last objection, opening, as it does, the whole question of how far fervent moral purpose injures the work of the true artist, is a matter of such living importance in the present state of our art, particularly of our literary art ; it so completely sums up all these contributory items of thought which have been gradually emerging in these lectures regarding the growth of human personality together with the correlative development of the novel ; and the discussions concerning it are conducted upon such small planes and from such low and confusing points of view : that I will ask to devote my next lecture to a faithful endeavor to get all the light possible upon the vexed matter of Art for Art's sake, and to showing how triumphantly George Eliot's *Daniel Deronda* seems to settle that entire debate with the most practical of answers.

Meantime in discussing the other class of objections which we managed to generalize, to wit that the three main characters in *Daniel Deronda* are prigs, a serious difficulty lies in the impossibility of learning from these objectors exactly what *is* a prig.   And I confess I should be warned off from any attempt at discussion by this initial difficulty if I did not find great light thrown on the subject by discovering that the two objections of prig-ism and that of didacticism already formulated are really founded upon the same cunning weakness in our current culture.   The truth is, George Eliot's book, *Daniel Deronda*, is so sharp a sermon that it has made the whole English contemporary society uncomfortable.

It is curious and instructive to see how unable all the objectors have been to put their fingers upon the exact source of this discomfort; so that in their bewilderment one lays it to prig-ism, another to didacticism, and so on. That a state of society should exist in which such a piece of corruption as Grandcourt should be not only the leader but the crazing fascination and ideal of the most delicate and fastidious young women in that society; that a state of society should exist in which those pure young girls whom George Eliot describes as "the delicate vessels in which man's affections are hoarded through the ages," should be found manœuvring for this Grandcourt infamy, plotting to be Grandcourt's wife, instead of flying from him in horror; that a state of society should exist in which such a thing was possible as a marriage between a Gwendolen Harleth and a Grandcourt: this was enough to irritate even the thickest skinned Philistine, and this George Eliot's book showed with a terrible conclusiveness. Yet the showing was made so daintily and with so light a hand that, as I have said, current society did not know, and has not yet recognized, where or how the wound was. We have all read of the miraculous sword in the German fable whose blade was so keen that when, upon a certain occasion, its owner smote a warrior with it from crown to crotch, the warrior nevertheless rode home and was scarcely aware he had been wounded until, upon his wife opening the door, he attempted to embrace her and fell into two pieces. Now, as I said, just as *Daniel Deronda* made people feel uncomfortable by even vaguely revealing a sharp truth — so, a prig, so far as I can make out, is a person whose goodness is so genuine, essential and ever-present that all ungenuine people have a certain sense of discomfort when brought in contact with it. If the prig-

hater be questioned he will not deny the real goodness of
the *Daniel Deronda* people; he dare not — no one in
this age dares — to wish explicitly that Mirah and Daniel
Deronda might be less good; but as nearly as anything
definite can be obtained what he desires is that the prig
should be good in some oily and lubricative way so as
not to jar the nerves of those who are less good. Conform, conform! seems to be the essential cry of the prig-
haters; if you go to an evening party you wear your
dress coat and look like every other man; but here your
goodness amounts to a hump, a deformity: we do not
ask you to cut it off, but at least pad it; if every one
grows as big as you we shall have to enlarge all our draw-
ing-rooms and society will be disorganized. In short,
the cry against the prig turns out to be nothing more
than the old claim for conformity and the conventional.
For one, I never hear these admonitions to conformity
without recalling a comical passage of Tom Hood's in
which the fellows of a Zoölogical society propose to
remedy the natural defects of animal morphology, such
as the humps of dromedaries and the overgrowth of hair
upon lions, so as to bring all the grotesqueness of the
animal creation into more conformity with conventional
ideas of proportion. The passage occurs in a pretended
report from the keeper of the animals to the President of
the society. After describing the condition of the various beasts the keeper proceeds:

Honnerd Sur, — Their is an aggitating skeem of witch I
humbly approve very hiley. The plan is owen to sum of the
Femail Fellers, —. . . For instances the Buffloo and Fallo
dears and cetra to have their horns Gildid and Sheaps is to
hav Pink ribbings round there nex. The Ostreaches is to
have their plums stuck in their heds, and the Pecox tales
will be always spred out on fraime wurks like the hispaliers.

All the Bares is to be tort to Dance to Wippert's Quadrils and the Lions manes is to be subjective to pappers and the curling tongues.   The gould and silver Fesants is to be Polisht every day with Plait Powder and the Cammils and Drumdearis and other defourmed anymills is to be paddid to hide their Crukidnes.   Mr. Howard is to file down the tusks of the wild Bores, and the Spoons of the Spoonbills is to be maid as like the King's Patten as posible.   The elifunt will be himbelisht with a Sugger candid Castle maid by Gunter and the Flaminggoes will be touched up with Frentch ruge.   The Sloath is propos'd to have an ellegunt Stait Bed — and the Bever is to ware one of Perren's lite Warter Proof Hats — and the Balld Vulters baldnes will be hided by a small Whig from Trewfits.   The Crains will be put into trousirs and the Hippotamus tite laced for a waste.   Experience will dictait menny more imbellishing modes, with witch I conclud that I am

   Your Honners,
    Very obleeged and humbel former servant,
     STEPHEN HUMPHREYS.

Such is the ideal to which the prig is asked to conform, but after the first six lectures of this course we are specially in position to see in all this cry nothing but the old clamor against personality.   Upon us who have traced the growth of personality from Æschylus to George Eliot, and who have found that growth to be the one direction for the advance of our species, this cry comes with little impressiveness.

XII

IN the last lecture we obtained a view of George Eliot's *Daniel Deronda* as containing two distinct stories, one of which might have been called *The Repentance of Gwendolen Harleth*, and the other, *The Mission of Daniel Deronda;* and we generalized the principal objections against the work into two: namely, that the main characters were prigs and that the artistic value of the book was spoiled by its moral purpose. In discussing the first of these objections we found that probably both of them might be referred to a common origin; for examination of precisely what is meant by a prig revealed that he is a person whose goodness is so downright, so unconforming and so radical that it makes the mass of us uncomfortable. Now there can be no question that so far as the charge of being overloaded with moral purpose is brought against *Daniel Deronda*, as distinguished from George Eliot's other works, it is so palpably contrary to all facts in the case that we may clearly refer it to some fact outside the case: and I readily find this outside fact in that peculiar home-thrust of the moral of *Daniel Deronda* which has rendered it more tangible than that of any preceding work which concerned time past. You will remember we found that it was only in *Daniel Deronda*, written in 1876, after thirty years of study and of production, that George Eliot allowed herself to treat current English society; you will remember too how we found that this first treatment revealed among other things a picture of an unspeakable brute, Grandcourt, throned like the Indian Lama above the multitude, and receiving with a blasé stare the special adoration of the most refined young English girls : a picture which made the worship of the golden calf or the savage dance around a merely impotent wooden idol, fade into tame blasphemy. No man could deny the truth of the picture ; the galled jade was obliged to wince ; this time it was *my* withers that were wrung. Thus the moral purpose of *Daniel Deronda*, which is certainly beyond all comparison less obtrusive than that of any other book written by George Eliot, grew, by its very nearness, out of all perspective. Though a mere gnat, it sat on the very eyelash of society and seemed a monster.

In speaking of George Eliot's earlier stories I was at pains to show how explicitly she avowed their moral purpose ; in *Amos Barton*, in *Janet's Repentance*, in *Adam Bede*, everywhere there is the fullest avowal of didacticism ; on almost every other page one meets those direct appeals from the author in her own person to the reader in which George Eliot indulged more freely than any novelist I know, enforcing this or that moral view in plain terms of preaching. But it curiously happens that even these moral "asides" are conspicuously absent in *Daniel Deronda ;* the most cursory comparison of it in this particular with *Adam Bede*, for example, reveals an enormous disproportion in favor of *Deronda* as to the weight of this criticism. Yet people who had enthusiastically accepted and extolled *Adam Bede*, with all its explicitly moralizing passages and its professedly preaching characters, suddenly found that *Daniel Deronda* was intolerably priggish and didactic. But resting thus on the facts in the case — easily provable by comparing *Daniel Deronda* with any previous work — to show how this censure of didacticism loses all momentum as against this particular book : let us advance to the more interesting, because more general, fact that many people — some in great sincerity — have preferred this censure against all of George Eliot's work and against all didactic novels in general. The objection involves many shades of opinion, and is urged with the most diverse motives and manner. At one extreme we have the *Saturday Review* huskily growling — as in the extract quoted in my last lecture — that the office of the novelist is to amuse, never to instruct, that George Eliot, in seeking the latter has even forfeited the former, and that *Daniel Deronda* neither amuses nor instructs ; whereupon George Eliot is derisively bid, in substance, to put on the cap and bells again and leave teaching to her betters ; with a voice, by the way, wondrously like that with which the *Edinburgh Review* some years ago cried out to our adorable John Keats, " Back to your gallipots, young man ! " From this extreme we have all shades of opinion to that vague and moderate apprehension much current among young persons influenced by a certain smart sound in the modern French phrase *l'Art pour l'Art* — or by the German nickname of " tendency-books " — that a moral intention on the part of an artist is apt to interfere with the naturalness or intrinsic beauty of his work, that in art the controlling consideration must always be artistic beauty, and that artistic beauty is not only distinct from but often opposed to moral beauty. Now, to discuss this question *a priori :* to go forward and establish an æsthetic basis for beauty, involving an examination which must range from Aristotle to Kant and Burke and Mr. Grant Allen's physiological theories, would require another course of lectures quite as long as that which is now ending ; so that all I can hope to do is but to throw, if I can,

some light upon this question. And so, to proceed immediately to that work with some system : permit me to
recall to you in the first place that the requirement has
been from time immemorial that wherever there is
contest as between artistic and moral beauty, unless the
moral side prevail, all is lost. Let any sculptor hew us
out the most ravishing combination of tender curves and
spheric softness that ever stood for woman ; yet if the
lip have a certain fullness that hints of the flesh, if the
brow be insincere, if in the minutest particular the physical beauty suggest a moral ugliness, that sculptor —
unless he be portraying a moral ugliness for a moral purpose — may as well give over his marble for paving-stones.
Time, whose judgments are inexorably moral, will not
accept his work. For indeed we may say that he who
has not yet perceived how artistic beauty and moral
beauty are convergent lines which run back into a common
ideal origin, and who therefore is not afire with moral
beauty just as with artistic beauty, — that he, in short,
who has not come to that stage of quiet and eternal
frenzy in which the beauty of holiness and the holiness of
beauty mean one thing, burn as one fire, shine as one light,
within him ; — he is not yet the great artist. Here it is
most instructive to note how the fine and beautiful souls
of time appear after awhile to lose all sense of distinction
between these terms, Beauty, Truth, Love, Wisdom,
Goodness, and the like. Hear some testimony upon this
point : this is a case for witnesses. Let us call, first,
Keats. Keats does not hesitate to draw a moral even
from his Grecian Urn, and even in the very climacteric
of his most "high sorrowful" song ; and that moral
effaces the distinction between truth and beauty. "Cold
pastoral !" he cries, at the end of the *Ode on a Grecian
Urn,*

" When old age shall this generation waste,
  Thou shalt remain in midst of other woe
  Than ours, a friend to man to whom thou say'st
  ' Beauty is truth, truth, beauty,' — that is all
  Ye know on earth, and all ye need to know."

Again, bearing in mind this identity of truth and
beauty in Keats's view, observe how Emerson, by strange
turns of thought, subtly refers both truth and beauty to
a common principle of the essential relation of each thing
to all things in the universe. Here are the beginning
and end of Emerson's poem called *Each and All :*

" Little thinks in the field yon red-cloaked clown
  Of thee from the hill-top looking down ;
  The sexton tolling his bell at noon
  Deems not that great Napoleon
  Stops his horse and lists with delight
  While his files sweep round yon Alpine height ;
  Nor knowest thou what argument
  Thy life to thy neighbor's creed has lent.
  All are needed by each one ;
  Nothing is fair or good alone."

Nothing is fair or good alone : that is to say fairness,
or beauty, and goodness depend upon relations between
creatures ; and so in the end of the poem, after telling
us how he learned this lesson by finding that the bird-
song was not beautiful when away from its proper relation to the sky and the river and so on, we have this :

" Then I said ' I covet truth ;
  Beauty is unripe childhood's cheat ;
  I leave it behind with the games of youth.'
  As I spoke, beneath my feet
  The ground-pine curled its pretty wreath,
  Running over the club-moss burs ;
  I inhaled the violet's breath ;
  Around me stood the oaks and firs ;

> Pine cones and acorns lay on the ground;
> Over me soared the eternal sky,
> Full of light and of deity;
> Again I saw, again I heard
> The rolling river, the morning bird;
> Beauty through all my senses stole,
> I yielded myself to the perfect whole."

But again, here Mrs. Browning, speaking by the mouth of Adam in *The Drama of Exile*, so far identifies beauty and love as to make the former depend on the latter; insomuch that Satan, created the most beautiful of all angels, becomes the most repulsive of all angels from lack of love, though retaining all his original outfit of beauty. In *The Drama of Exile*, after Adam and Eve have become wise with the great lessons of grief, love and forgiveness, to them comes Satan, with such talk as if he would mock them back into their misery; but it is fine to see how the father of men now instructs the prince of the angels upon this matter of love and beauty.

Eve. — Speak no more with him,
　　　Beloved! it is not good to speak with him.
　　　Go from us, Lucifer, and speak no more!
　　　We have no pardon which thou dost not scorn,
　　　Nor any bliss, thou seest, for coveting,
　　　Nor innocence for staining. Being bereft,
　　　We would be alone. Go.
Luc. — 　　　　　　　　　Ah! ye talk the same,
　　　All of you — spirits and clay — go, and depart!
　　　In Heaven they said so; and at Eden's gate, —
　　　And here, reiterant, in the wilderness.
　　　None saith, Stay with me, for thy face is fair!
　　　None saith, Stay with me, for thy voice is sweet!
　　　And yet I was not fashioned out of clay.
　　　Look on me, woman! Am I beautiful?
Eve. — Thou hast a glorious darkness.
Luc. — 　　　　　　　　　Nothing more?
Eve. — I think, no more.

Luc. —   False Heart — thou thinkest more!
Thou canst not choose but think, . . . that I stand
Most absolute in beauty.   As yourselves
Were fashioned very good at best, so *we*
Sprang very beauteous from the creant Word
Which thrilled behind us, God Himself being moved
When that august work of a perfect shape, —
His dignities of sovran angel-hood, —
Swept out into the universe, — divine
With thunderous movements, earnest looks of gods,
And silver-solemn clash of cymbal-wings !
Whereof was I, in motion and in form,
A part not poorest.   And yet, — yet, perhaps,
This beauty which I speak of is not here,
As God's voice is not here, nor even my crown —
I do not know.   What is this thought or thing
Which I call beauty ? is it thought or thing ?
Is it a thought accepted for a thing ?
Or both ? or neither ? — a pretext — a word ?
Its meaning flutters in me like a flame
Under my own breath : my perceptions reel
For evermore around it, and fall off,
As if it, too, were holy.
Eve. —   Which it is.
Adam. — The essence of all beauty, I call love.
The attribute, the evidence, the end,
The consummation to the inward sense
Of beauty apprehended from without,
I still call love.   As form when colorless
Is nothing to the eye, — that pine-tree there,
Without its black and green, being all a blank, —
So, without love, is beauty undiscerned,
In man or angel.   Angel ! rather ask
What love is in thee, what love moves to thee,
And what collateral love moves on with thee ;
Then shalt thou know if thou art beautiful.

Luc. — Love ! what is love ?   I lose it.   Beauty and love
I darken to the image.   Beauty — love !   (*He disappears.*)

Let us now carry forward this connection between
love and beauty in listening to a further testimony of

Emerson's in a poem called *The Celestial Love*, where, instead of identifying beauty and truth with Keats, we find him making love and truth to be one:

> " Love's hearts are faithful, but not fond,
> Bound for the just but not beyond;
> Not glad, as the low-loving herd,
> Of self in other still preferred,
> But they have heartily designed
> The benefit of broad mankind.
> And they serve men austerely,
> After their own genius, clearly,
> Without a false humility;
> For this is love's nobility, —
> Not to scatter bread and gold,
> Goods and raiment bought and sold;
> But to hold fast his simple sense,
> And speak the speech of innocence,
> And with hand, and body, and blood,
> To make his bosom-counsel good.
> For he that feeds men serveth few;
> He serves all that dares be true."

And in connection with these lines:

> " Not glad, as the low-loving herd,
> Of self in other still preferred," —

I must here beg you to observe the quite incalculable advance in the ideal of love here presented by Emerson and the ideal which was thought to be the crown and boast of the classic novel a hundred years ago, and which is still pointed to with exultation by thoughtless people. This ideal, by universal voice, was held to have been consummated by Fielding in his character of Squire Allworthy, in the famous novel, *Tom Jones*. And here it is: we have a dramatic presentation of Squire Allworthy, early on a May morning pacing the terrace before his mansion which commanded a noble stretch of coun-

try, and then Fielding glows thus: "In the full blaze
of his majesty up rose the sun, than which one object
alone in this lower creation could be more glorious, and
that Mr. Allworthy himself presented — a human being
replete with benevolence, meditating in what manner he
might render himself most acceptable to his Creator by
doing most good to his creatures." Here Mr. Allworthy's
benevolence has for its object to render himself most
acceptable to his Creator; his love, in other words, is
only another term for increasing his account in the Bank
of Heaven; a perfect example, in short, of that love of
the low-loving herd which is self in other still preferred.

But now let me once more turn the tube and gain.
another radiant arrangement of these kaleidoscopic
elements, beauty and love and the like. In Emerson's
poem called *Beauty* (which must be distinguished from
the *Ode to Beauty*) the relation between love and beauty
takes this turn: "Seyd," he says, "chased beauty

> everywhere,
> In flame, in storm, in clouds of air.
> He smote the lake to feed his eye
> With the beryl beam of the broken wave;
> He flung in pebbles well to hear
> The moment's music which they gave.
> Oft pealed for him a lofty tone
> From nodding pole and belting zone.

> "He heard a voice none else could hear
> From centred and from errant sphere.
> The quaking earth did quake in rhyme,
> Seas ebbed and flowed in epic chime.
> In dens of passion, pits of woe,
> He saw strong Eros struggling through,
> To sum the doubt and solve the curse
> And beam to the bounds of the universe.
> While thus to love he gave his days
> In loyal worship, scorning praise,"

(where, you observe, love is substituted for beauty, as
that to which he gave his days, in the most naïve assumption that the one involves the other,)

> " While thus to love he gave his days
> In loyal worship, scorning praise,
> How spread their lures for him in vain
> Thieving ambition and paltering gain !
> He thought it happier to be dead,
> To die for Beauty, — than live for bread."

George Eliot has somewhere called this word love
a word-of-all-work.   If with another turn I add to these
testimonies one from Swedenborg, in which this same
love — which we have just seen to be beauty — which
beauty we just before saw to be truth — is now identified
with *wisdom :* we prove the justice of George Eliot's
phrase.   In Section X of his work on the Divine Provi-
dence Swedenborg says : " The good of love is not good
any further than it is united to the truth of wisdom ; and
the truth of wisdom is not truth any further than it is
united to the good of love ; " and he continues in Section
XIII : " Now because truth is from good, as wisdom is
from love, therefore both taken together are called love
or good ; for love in its form is wisdom, and good in its
form is truth."

And finally does not David practically confirm this
view where, in Psalm CXIX, he involves the love of the
law of God with wisdom in the verse : " I understand
more than the ancients because I keep thy precepts " ?

I grieve that there is no time to call more witnesses ;
for I love to assemble these lofty spirits and hear them
speak upon one topic.   Is it not clear that in the minds
of these serious thinkers truth, beauty, wisdom, goodness, love, appear as if they were but avatars of one and
the same essential God ?

And if this be true cannot one say with authority to the young artist, — whether working in stone, in color, in tones or in character-forms of the novel : so far from dreading that your moral purpose will interfere with your beautiful creation, go forward in the clear conviction that unless you are suffused — soul and body, one might say — with that moral purpose which finds its largest expression in love — that is, the love of all things in their proper relation — unless you are suffused with this love, do not dare to meddle with beauty, unless you are suffused with beauty, do not dare to meddle with love, unless you are suffused with truth, do not dare to meddle with goodness, — in a word, unless you are suffused with beauty, truth, wisdom, goodness *and* love, abandon the hope that the ages will accept you as an artist.

Of course I leave out of view here all that field of artistic activity which is merely neutral, which is — not immoral but — merely *un*moral. The situations in Scott's novels for instance do not in general put us upon any moral question as between man and man. Or when our own Mr. Way paints his luminous bunches of grapes, one of which will feed the palates of a thousand souls though it is never eaten, and thus shows us how Art repeats the miracle of the loaves and fishes, feeding the multitude and leaving more of the original provision than was at first, — we have most delightful unmoral art. This is not only legitimate, but I think among the most beneficent energies of art : it rests our hearts, it gives us holiday from the Eternal Debate, it re-creates us for all work.

But now secondly, as to the influence of moral purpose in art : we have been in the habit, as you will remember, of passing at the earliest possible moment from abstract discussion to the concrete instance ; and if we now follow that course and inquire, — not whether moral

purpose *may* interfere with artistic creation, — but whether
moral purpose *has* interfered with artistic creation, as a
matter of fact, in the works of those whom the ages have
set in the highest heaven of art, we get a verdict which
seems to leave little room for question.   At the beginning we are met with the fact that the greatest work has
always gone hand in hand with the most fervent moral
purpose.   For example, the most poetical poetry of
which we know anything is that of the author of *Job*,
and of David and his fellow psalm-writers.   I have used
the expression " most poetical " here with design ; for
regarded as pure literature these poems in this particular
of poeticalness, of pure spirituality, lift themselves into a
plane not reached by any others.   A single fact in proof
of this exceeding poeticalness will suffice : it is the fact
that these poems alone, of all ever written, bear translation
from one language into another without hurt.   Surely
this can be said of no other poetic work.   If we strike
away all allowances of amateurishness and good fellowship, and judge with the uncompromising truth of the
pious artist : how pitiful is Homer as he appears in even
Pope's English ; or how subtly does the simplicity of
Dante sink into childishness even with Mr. Longfellow
guiding ; or how tedious and flat fall the cultured sentences of Goethe even in Taylor's version, which has by
many been declared the most successful translation ever
made, not only of *Faust* but of any foreign poem ; nay,
how completely the charm of Chaucer exhales away
even when redacted merely from an older dialect into a
later one, by hands so skillful as those of Dryden and
Wordsworth !

Now, it is words and their associations which are
untranslatable, not ideas ; there is no idea, whether
originating in a Hebrew, Greek or other mind, which

cannot be adequately produced as idea in English words ; the reason why Shakspere and Dante are practically untranslatable is that, recognizing how every word means more than itself to its native users, — how every word is like the bright head of a comet drawing behind it a less luminous train of vague associations which are associations only to those who have used such words from infancy, — Shakspere and Dante, I say, have used this fact and have constructed poems which necessarily mean more to native hearers than they can possibly mean to any foreign ear.

But this Hebrew poetry which I have mentioned is so purely composed of ideas which are universal, essential, fundamental to the personality of man, instantly recognizable by every soul of every race, — that they remain absolutely great, absolutely artistic, in whatever language they are couched.

For example : if one climbs up for a moment out of that vagueness with which Biblical expressions, for various reasons, are apt to fall upon many ears, so that one may consider the clean and virgin quality of ideas clarified from all factitious charm of word and of association, — what could be more nearly perfect as pure literature than this :

> " The entrance of Thy words giveth light ;
> it giveth understanding unto the simple.
> " I opened my mouth and panted :
> for I longed for Thy commandments.
> " Deliver me from the oppression of man :
> so will I keep Thy precepts.
> " Order my steps in Thy word,
> and let not any iniquity have dominion over me.
> " Make Thy face to shine upon Thy servant;
> and teach me Thy statutes.
> " Rivers of waters run down my eyes,
> because they keep not Thy law."

Or this :

> " I will lift up mine eyes to the hills,
> whence cometh my help.
> " My help cometh from the Lord,
> which made heaven and earth.
> " The Lord is thy keeper : the Lord is thy shade
> upon thy right hand.
> " The sun shall not smite thee by day,
> nor the moon by night.
> " The Lord shall preserve thee from all evil :
> He shall preserve thy soul.
> " The Lord shall preserve thy going out
> and thy coming in from this time forth,
> and even for evermore."

Or this, of Isaiah's :

" Then the eyes of the blind shall be opened and the ears of the deaf unstopped.

" Then the lame shall leap as an hart, and the tongue of the dumb *shall* sing : for in the wilderness shall waters break out, and streams in the desert. And the parched ground shall become a pool, and the thirsty land springs of water.

" In the habitations of dragons where each lay shall be grass with reeds and rushes. . . . No lion shall be there, nor any ravenous beast shall go up thereon, it shall not be found there ; but the redeemed shall walk there ;

" And the ransomed of the Lord shall return and come to Zion with songs of everlasting joy upon their heads: they shall obtain joy and gladness, and sorrow and sighing shall flee away."

Or this, from the author of *Job:*

" Surely there is a vein for the silver and a place for gold where they fine it. . .

" As for the earth, out of it cometh bread : and under it is turned up as it were fire. . . .

" But where shall wisdom be found ?

" And where is the place of understanding ?

" . . . The depth saith, it is not in me : and the sea saith, it is not with me.

" . . . Destruction and death say, we have heard the fame thereof with our ears ; God understandeth the way thereof and he knoweth the place thereof. For he looketh to the ends of the earth, and seeth under the *whole* heaven ;

" . . . When He made a decree for the rain and a way for the lightning of the thunder :

> "Then did He see it and declare it;
> He prepared it, yea, and searched it out.
> And unto man He said : ' Behold the fear of the Lord, that
>   is wisdom ; and to depart from evil is understanding.' "

Here it is apparent enough that the moral purpose with which these writers were beyond all question surcharged, instead of interfering with the artistic value of their product has spiritualized the art of it into an intensity which burns away all limitations of language, and sets their poems as indestructible monuments in the hearts of the whole human race.

If we descend to the next rank of poetry I have only to ask you to observe how, in Shakspere, just as the moral purpose becomes loftier the artistic creations become lovelier. Compare, for example, the forgiveness and reconciliation group of plays, as they have been called, — *Winter's Tale, Henry VIII,* and *The Tempest* (which must have been written late in Shakspere's life, when the moral beauty of large forgiveness seems to have taken full possession of his fancy, and when the moral purpose of displaying that beauty to his fellow-men seemed to have reigned over his creative energy) : compare, I say, these plays with earlier ones, and it seems to me that all the main creations are more distinctly artistic, more spiritually beautiful, lifted up into a plane of holy ravishment which is far above that of all the earlier plays. Think of the dignity and endless womanly patience of Hermione, of the heavenly freshness and morning quality of Perdita, of the captivating roguery of Autolycus in *Winter's Tale*, of the colossal forgiveness of Queen Katherine in *Henry VIII*, of the equally colossal pardon of Prospero, of the dewy innocence of Miranda, of the gracious and graceful ministrations of Ariel, of the grotesquerie of Caliban and Trinculo, of the play of ever-fresh delights and surprises which make the drama of *The Tempest* itself a lone and music-haunted island among dramas! Everywhere in these latter plays I seem to feel the brooding of a certain sanctity which breathes out of the larger moral purpose of the period.

Leaving these illustrations, for which time fails, it seems to me that we have fairly made out our case against these objectors if, after this review of the connection between moral purpose and artistic creation, we advance thirdly to the fact — of which these objectors seem profoundly oblivious — that the English novel at its very beginning announces itself as the vehicle of moral purpose. You will remember that when discussing Richardson and Fielding, the first English novelists, I was at pains to show how carefully they sheltered their works behind the claim of this very didacticism. Everywhere in *Pamela, Clarissa Harlowe, Tom Jones,* — in the preface, sometimes in the very titlepage, — it is ostentatiously set up that the object of the book is to improve men's *moral* condition by setting before them plain examples of vice and virtue.

Passing by, therefore, the grinning absurdity of the *Saturday Review's* declaration that the proper office of the novelist is to amuse, and that when George Eliot pretended to do more, and to instruct, she necessarily failed to do either, — it is almost as odd to find that the very objectors who urge the injurious effect of George Eliot's moral purpose upon her work are people who swear by Richardson and Fielding, utterly forgetting that if moral purpose is a detriment to *Daniel Deronda*, it is simply destruction to *Clarissa Harlowe* and *Tom Jones*.

And lastly upon this point, when I think of the crude and hasty criticism which confines this moral purpose in *Daniel Deronda* to the pushing forward of Deronda's so-called religious patriotism in endeavoring to re-establish his people in the ancient seat of the Hebrews, — a view which I call crude and hasty because it completely loses sight of the much more prominent and important moral purpose of the book, namely, the setting forth of Gwendolen Harleth's repentance ; when, I say, I hear these critics not only assume that Deronda's mission is *the* moral purpose of this book, but even belittle that by declaring that George Eliot's enthusiasm for the rehabilitation of the Jews must have been due to a chance personal acquaintance of hers with some fervid Jew who led her off into these chimerical fancies ; and when I find this tone prevailing not only with the Philistines but among a great part of George Eliot's otherwise friends and lovers : then I am in a state of amazement which precludes anything like critical judgment on my part.   As for me, no Jew — not even the poorest shambling clothes-dealer in Harrison street — but startles me effectually out of this work-a-day world : when I look upon the face of a Jew, I seem to feel a little wind fresh from off the sea of Tiberias, I seem to receive a message which has come under the whole sea of time from the further shore of it : this wandering person, who without a home in any nation has yet made a literature which is at home in every nation, carries me in one direction to my mysterious brethren the cave-men and the lake dwellers, in the other direction to the masterful carpenter of Bethlehem, climax of our race. Until you can bring me a statesman more comprehensive in view and more diligent in detail than Moses, until you can bring me poets more spiritual than David and him who wrote Job, until you can bring me a lover more pure or a mystic more rapt than John, until you can bring me a man more dear and friendly and helpful and strong and human and Christly than Jesus, — do not speak to me slightingly of the Jew. And now, to gather together these people from the four ends of the earth, to rehabilitate them in their thousand-fold consecrated home after so many ages of wandering, to re-make them into a homologous nation at once the newest and the oldest upon the earth, to endow the nineteenth century with that prodigious momentum which all the old Jewish fervor and spirituality and tenacity would acquire in the backward spring from such long ages of restraint and oppression, and with the mighty accumulation of cosmopolitan experiences ; the bare suggestion would seem enough to stir the blood of the most ungentle Gentile. And if, anticipating a certain shame in their attitude, these objectors add that Deronda's mission was chimerical, I reply that since we have seen the telegraph and the photophone and the railway and Benjamin Disraeli prime minister of England, the word chimerical has ceased to have a meaning. Somewhere in this same book we are discussing George Eliot says : "There is a sort of human paste that when it comes near the fire of enthusiasm is only baked into harder shape." Such seem to me those who remain sardonically unaffected by the idea of Jewish restoration. As for me : the movement seems so noble and captivating that to fail in it appears finer than to succeed in most

of the promising projects of this world; and one almost
wishes one were a Jew, that one might begin it without
loss of time.

But I must hasten to complete the account of George
Eliot's personal existence which we suspended at the
point where she had come to London in 1851.

She had been persuaded to this step by Dr. Chapman,
who was at that time editor of the *Westminster Review*,
and who asked her to come and help him to conduct
that publication.   At this time she must have been one
of the most captivating companions imaginable.   She
knew French, German and Italian, and had besides a
good knowledge of Latin, Greek, Russian and Hebrew.
She was a really good player of the piano, and had some
proficiency on the organ; she had already mixed in
some of the best society of the world, for, in 1841, her
father had moved to Foleshill, near Coventry, and here
she quickly became intimate in the household of Mr.
and Mrs. Charles Bray, where she met such people as
Emerson, George Combe, Mr. Froude, and many other
noted ones of the literary circles which the Brays
delighted in drawing about them; her mind had been
enlarged by the treasures of the Continent which she
visited with her life-long friends, the Brays, in 1849,
after the death of her father, remaining at Geneva after
the Brays returned to England; she had all that homely
lore which comes with the successful administration of
breakfast, dinner and supper, for her sisters and brothers
had all married, and she lived alone with her father after
his removal to Coventry in 1841, and kept his house for
him from that time until his death, not only with great
daughterly devotion but, it is said, with great success as
a domestic manager; besides thus knowing the mysteries of good coffee and good bread she was widely

versed in theology, philosophy and the movements of modern science : all of which equipment was permeated with a certain intensity which struck every one who came near her. With this endowment she came to London in 1851, as I have said, by Dr. Chapman's invitation, and took up her residence at Dr. Chapman's house. Here she immediately began to meet George H. Lewes, Carlyle, Mill and Herbert Spencer. Of her relations to Lewes it seems to me discussion is not now possible. It is known that Lewes's wife had once left him, that he had generously condoned the offence and received her again, and that in a year she again eloped ; the laws of England make such a condonation preclude divorce ; Lewes was thus prevented from legally marrying again by a technicality of the law which converted his own generosity into a penalty ; under these circumstances George Eliot, moved surely by pure love, took up her residence with him, and according to universal account, not only was a faithful wife to him for twenty years until his death, but was a devoted mother to his children. That her failure to go through the form of marriage was not due to any contempt for that form, as has sometimes been absurdly alleged, is conclusively shown by the fact that when she married Mr. Cross, a year and a half after Lewes's death, the ceremony was performed according to the regular rites of the Church of England.

The most congenial of George Eliot's acquaintances during these early days at the Chapmans' in London was Mr. Herbert Spencer. For a long time indeed the story went the rounds that Mr. Spencer had been George Eliot's tutor ; but you easily observe that when she met him at this time in London she was already thirty-one years old, long past her days of tutorship. The story however has authoritatively been denied by Mr. Spencer himself. That George Eliot took pleasure in his philosophy, that she was especially conversant with his *Principles of Psychology*, and that they were mutually-admiring and mutually-profitable friends, seems clear enough ; but I cannot help regarding it a serious mistake to suppose that her novels were largely determined by Mr. Spencer's theory of evolution, as I find asserted by a recent critic who ends an article with the declaration that "the writings of George Eliot must be regarded, I think, as one of the earliest triumphs of the Spencerian method of studying personal character and the laws of social life."

This seems to me so far from being true that many of George Eliot's characters appear like living objections to the theory of evolution. How could you, according to this theory, evolve the moral stoutness and sobriety of Adam Bede, for example, from *his* precedent conditions, to wit, his drunken father and querulous mother? How could you evolve the intensity and intellectual alertness of Maggie Tulliver from *her* precedent conditions, to wit, a flaccid mother, and a father wooden by nature and sodden by misfortune? Though surely influenced by circumstances her characters everywhere seem to flout evolution in the face.

But the most pleasant feature connected with the intercourse of George Eliot and Herbert Spencer is that it appears to have been Mr. Spencer who first influenced her to write novels instead of heavy essays in *The Westminster*. It is most instructive to note that this was done with much difficulty. Only after long resistance, after careful thought, and indeed after actual trial was George Eliot persuaded that her gift lay in fiction and not in philosophy; for it was pending the argument about the matter that she quietly wrote *Scenes of Clerical Life* and caused them to be published with all the precaution of anonymousness, by way of actual test.

As to her personal habits I have gleaned that her manuscript was wonderfully beautiful and perfect, a delight to
the printers, without blot or erasure, every letter carefully
formed ; that she read the Bible every day and that one
of her favorite books was Thomas à Kempis on *The Imitation of Christ;* that she took no knowledge at second-
hand ; that she had a great grasp of business ; that she
worked slowly and with infinite pains, meditating long
over her subject before beginning ; that she was intensely
sensitive to criticism ; that she believed herself a poet in
opposition to the almost unanimous verdict of criticism
which had pronounced *The Spanish Gypsy, Agatha* and
The Legend of Jubal as failing in the gift of song, though
highly poetic ; that the very best society in London —
that is to say in the world — was to be found at her Sunday afternoon receptions at the Priory, Regent's Park,
where she and Mr. Lewes lived so long ; and that she
rarely left her own home except when tempted by a fine
painting or some unusually good performance of music.

I have given here a list of her complete works, with
dates of publication so far as I have been able to gather.
I believe this is nearly complete.

Translation of Strauss' *Leben Jesu,* 1846 ; contributions
to *The Westminster Review,* from about 1850, during sev-
eral years ; translation of Feuerbach's *Essence of Chris-
tianity,* 1854 ; *Scenes of Clerical Life, Blackwood's Mag-
azine,* 1857, — book-form, 1858 ; *Adam Bede,* 1859 ; *The
Mill on the Floss,* 1860 ; *The Lifted Veil, Blackwood's
Magazine,* 1860 : *Silas Marner,* 1861 ; *Romola, Cornhill
Magazine,* book-form, 1863 ; *Felix Holt,* 1866 ; *The
Spanish Gypsy,* 1868 ; *Address to Workmen, Blackwood's
Magazine,* 1868 ; *Agatha,* 1869 ; *How Lisa loved the king,
Blackwood's Magazine,* 1869 ; *Middlemarch,* 1871 ; *The
Legend of Jubal,* 1874 ; *Daniel Deronda,* 1876 ; The *Im-*

pressions of Theophrastus Such, 1879 ; and said to have left a translation of Spinoza's *Ethics*, not yet published.

As the mind runs along these brief phrases in which I have with a purposed brevity endeavored to flash the whole woman before you, and as you supplement that view with this rapid summary of her literary product,— the details of fact seem to bring out the extraordinary nature of this woman's endowment in such a way that to add any general eulogium would be necessarily to weaken the picture. There is but one fact remaining so strong and high as not to be liable to this objection, which seems to me so characteristic that I cannot do better than close this study with it. During all her later life the central and organic idea which gave unity to her existence was a burning love for her fellow-men. I have somewhere seen that in conversation she once said to a friend : " What I look to is a time when the impulse to help our fellows shall be as immediate and as irresistible as that which I feel to grasp something firm if I am falling ; " and the narrator of this speech adds that at the end of it she grasped the mantel-piece as if actually saving herself from a fall, with an intensity which made the gesture most eloquent.

You will observe that of the two commandments in which the Master summed up all duty and happiness, — namely, to love the Lord with all our heart, soul and mind and to love our neighbor as ourself, George Eliot's whole life and work were devoted to the exposition of the latter. She has been blamed for devoting so little attention to the former ; as for me, I am too heartily grateful for the stimulus of human love which radiates from all her works to feel any sense of lack or regret. This, after all — the general stimulus along the line of one's whole nature — is the only true benefit of contact with the great. More

than this is hurtful.   Nowadays, you do not want an
author to tell you how many times a day to pray, to
prescribe how many inches wide shall be the hem of your
garment.   This the Master never did ; too well He knew
the growth of personality which *would* settle these matters, each for itself; too well He knew the subtle hurt
of all such violations of modern individualism ; and after
our many glimpses of the heartiness with which George
Eliot recognized the fact and function of human personality one may easily expect that she never attempted to
teach the world with a rule and square, but desired only
to embody in living forms those prodigious generalizations in which the Master's philosophy, considered
purely as a philosophy, surely excelled all other systems.

In fine, if I try to sum up the whole work of this
great and beautiful spirit which has just left us, in the
light of all the various views I have presented in these
lectures, where we have been tracing the growth of
human personality from Æschylus, through Plato,
Socrates, the contemporary Greek mind,— through the
Renaissance, Shakspere, Richardson and Fielding,
down to Dickens and our author; I find all the
numerous threads of thought which have been put before
you gathered into one, if I say that George Eliot shows
man what he may be, in terms of what he is.

www.ingramcontent.com/pod-product-compliance
Lightning Source LLC
Chambersburg PA
CBHW060541030726
47498CB00004B/1277